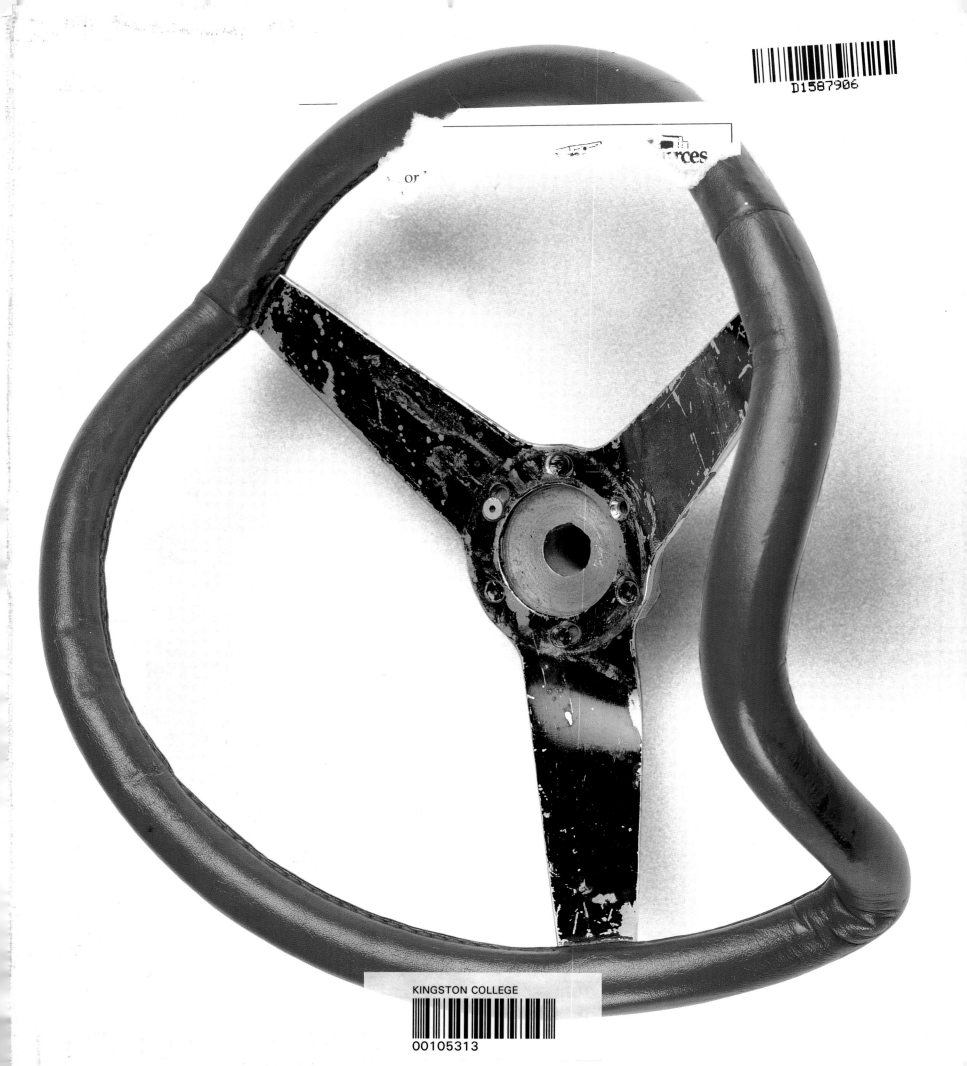

STIRLING MOSS

THE AUTHORISED BIOGRAPHY

ROBERT EDWARDS

CASSELL&CO

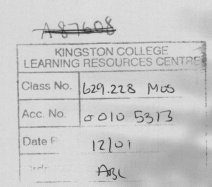

STIRLING MOSS

Introduction

Stirling Moss is still one of Britain's best-known sports stars and one of motor racing's most durable figures despite the passing of nearly forty years since his unavoidable retirement from motor racing. There are people who drift in and out of public awareness, and then there are others whose impact is so fundamental, so definitive, that people simply never forget them – such a man is Stirling Moss. Most importantly, he taught his country how to win and lose with equal grace. In the dire post-war gloom of Britain, there was a sense of anti-climax for the long-suffering population, and the rise of Moss, the boy wonder, cemented him firmly in the minds of at least two generations.

I set about writing this book with some trepidation; after all, a reputation is no small thing and while Stirling's is very robust, it is all too easy to fall into journalistic traps. The assumption that everyone has total recall is an easy one to make, as is the even commoner one that genius must, in some way, be flawed. This is a very British fault, nothing less than a national weakness.

As you read this book, you may find in it things that are new; I certainly hope so. This does not mean that everything that went before is to be discounted, as there have been several fine books about Stirling. The two which spring quickest to my mind are Doug Nye's marvellous study of the Moss racing résumé, *My Cars, My Career* (Haynes, 1987) and the late Ken Purdy's *All But My Life* (William Kimber, 1963). This latter book broke much new ground in both its approach and its candour, although there is almost as much about its author as there is about his subject. A fine read though, with elegant discourses concerning sport, art, risk and temperament.

Several publishers were keen to look at this book as a ghosted autobiography; Stirling disagreed for reasons that became clear only after we had started the project. Once I realised that there were things he wished to reveal which might perhaps appear gauche if stated in the first person, I quite understood his point of view, that the ghosted book often more properly belongs in the genre of fiction. While there are elements of Stirling's life that would leave many a fiction writer gasping, all involved felt that the time was right to tell the story, correct a few misunderstandings and set the record straight on a number of key issues. These motives provide a powerful picture of why he was the supreme driver of his generation and why the reverence in which he is held by

his circle of friends is genuine. There may be information that is new to them too. Some of it has not been easy for Stirling to relate, and not merely because of his famously terrible memory, either.

For the large community of people who follow or have followed motor racing (and many others who do not), the news in 1999 that Stirling Moss was to receive a knighthood in the New Year's Honours List was probably a high point of their year. It was certainly the high point of his, but when I heard him commenting on the radio from his cruise liner in the Caribbean that he was pleased to be 'accepted' after so long, I thought it a rather strange form of words for him to use until he told me about his schooldays.

Stirling Moss became an important public figure at more than one simple level. When leafing through his scrapbooks, I found an item which would move even the flintiest heart – it was a cheap envelope, addressed in child-like calligraphy, bearing a 3d stamp and an April 1962 postmark. It is addressed with all the confidence of youth, very simply and very firmly:

> To: *The great and wonderful Stirling Moss.*
> *I don't know which hospital he is in,*
> *but please deliver this to him.*

Well, it found him, as did thousands more. He still gets many in a similar vein – Stirling Moss, England – which is ironic, given that he has been in the telephone book at the same address for nearly forty years. He remains as accessible today as he had been in the paddock at Goodwood on the morning of St George's Day, 1962. He achieved a level of importance that was unmatched at the time, and indeed for many years afterwards. To the public he was quite simply a hero. He did what sports stars do, which is to point out by their example the implicit shortcomings of everybody else. It is not a conscious, court-jester way of behaving, but that is the effect it has on others; it is why he is treasured.

Stirling has said that he has never driven a perfect lap. Many people disagree and would go so far as to say that it was not his place to comment, that he should let others be the judge of that. They are wrong, of course, because the pleasure we get from watching a Moss, a Senna, an Ali or a Nureyev at work is to know that at that moment, in that sliver of time, they are giving their best, and that the inconsistencies which the rest of us suffer are apparently unknown to them. That is our perception and we should hug it close.

The way in which the Stirling Moss machine – him, his father Alfred and his manager Ken Gregory, assisted by a succession of able and talented staff – redefined the role of

Facing page: A study in concentration.

Overleaf: Laurels. Stirling's win at the 1959 Italian *Grand Prix* gave Cooper its first Constructor's Championship.

their boy, is an object lesson in what would be called brand management today. This was done in a quite instinctive manner; there was no grand plan, it simply happened.

Stirling has had an exciting and often violent life. He raced in 529 competitive events and won over 40 per cent of them. He placed either first, second or third in 65 per cent of these races, which is even more extraordinary. He has had crashes – sometimes the injuries he sustained would have killed other men, sometimes he was not hurt at all. He has lost many, many friends. He is remarkable from an actuarial point of view as much as anything else. He thinks he is lucky.

Compared with many, he is. Motor racing, when Stirling was its senior exponent, was an astonishingly dangerous sport. Post-war, there was a cavalier disregard for danger, not to mention a total inability to afford safety. That state would continue into the 1960s when Jackie Stewart and others addressed it. No one was very surprised if three or four top-line drivers died in a single season, for example, and many more would be killed or hurt in minor races. As Stirling has related his remarkable life story to me, I thought that it was extraordinary that there were not even more fatalities. George Abecassis, the ex-RAF bomber command squadron leader who co-owned Hersham and Walton Motors (HWM), airily dismissed such concerns: 'At least nobody was shooting at us.'

But, statistically, they might as well have been. The cars were unsafe and the circuits were even worse. When the cars improved, the circuits were much slower to change, and their capacity to contain the exponential performance growth was found wanting. The dreadful Le Mans tragedy of 1955 was the worst but was only one of a succession of disasters that would eventually result in a persistent lobby for circuit safety. It would take the deaths of many, many drivers and spectators before the issues of both car and circuit safety were addressed fully. During Stirling Moss's career, motor racing was, short of war, the most dangerous activity on the planet.

The sport that he still loves has nearly been the end of him on many occasions: at Naples, Castle Combe, Silverstone, Caracas, Monza, Spa, Zandvoort and, most famously, his adored Goodwood. He is philosophical about it, maintaining that racing drivers may very well crash if they do their jobs properly. He further maintains that he, as a driver, always held something in reserve, so that if required to go even faster, he could reach deeper within himself rather than asking more of the car. He certainly did demand much from his machinery, but that is what it was designed for. If an engine is intended to offer 7200 rpm, then it should. If it breaks down at a slower speed, then the driver is hardly at fault. Other components were less easy to measure.

One of the main reasons for frequent technical failure was that excessive loads were imposed upon vital components by developments in peripherals such as tyres and brakes. Unavoidable Newtonian laws of physics meant that the increased grip offered by new compounds and structures from Pirelli, Dunlop, Avon and the like almost ensured that the strain put on parts of frequently humble origin began to exert a terrible penalty. Just as downforce would be misunderstood later on, so the massive strains put on these vital little pieces of metal – track rods, bearings, hubs and steering racks – would trigger a high casualty rate, particularly among the early British specials.

It would be a mistake to compare racing in Stirling's time with its modern equivalent; comparisons between, say, Ayrton Senna and Juan Manuel Fangio are fruitless, for the simple reason that Senna was a Formula One driver, whereas Fangio was a generalist. While it is undoubtedly the case that Senna would happily have driven other classes of machine, the organisation of the sport prevented him from doing so. This leads us to the unavoidable conclusion that you can compare and contrast only on a level playing field. Charles Anthony Standish Brooks, Stirling's team mate at both Vanwall and Aston Martin, kindly did so for me with the following remark: 'Stirling was, in my book, the best all-round driver we have ever seen. There can be no argument that he was the best driver ever in terms of versatility.' If that is true (and it is by no means a rare opinion) then Tony Brooks must himself be very close behind Stirling indeed.

The irony of writing a biography of a man who does not read very much is clear to me; but if you made your living as well as your reputation by threading a howling, obsolete racing car around the streets of Monaco, holding your line to a centimetre, compensating for the lightening fuel load, the wear on the tyres, even your own loss of weight, while being harried by the entire Ferrari works team, then merely reading a book – whoever wrote it – could seem a very minor thing by comparison.

But Stirling Moss regrets that he is not as well-read as other men – he feels that he is culturally worse off for it. However, when he started to explain to me the dynamics, both personal and technical, of actually driving a racing car, it became evident to me that it was the hydrostatistician talking to the plumber. Both work with water – indeed, I even have a driving licence and have owned and driven some marvellous cars – but there ends the shared experience. The result has

Facing page: Full participation; Stirling refuels the HWM.

Previous pages: Stirling Moss at Goodwood, 1958. Pushing hard, the nose of his Cooper-Climax lifts under power.

been a remarkable series of conversations, at least from my point of view. In my circle of acquaintances there are several academics; few of them hesitated in stating that they would swap their enviable educational qualifications for a tenth of Stirling Moss's talents, and many of them have absolutely no interest in motor racing or even cars. They simply know how exceptional he is.

So this book is not a race résumé, quite simply because Stirling and Doug Nye have already produced one; it is not particularly a motor racing book either, although racing cars and races feature in it, and while that fact is visually pleasing it is not why I wrote it. In essence, I regard it as the biography of a complex and enigmatic man whose contribution to both his sport and the fabric of his country is unequalled.

Apart from Sir Stirling and Lady Moss, both of whom put up with my often impertinent questioning with great aplomb and candour, I would also like to thank Berenice Krikler, Annie Strudwick, Sarah Wilkes (*née* Hobson), David Haynes, Pat Carlsson, Andrew Frankel, Mick Walsh, Duncan Rabagliatti, Stanley Moss, Elliot Moss, John Craufurd, Herb Jones, Jim Heaton, Ted Croucher, Tony Brooks, John Horsman, Tony Rudd, Gordon Cruickshank, Peter Jackson, Nigel Roebuck, Andrew Hambling, Valerie Pirie, the late John Cooper, Doug Nye, Rob Walker, Betty Walker, Brian Lister, Donn Gurney, Chris Nixon, Ken Gregory, Kate Earl, David Venables, the Jewish College, Hendon, the British Automobile Racing Club, the BBC, the House of Commons Library, the Public Records Office at Kew and Goodwood Circuit. Without their enthusiasm and willingness, this book would not have happened. Similarly, at Cassell and Co., I owe a great debt of gratitude to my publisher, Michael Dover, my editor, Marilyn Inglis and to Matthew Lowing, who pulled much of the material together. Thanks too, to David Costa and his team for the design. Their evident commitment and support has been invaluable. I must add, that despite the authoratative input of all the above, that any errors present in this story are entirely mine.

Left: Movement is tranquillity. Moss in the Maserati that would transform his career.

① A Very Singular Child

No historian has to kick the tyres of a history of Scotland very hard before encountering a Craufurd. Intensely political, frequently violent and possessed of an extraordinary capacity for survival even when wrong-footed by events, the Craufurd clan was both influential and extensive. The mother of William Wallace was a Craufurd and her brother was the Sheriff of Ayr, which meant rather more then than it might now; Mary, Queen of Scots' go-between was a Craufurd, suggesting that the efforts of the clan to establish themselves in the thirteenth century had paid dividends, albeit dubious ones, by the sixteenth century. By 1500 the extended family had spread. A grant of land from Robert the Bruce had established the senior branch, the Crawfords of Auchinames. The second branch, the Craufurds of Craufurdland, settled on territory gifted by King Robert III. The third branch, the Craufurds of Kilburnie, came about in 1499 as a result of Sir John Craufurd acquiring lands there.

By the eighteenth century, there was a baronetcy for the senior male in the Kilburnie branch and in 1764 Robert Craufurd was born, the third son of the first baronet. Probably the most famous of the entire clan, Craufurd, who as a third son was effectively quite poor, joined the Army in 1779. He commanded the Light Division from 1807, which, after interesting service in South America, he took to Spain in 1809. He distinguished himself, covering the retreats to both Coruña in 1809 and Torres Vedras the next year. He was astonishingly brave, but displayed some of the lack of imagination that can often accompany that characteristic. He was also an inveterate diarist and scribbler, as well as being ferociously bad-tempered. He was known throughout the Army as 'Black Bob'.

His methods of exercising discipline over his force seem needlessly cruel to modern eyes; he was a flogger, a brutal disciplinarian and displayed a total contempt for danger (or popularity, come to that) which was rare even then. Perversely, his men loved him, although the apparent delight he took in humiliating those officers (in front of the men – almost unheard-of) whom he regarded as slackers and 'croakers' may well have contributed to that. He became almost as much a mascot as commander. His men would follow him anywhere.

His efforts earned him a major-generalship in late 1811, but he was to have little time to enjoy it. In January 1812 he led the Light Division's 'Forlorn Hope' in the assault on the breach of Cuidad Rodrigo, was critically wounded by canister shot and died five days later. He was forty-eight. To the Light Division, slackers aside, his death was nothing less than a total disaster, an unimaginable hammer blow. His memory was and is treasured.

By the time Aileen Craufurd was born on 7 July, 1897, the memory of her great-great uncle was a dim one. The Craufurds had spread out again, this time southward, so although Aileen had been born in Stirling, by the time the Great War was over she was living in Berkshire. Whereas her illustrious ancestor had been the prototypical infantryman, eschewing the saddle while his men walked, Aileen grew up besotted by horses. She was indulged, too, and became an excellent horsewoman.

As 'Black Bob' Craufurd was flogging the exhausted, starving, tattered but loyal remnants of his beloved Light Division towards Coruña, little Abraham Moses was growing up in north London. He came from a long line of industrious businessmen and in 1832 produced a son, Nathan, who grew up to become something of an engineer, specialising in new-fangled cycles. Nathan was rather hastily married to Phoebe Abrahams at the Jewish College in Leadenhall Street, London on 29 August, 1852. The reason for the unseemly haste popped out before the end of the year. Named after his grandfather, Abraham (Abe to his later family) grew into a very fine-looking young man and after completing his education, became involved in the planning and construction of commercial

Previous page: Aileen and Alfred at a North West Motor Club Trial, December 1935. The car is a Singer.

This page, top: Stirling's grandfather Abe, c. 1912; middle: Stirling's father Alfred Moss as a schoolboy, c. 1912; bottom: Sarah-Jane Moss, née Durtnall (Stirling's grandmother, c. 1912.

Facing page: A confident Alfred at Brooklands, c. 1923. The car is a 'Sporting' 12-hp Crouch.

Overleaf: Moss family and friends on the river at Thames Ditton.

property, not as an architect, but as a businessman. As the capital expanded in all directions in the last quarter of the nineteenth century, with new suburbs sprouting wherever the growth of railways permitted them, it was frequently Abraham who built the commercial real estate infrastructure which went hand in hand with the new housing. Unsurprisingly, he prospered.

He married in November 1878. He was twenty-six, his bride Sarah Jane Durtnall was just eighteen. She was to give him five children – the first of these also arrived suspiciously early in 1879 and Abe named him, perhaps appropriately, after Nathan. Two daughters, Martha and Evelyn, followed in 1881 and 1882, followed by Ardon in 1887 and Alfred in 1896. Perhaps because Abe had married outside the faith, he gave much thought to anglicising his name. Naturally, because Sarah Jane was a Christian, none of his children could be

happy in England, the massive influx of Ashkenazi Jews from Poland and Russia at the end of the nineteenth century gave Abraham (and many others like him) some pause for thought. Theodor Herzl had not been discussing the situation of the comfortable Jewish middle classes in England; he had been railing at the plight of the dispossessed hordes who had, under Cossack whips, been forced to flee westward to save themselves.

These proud, long-established English families of European Jewish origin, many of whom had arrived as far back as 1656, were keen to distance themselves from the obviously foreign immigrants who began to arrive in large numbers in the wake of the ferocious pogroms in Russia, Carpathia and Poland after 1881. It was not purely a matter of snobbery (although there must have been an element of that); it was a matter of declaration, of choosing sides. Only with the arrival of this

It was almost as if Judaism was considered a subset of Protestantism...

brought up as Jewish without converting back to the faith, and a quick glance at the goings-on in Europe may well have triggered his decision to act.

The issue of Judaism was something of a hot potato in Europe, particularly after the fiasco of the Dreyfus affair in France. The story is well-known, but the outrage of the Liberal Left had a far-reaching effect, even in England. In 1896, the Austrian Theodor Herzl published his influential work *The Jewish State: A Modern Solution to the Jewish Question* which concluded that assimilation did not necessarily work and that the Jews needed a homeland of their own. Herzl's book was to be the midwife at the birth of Zionism, but that was not a conclusion that everybody reached, particularly if they were settled where they were. Records show an acceleration in applications by British Ashkenazi Jewish families to change their names in light of the Dreyfus scandal and its attendant fall-out. It was a trend that Abraham Moses and many others joined. But there were other, earlier reasons.

The Moses family were originally Ashkenazi Jews from the Rhineland, and although they were long-established and very

Eastern European influx did the more established families feel any real need to anglicise their names. It was ironic that they felt forced to do this in order to protect their identities, but assimilation of one culture into another is never a quick thing and as the Jewish population of Britain rose meteorically, so perhaps did the risk of some sort of backlash.

So these English Jews were not hiding, rather they were committing themselves as well as firmly differentiating themselves from what some considered to be uncouth new arrivals. Many of the new immigrants had suffered appallingly in their native countries, particularly Russia. The newcomers were frequently uneducated (as a result of Imperial decree), often hungry, almost certainly penniless, and very few spoke any English. From the point of view of at least some of the older-established English Jewish families, these new arrivals might as well have been from Mars.

For some it was a difficult decision, but they also had families and businesses to protect in an England that was (for the moment) free of the appalling visitations that were clearly matters of government policy elsewhere in Europe. It cannot have felt like a time of great security.

By the last quarter of the nineteenth century it was almost as if Judaism was considered in England to be a subset of Protestantism – really just another non-Catholic sect – and there was hardly any evidence of establishment ill-feeling

Facing page: Alfred as a man of his hands pitched in to fettle the Frontenac-Fords. Here he is with a modified Model-T Ford gearbox.

Previous page: Henry Ford sits in Alfred's car, the Frontenac-Ford 'Barber Warnock Special' at Indianapolis in 1924.

Registered Dentist of London To' Pilot Car At Indianapolis

ALFRED E MOSS

AIN'T WE GOT FUN?

towards Jewish people. After all, the first Jewish peer had been created a hundred years before at the end of the eighteenth century, and in reality there was still rather more anti-Catholic sentiment about. The risk that this state might not necessarily persist in the face of the huge influx forced the hands of Abraham and others like him. He opted to drop the 'e' from the family name and became, overnight, Abraham Moss. For Abe this was an easier decision than for some; he had happily married outside the faith, so there was little point in exposing his burgeoning family to needless social risk.

In recognition of this decision to thoroughly integrate his family into mainstream Britain, he decided to give his youngest son a thoroughly British moniker. To make sure that no one would be in any doubt that the family Moss was now

Above: Alfred also had an eye for publicity. The media clearly saw some novelty value in a racing dentist.

Facing page: Aileen's best-known car, the very pretty 1½-litre Marendaz.

Overleaf: Aileen and Alfred with a larger 2-litre Marendaz.

indisputably English, he perhaps over-egged the pudding a little; the new arrival was named Alfred Ethelbert.

There is little doubt that Alfred was something of a scamp. While he had inherited his grandfather Nathan's manual dexterity, he had also picked up more than his fair share of *chutzpah*; he was to demonstrate this relatively quickly. Dentistry was a matter of apprenticeship, coupled with blood-curdling trial and error. Alfred had learned this when seconded as an apprentice dentist to the war effort and he had seen the state of the nation's teeth. In the early 1920s, as Alfred entered the profession, it was quite common, in England at least, for women to have all their teeth removed prior to marriage in order to save their future husbands the ruinous expense of dentists' bills. Men would quite often have no teeth of their own past the age of forty, for the neatly paired reasons of painlessness and economy. Alfred was to develop the largest practice in the country, combining both a professional inventiveness and a sound head for business. He would prosper, but not before he had worked a few passions out of his system.

One passion was the motor car. His first conveyance, as ill-advised as any young man's, was an AV Monocar, a curious device with the seats staggered in tandem. By 1923 he had graduated to a more promising machine, a Crouch, powered by an Anzani motor. He actually raced this car at Brooklands that year and even won a race.

Despite the Doc Holliday heritage American dentistry was ahead of its British equivalent by a large margin; one of the finest places of learning was the School of Dental Medicine at the University of Indiana. The fact that conveniently close by was 'The Brickyard', site of the Indianapolis 500, may well have been lost on Abe, but was certainly not lost on Alfred. He suggested to his father that a spell there might be useful.

He arrived at the University of Indiana in the autumn of 1923, fresh from his success at Brooklands, and set about establishing himself as a potential entrant to the 1924 Indianapolis 500. The Great Motor Race would be held on Memorial Day, 30 May which was also Alfred's birthday. He was armed with a letter of introduction from the Mercedes agent in Britain; his original intention had been to get aboard a Mercedes, but as they would not be contenders that year he had to look elsewhere.

History does not record the level of his commitment to the curriculum of the Dental School; it does record that he entered the 1924 Indy 500 aboard a Barber-Warnock Special. It was, in fact, a Frontenac-Ford designed by Louis Chevrolet, entered by a local Ford dealer, financed by Henry Ford himself and in many ways the Maserati 250 of its day, although its high point had been some years before. Although it was based on a

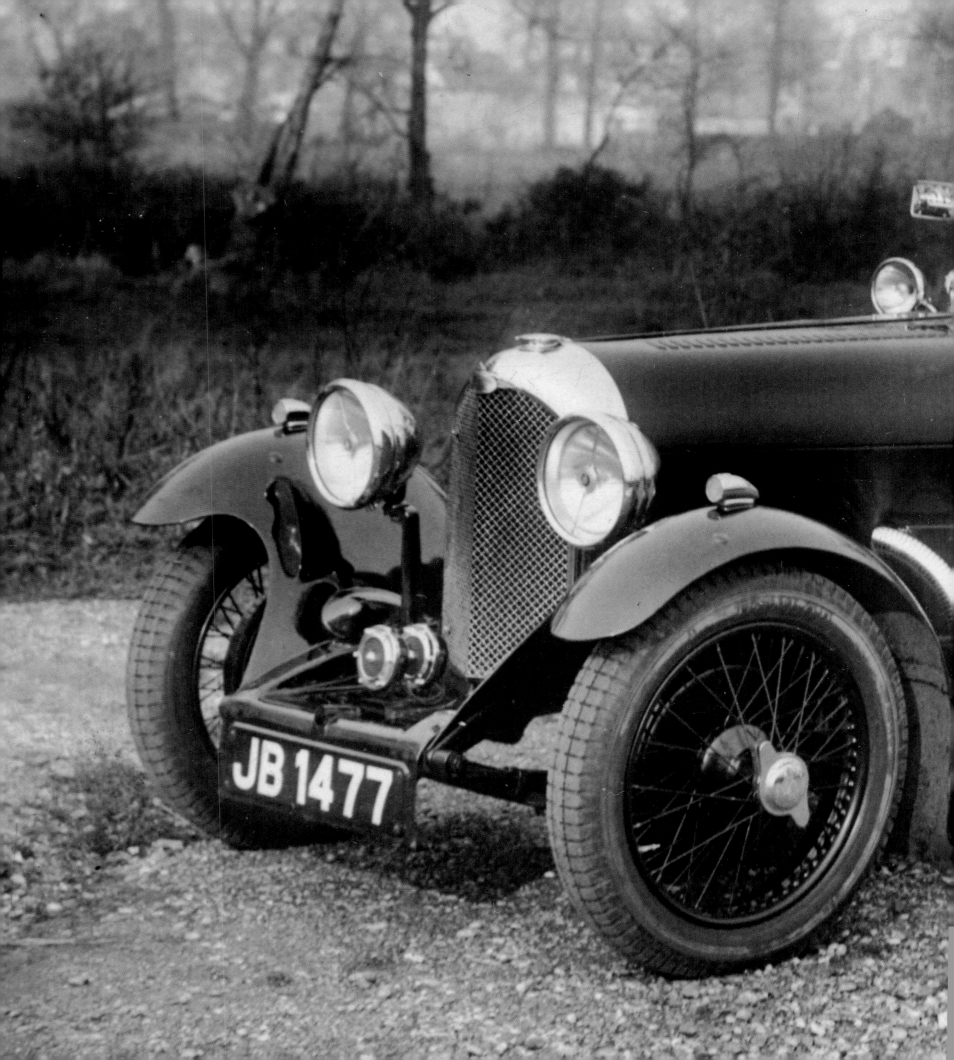

relatively humble Ford Model T chassis, the cylinder head was where the value was added. Stripped-down bodywork and a tradition of reliability (encouraged by Chevrolet's insistence that every load-bearing nut and bolt should be welded solid) allowed Alfred to finish sixteenth at 84 mph. He won $900, which was a substantial sum. It transpired that his car had also been the 1922 winner and had not been touched since, which is presumably why a tyre suddenly let go its two-year-old air in practice and bounced him off both walls of the Brickyard.

Alfred brought back to England an agency for Barber-Warnock and set himself up in business with his brother-in-law Michael Lawson in Thornton Heath, Surrey, whence he re-entered the lists at Brooklands, driving what was by now a totally outdated machine, but with some success. But the business did not really prosper and after two years Alfred reverted to his dental qualifications and established his first dental practice, Moss and Roberts, shortly afterwards.

Alfred Moss met Aileen Craufurd at Brooklands in 1926. She had diversified from horses somewhat (although her love for them would never leave her) and developed something of a passion for the motor car after having served as an ambulance driver in the Royal Flying Corps during the Great War. The pair married in 1927 and the first fruit of their union arrived on 17 September, 1929, a month before the Wall Street Crash.

Upon marriage Alfred decided to stop racing altogether, although he willingly accompanied Aileen as she developed her own interest in the sport. She worked hard at it too, and campaigned in a series of cars, culminating in an elegant Marendaz Special, in which she later received recognition as the Ladies' Trials Champion of England. Trials driving was not as dangerous as circuit racing, but it was certainly competitive, and it was that element which attracted her. Aileen, like Alfred, rather liked to win, a tendency that their son would inherit, in spades.

Aileen was initially minded to call their son Hamish but Alfred felt that it was probably too Scottish. A compromise was reached – Stirling was the place of Aileen's birth, and so Stirling Craufurd Moss he was duly named. He was never actually christened; Alfred had little time for the rites of any organised religion, not necessarily because of any cultural confusion on his part, but more because he viewed his family as a unit in and of itself.

The family lived in a modest house in Thames Ditton. They employed no servants as such, but they did have Nanny Brooks, whose presence allowed Alfred and Aileen ample time

for trials driving. But when Aileen became pregnant for the second time, Alfred decided to relocate. He had seen a house at Bray, a long way up the Thames, which might do very well. He took a fourteen-year lease on it and installed the family there in 1936, just in time for the arrival of Patricia Ann, a sister for Stirling. The house was called the Long White Cloud and it would be the family home until 1950. Attached to it was a modest acreage that allowed a degree of hobby farming for Alfred as well as enough space for a small menagerie of pets. Little Stirling's favourite pet was a crow that he had discovered flat on its back with a broken wing. He named it Cecil and nursed it back to health. Pleasingly, the bird decided to stay on once recovered and became a permanent fixture.

Alfred Moss knew that his son was unlikely to be poor, but he was an imaginative and observant enough man to realise three important things: that wealth can often be as much of a challenge as poverty; that it is infinitely worse to be newly poor than newly rich; and that the former is very much easier to achieve than the latter. Alfred's strict insistence upon Stirling developing a sense of financial values was purely in order to protect his son from the perils of affluence, which can be very real, particularly among inheritors.

His view was that any tendency towards Stirling becoming a spendthrift must be curtailed, and his method was to inculcate in his young son a healthy respect for the value of money. Things therefore became to young Stirling worth exactly what he was prepared to give up in order to have them. To an economist this equation merely defines price, but it is not necessarily always defined as simply as that in the minds of children. It was a lesson that was never to leave Stirling, but not one that would necessarily serve him well in all situations or in all his relationships. He kicked against it, of course, but his father would brook no arguments. He was firm; Stirling would not grow up be financially illiterate. It must be said, nor did he.

But Alfred was a generous and easy-going man in all other ways; he was a plain dealer, a generous father and an indulgent friend. He also had very well-developed ideas about how his son would be raised; he would certainly be well educated, but just as important he would be sporty. Accordingly, Stirling was learning to box by the age of three. On family holidays, generally taken on the Essex coast, Alfred actively encouraged his son to take on all comers at the boxing booths that were commonly found there. Ciné film of his ferocious attack on a punch-ball that stood taller than himself reveals a character trait that emerged early and stayed with him – determination bordering on bloody-mindedness; Britishness, if you like.

Alfred's reasoning was not entirely objective; he had been attacked more than once on the way back from one of his far-flung surgeries and had taken to carrying a set of brass knuckles with which to even the odds a little. Street crime often marches in step with economic conditions, and in the teeth of the Depression this was the case. East London was quite often not a safe place at all, even before the presence of the British Union of Fascists. Happily, one of Alfred's regular patients was a leading figure in the small but active criminal *demi-monde* around the Mile End Road and thus he was able, with no great finesse but great discretion, to arrange matters so that Alfred was not 'bovvered' again.

So for Alfred it was a matter of common sense that young Stirling should take up a martial art, but he was not to know that his son would need his skills depressingly early in life. Or perhaps he did? Having addressed the issue of his son's physical fitness and ability to defend himself, he then turned to the matter of his education.

Oscar Wilde had famously, and with an outsider's accuracy, observed only two generations earlier, that English public schools are not for the sons of gentlemen, but rather for the fathers of them. Alfred, who was already a gentleman and certainly no social climber, simply wanted a decent all-round (but particularly an *English*) education for Stirling, in line with Abe's original strategy. And he certainly got one, but while Alfred would never regret it, Stirling certainly would. After a happy spell in a little pre-prep school called Shrewsbury House, Stirling was entered for Clewer Manor, a proper preparatory school that was the main junior feeder school for the Imperial Service College in Windsor. He arrived there in 1936, the year his little sister Pat was born.

The head of Clewer Manor sounds like a very good egg indeed. Sidney Beckwith was the exemplar of a good prep-school headmaster and a competitive and enthusiastic sportsman. His demonstration of the correct way to hammer a rugby ball from one end of a pitch to the other is a memory that has never left Stirling. Particularly impressive to a seven-year-old was the fact that Beckwith did this barefoot. If you are only seven a rugby pitch is a very long thing indeed. From that moment on, rugby became a mild obsession and Sidney Beckwith became something of a hero.

Perhaps in response to Stirling's clear enthusiasm for his new mentor, Alfred turned to his manual skills and, quite unannounced, whipped up a splendid suit of armour for Stirling's amusement. Lovingly assembled from tinplate and solder, it reflected both Alfred's extraordinary craftsmanship and design ability as well as his heartfelt belief that he could probably knock up a better one than any toyshop, or any prep-school headmaster, come to that. The fact that he made it himself, rather than simply buying it, was very significant. It took a lot of time and he was a very busy man. He was, as his

son would become, a man of his hands.

By 1939 Alfred was also a successful man. The series of partnerships that he started had prospered; he was fast becoming a participant in one of the largest chains of practices in England – post-war, it would be the biggest. He splashed out on a brand-new 4¼-litre Bentley. He was inordinately proud of it, but disappointed that it would not do the well-advertised ton; 98 mph was the flat-out maximum.

For an eleven-year-old schoolboy, 1940 was a hugely entertaining, even an idyllic time. The worst thing to happen that year for the young Stirling was not Dunkirk but the death of his grandfather Abe. The war was remote, almost an abstraction, constructed from radio broadcasts, model Spitfires, vapour trails, stray cartridge cases and bits of aeroplane that obligingly dropped from the sky, to be scooped up like seashells, traded, swapped and treasured. The most popular book on sale was an economy edition by Penguin entitled *Aircraft Recognition*. The conflict might well have been remote but its day-to-day impact was not, as a frustrated generation of boys, teetering on the edge of puberty, could only be spectators as the events of 1940 unfolded. This experience would produce an aggressive generation.

Alfred's contribution to the war effort was a little more direct. All the ingenuity he could muster went towards inventions that might be useful. One that succeeded was a form of air-raid shelter that could double as a table. It was entirely modular and bolted together, even to the point of having more than one storey. Effectively a fabricated steel cage with side panels of stout mesh, it allowed its inhabitants to stay indoors during a bombing raid. Modelled on the protective cages used in hospitals to protect fractured limbs, it found immediate favour with the Ministry of Supply; it was promptly renamed the Morrison shelter after the Secretary of State, Herbert. Other design efforts were more radical; a downwards-firing rocket that could be triggered by an enemy aeroplane snagging the cable of a barrage balloon was certainly imaginatively aggressive, but the risk that it might miss its target and effectively destroy what the bomber had missed underneath was wisely considered to be a risk too far.

At Clewer Manor Stirling was, despite his contentment, plagued by assorted illnesses – scarlet fever, appendicitis and nephritis in quick succession. As a result, his schoolwork, which was not exactly a model of diligence in the first place, started to suffer somewhat. His later academic accomplishments, at best modest, were always held by his mother to be the result of these illnesses, but one suspects that this was

Facing page: Moss's childhood home, the Long White Cloud.

parental indulgence. A simpler explanation was that he was basically not interested. He was and is a person of movement and competition, and his ability to apply himself has always been a function of a definable and foreseeable end result; Stirling was not, even as a schoolboy, remotely interested in abstractions. But he was blissfully happy. As a weekly boarder he enjoyed the best of both worlds; plentiful food at weekends, coupled with a suitably sporty regime at school. This pleased Aileen too, if only because she would have the opportunity to feed him up properly before plonking him on a horse, a process that he was starting to find tiresome. 'I've always hated riding; I only really ever bothered with it to please my mother.'

Stirling's view was that horses were fundamentally unreliable; whatever riding did for his balance, there was the downside that they bit, kicked and occasionally went their own way. Careering around the orchard in the dilapidated Austin 7 that Alfred had bought for him was a much more satisfying occupation. But he was a virtuoso equestrian despite his well-concealed distaste for it. Usefully, he also made money at it; winning at gymkhana might easily be worth five pounds or so as well as a trophy.

So it was not as a result of any unhappiness at Clewer Manor that he decided to attempt to reach America. The plan was simple enough; he and two friends, one of whose fathers was an officer on the *Queen Mary*, would borrow the Moss family dinghy from its boathouse, paddle it down the Thames

to the coast and follow the shoreline round to Southampton before stowing away on the great ship. The ill-prepared trio of Moss, Perry and Lowe sneaked out and headed for Bray across country. We can imagine the scene as they flitted from tree to tree, an ear cocked for pursuers. Unsurprisingly, upon reaching Long White Cloud, a startled Aileen spotted them as they headed for the boathouse. After a hastily devised explanation, they were delivered back into the care of Beckwith.

Anthony Perry remembered the event very well even in early 2001; he also remembered the warmth of the welcome he received when he and horse-boxes full of other undernourished prep-school boys were fed and watered, soup-kitchen style, by a bustling Aileen Moss. Unlike Stirling, Perry was utterly miserable at Clewer Manor. Whereas Stirling looked upon the proposed emigration as a great adventure, poor Perry probably looked upon it as a serious escape attempt, since Beckwith was something of a flogger.

Stirling had, under Sidney Beckwith's eye, rapidly developed into an excellent sportsman on the athletics track, on the rugger field and in the boxing ring. He had taken to boxing very easily; it not only suited his competitive nature, but also served to keep him very fit, which helped to counter a slight tendency towards chubbiness in his early years. When he entered public school, he had every reason to expect great things of it; the Imperial Service College (ISC) was, after all, a very sporty place. The fact that he was academically ill-prepared was, it was hoped, surmountable.

The ISC was no longer in Windsor when Stirling arrived there in 1943. For reasons of economy as much as anything else, it had been amalgamated with Haileybury College in Hertford, and the institutions were run in parallel from then on. The traditions of the ISC and those of Haileybury were not

Facing page: 'I only rode to please my mother' – but with some success. Stirling with a proud Alfred.

Above: 'Cousin John' as a toddler with family pet Basher.

so very dissimilar, so there was no particular cultural clash when the two were amalgamated, although for reasons of those traditions a mild apartheid existed between the two groups of boys in terms of dress, custom and privilege. Haileybury boys, for example, were compelled to take a cold shower each morning. Steeped in the dubious traditions of the White Man's Burden, neither of the two schools had radically changed since the previous century; indeed many of their type would not change for some time to come.

The ISC had been founded to supply the needs of a demanding Empire for well-educated young gentlemen to administer it, defend it and in the case of the Honourable East India Company, to make money out of it. The orthodoxy of proselytising muscular Christianity that was the perceived norm during the war years had naturally evolved into a general distrust of all things foreign. It was a mindset almost guaranteed to make the life of anyone who was only a little different from the ordinary an absolute misery. Stirling started

Semitism that can characterise the English boarding school flourished as much during the war as it had before it. If it was a matter of public knowledge that the plight of the Jews in Europe was dire, then nobody thought to tell the schoolboys and, even if they had, it is unlikely to have made much difference. Anti-Semitism, of the uniquely cruel schoolboy kind, was alive and well in Hertfordshire. And Stirling suffered from it very badly indeed. The name Moss had become a frequently used anglicisation of Moses and it was not long before Grandfather Abe's efforts were undone. Stirling had never even heard words like 'Yid', let alone 'Jew-boy' before. Such prejudices often only appear with puberty.

So, Stirling's keenly honed boxing skills came in rather handy, but frequently without gloves and not at all in the way that Alfred had anticipated. On a one-to-one basis he gave a very good account of himself, but against a gaggle of three or four, it was a rather different matter. Any outward manifestation of these fights was dismissed airily by Stirling as

Tellingly, Alfred was never to know of his son's humiliating torments

to suffer from the anti-Semitism that Abe had feared would appear and had so pragmatically sought to avoid.

It is ironic that the man whose very name would eventually become a byword for Britishness should have undergone such cruel treatment, and doubly ironic that within the year in the heart of Europe, Allied forces would discover the extent of the truth behind the rumours about the persecution of European Jewry. What they would find there would reduce battle-hardened veterans to speechless tears. For Stirling, the ill-treatment that was routinely handed out had a predictable effect: 'It was something I held against the Jewish religion – totally unfairly – for a long time, because of the persecution I suffered . . .bloody religion; who needs it?'

But Stirling wasn't Jewish officially, simply because Aileen wasn't; one can only assume that faith without conversion via one's mother. This was not a distinction familiar to the young thugs of the fifth form, but then neither would it have excused them had it been true. The Moss family was more or less agnostic, as the omission of any baptism rather suggests, and Stirling's view, that 'Dad was English and Mum was a Scot', had served him very well as an identifier, not least because it was true.

In truth, the persistent, bloody-minded racism and anti-

the result of over-enthusiasm in the more formal surroundings of the gym, and indeed Alfred may even have been delighted that his son was taking such an aggressive view of sporting endeavour. Had he known the truth, he would have been mortified. This early introduction to aches and pains (including many formal beatings), would serve Stirling well in later life.

There was at least more sport to participate in; he continued playing rugger as a Colts' XV wing three-quarter, and also took up rowing, in the coxless fours. Not only was it superb exercise, it was extremely competitive, and the upper body strength that it developed was always to be an asset.

Tellingly, Alfred was never to know of his son's humiliating torments, for neither Stirling nor anybody else ever told him. For small boys to put such a brave face on bullying is not particularly uncommon, but for Stirling to have even mentioned it would have been the cause of potential trouble on three fronts. Alfred, when roused, had a ferocious temper (as Stirling knew) and his reaction to this unwelcome

Facing page: Messing about on the river; Aileen and Alfred with toddler John Craufurd and dog Basher.

information might be unpredictable and therefore potentially embarrassing. The last thing Stirling wanted was Alfred charging in to see a startled headmaster. Second, and much more important for Stirling, was that to even mention the matter could imply criticism of his grandfather, for it was his religion that seemed to be the root of the problem and basically Stirling adored his grandfather. Third, there was the issue of simple (and understandable) pride. So he kept quiet and suffered. Already shy by nature, this experience served to make him even more so.

Naturally the food at Haileybury was dreadful, but there were ways to augment it. The boys would frequently patronise an establishment known as Mollie's, a small farmhouse that provided all-day breakfasts. It was one of the benefits of living in the countryside during wartime where the restrictions imposed by rationing were more easily circumvented. Without the fry-ups offered there, life would have been quite intolerable; they were well worth the beatings for breaking grounds, which often ensued. So bad was the food that Stirling would frequently complain about it to the head of Lawrence House, where he was quartered. On the basis of safety in numbers, a deputation, frequently led by Stirling, would knock on the door of 'Bat' Nichols, the housemaster, whereupon the group would melt away, leaving Stirling to make the complaint on his own. He became known, by Nichols at least, as 'the agitator'. But he had a point; he knew the rationing rules and if the boys did not receive their fair allotment, he felt quite justified in pointing it out. Like many boys who attended such establishments, he still eats rather quickly.

Sport and complaining aside, he joined the Cadets, but once he realised that the Lee-Enfield rifles with which the Corps was equipped were entirely without ammunition, he joined the band instead. A fife weighing a few ounces was much more portable than a weighty .303 rifle. The band uniform was also a good deal smarter.

The war years had also brought him another companion; his cousin John Craufurd, who was at boarding school in Cheltenham, spent his holidays at the Long White Cloud. Being four years older than Stirling, he made for interesting, if risky company. Cousin John was an inveterate experimenter who was fatally fascinated by pyrotechnics; the near-destruction of Stirling's tree house was the result of a quite large explosion. John Craufurd had built a sophisticated petrol bomb and when it exploded in Stirling's face (he had attempted to manoeuvre it with a broom handle), the results were predictably dire. Blazing, he plummeted straight to the

ground and was severely burned. The tree house survived, but Stirling was not able to enjoy it for some weeks.

Despite Alfred's insistence on financial discipline, which could be irksome, home life *chez* Moss was anything but stratified. Alfred believed in familial equality and was not a heavy-handed father. Lively debate among equals was the order of the day, particularly around the dining-table. Such liberal attitudes were rare in those days, and while they helped to nurture in Stirling a firm grasp of grown-up conversation and the good manners that go along with it, he also became quite assertive, which helped combat his natural shyness.

Aileen was as pleased with his progress in horsemanship as Alfred was with his progress as a pugilist. Unable to share with either parent the truth of what he was going through at school, Stirling grew a carapace, a scrupulously polite but rather deadpan mien that offered the world an air of intense keenness when a challenge was in the offing. Stirling had discovered that he had a competitive nature at a young age; polished in the gym and on the running track, not to mention in the saddle, it was to become a characteristic that later defined him.

A truly competitive nature is relatively rare and most people simply do not understand it. The desire to win can be seen on any prep school sports field, but for Stirling it became clear that winning was much more fun than merely taking part. It was not simply a matter of getting his own back on those who had been unpleasant to him (although that would always give him a particularly fierce satisfaction), but in doing his absolute and total best he was setting a yardstick against which he could lean. He began to view his own best efforts as an absolute measure of something, and this gave him comfort as well as confidence. This was also accompanied by a scrupulous sense of fairness, which, when all was said and done, came from Alfred rather than anywhere else. Certainly, Stirling's experiences at Haileybury seemed anything but fair.

But if you establish a standard that others find hard to approach, let alone equal, it is also true that you can afford to be as fair as you like. Stirling had not managed to do that just yet, but it would not take him very long. Again, it was to be a feature of his life and career; the strongest can always afford to be indulgent. In Stirling's case, this would evolve into a sense of general isolation from others and his natural shyness only served to intensify that. An interest in other people for their own sakes was something that he would always struggle to cultivate. He was left with a sense of profound respect for those who stood up for themselves, as he had learned very well that it is simpler merely to fit in at any cost. His relationships with some key figures in his life were to reflect this; they were not always associations necessarily warmed by great affection, but they were ones that he was to cherish.

Facing page: Stirling paddling, at around five years old.

If the ordeal of Haileybury left Stirling with little enthusiasm for academic work but a strong desire to prove himself in ways that can comfort the frequently bullied, then no one should be overly surprised. But for Alfred, who had worked very long and hard indeed to build up his dental practices as well as his other activities, Stirling's apparent indifference to scholarship was vexing, to say the least. It was Alfred's desire that he should bequeath to his son a thriving business, but to qualify as a dentist there were exams to be taken and passed.

Stirling managed distinctions in English and arithmetic when he took his School Certificate in the late summer of 1945, but little else, and it was with an almost audible sigh of relief that he left school after three fairly miserable years. Even with the aid of a crammer (Messrs. Davies, Lang and Dick), it was fairly clear that he was not destined for a medical or even a dental career. It was not an issue of intelligence, it was simply one of interest, or rather his total lack of it. School Certificate was to be the last examination Stirling Moss ever took, at least on paper.

Stirling's childhood was a brief one, not simply because the persecution he suffered at school had propelled him into early adulthood, but for a simpler and earthier reason; raging hormones. Texcess of testosterone in his system, which would before long lay waste his mop of wavy hair, kicked in relatively early. By sixteen he was putting away childish things. He had, with his habitual foresight, applied for his driving licence in August 1945 at the age of fifteen years and eleven months, assuming that it might take some time to arrive. He had miscalculated though; due to the post-war shortage of motor cars, the licensing authorities spent most of their time drumming their fingers. Pleased to have something to do, they leaped at his application and processed it none too carefully. He was surprised to receive it back almost by return post. It was a shame to waste such a precious thing as a driving licence and there was a perfectly serviceable Morgan three-wheeler sitting in the garage awaiting his sixteenth birthday. It had been acquired with £50 of his equestrian prize money and the Austin 7. Into it he hopped while Alfred turned a blind eye.

Now that he was a proper motorist, he could scan the pages of *Motor Sport* magazine with a different perspective, particularly with his savings burning a hole in his pocket. The advertisement he saw there was tempting; a new car was being developed. It was to be powered by a revolutionary new engine with rotary valves, known as the Aspin. The Aspin was something of a hot issue in the enthusiasts' press, which Stirling read avidly. It promised much, although this writer's researches have failed to discover a single example actually in the metal. The car was the product of the Cowell-Watson

Partnership and it must be said was a somewhat speculative venture. All the happy punter had to do was send £50 as a 10 per cent deposit and be patient, which is what Stirling did.

His scheme to buy his own racing car might well have prospered were it not for his habitual neatness. He was silly enough to record this transaction on the stub of his chequebook; when Alfred saw it he was very, very angry. The issue of giving money to complete strangers was as bad as the fact that Stirling had not consulted him.

Alfred's first act was to confiscate the Morgan, which was disheartening. From our perspective this may seem high-handed, but then Alfred saw himself as a patriarch, with all the responsibilities and duties that went with that role. His immediate reaction to the thought of his only son racing cars was one of horror. Not only was it supremely dangerous, as he himself had learned, but it was, even worse, uneconomical. His view was that no one could really make a living at racing; it was something you paid to do rather than got paid for doing, and besides Stirling was supposed to be concentrating on retaking his School Certificate. Aileen dutifully agreed.

Stirling's contention, both uninformed and naïve at the time, that he might make a living at it, as opposed to running the dentistry business or doing anything else, enraged Alfred. It was an absurd proposition from Alfred's point of view, although he did concede that it was enjoyable. Basically, it was a hobby, not a business. There was a whiff of hypocrisy here. Alfred knew quite well that there were drivers in America, Barney Oldfield, Jimmy Murphy and Frank Lockhart, for example, who had made a great deal of money from racing as the motor industry started to cough up the resources necessary to fund the sport properly. He also knew that they generally managed to hold on to very little of it, but anyway, they were exceptional men. Further, his own little deceits in opting for the Indianapolis Dental School were conveniently forgotten. He also chose to ignore the fact that his son had made a decent enough sum of money from competing on a horse; enough, indeed, to buy the Morgan that Alfred was now confiscating. His immediate action was to call the hapless manufacturers and demand Stirling's money back. His son was a minor and therefore the contract was null and void.

After a token interval, during which Stirling was reduced to using a bicycle for transport ('totally humiliating'), Alfred relented. He had made his point. After a potentially dangerous accident in the Morgan, when the single rear tyre deflated, it was exchanged for a 1940 MG TB coupé. For Stirling, the new car was a great improvement, as the difficulties of canoodling in the narrow (and open) Morgan were something he had already encountered. The MG at least offered some protection from the weather.

UY 9599

Above: This Morgan was the first car that Aileen owned. Two years later she was winning races and rallies. A tiny Stirling looks out over the windscreen.

Stirling's plans for an elegant consummation of his first serious relationship with Sylvia, a local dental receptionist, were thwarted by the confines of the car, so he was pleased to be approached by the groom at the Long White Cloud, Bob Cowan, who had a desperate need to nip into Bray to buy some cigarettes. Could he perhaps borrow Stirling's new MG? Well, a thing is worth whatever you are prepared to give up for it, so the answer was an enthusiastic affirmative, with the rider that the price for the use of the car was the use of Bob's little

flat over the stables. Swiftly, the pair swapped keys, Cowan in a frenzy of nicotine deprivation, Stirling in the grip of something just as urgent, but rather more fundamental.

'But don't take the main road, you might meet my mother.'
'Fine, fine.'

So Bob didn't take the main road, he took the bumpier, unmade drive. And Sod's law dictated that he came upon Aileen, returning late from a shopping trip. After a flurry of interrogation, the reason for Bob being in Stirling's new car gradually emerged. Ruefully, he confessed all; Stirling was at that very moment preparing himself for the long-awaited denouement of his burgeoning relationship. Now, Aileen Moss was a rally driver. Whatever the unofficial course record for

the negotiation of that bumpy drive, she probably smashed it, reaching the stable yard in an elegant four-wheel drift just in time to interrupt events. The mixed feelings of a mother encountering her adored firstborn in a potential leg-over situation were quickly swept aside. The hapless Sylvia, *en deshabillée*, was questioned very closely as to whether this was really an 'appropriate way for a young lady to behave?' Bravely, Stirling stepped to the fore. Physically shielding the now-quaking target of his previously amorous attentions, he announced importantly: 'If you wish to speak with Sylvia, then I would prefer it if you spoke to me.'

If the instinctive negotiation for the real estate for this touching little tryst had been pure Alfred, then Stirling's defence of his rather compromised position was pure Ronald Colman. But Stirling did not (indeed does not) embarrass easily. Aileen was not by any measure a snob, but her son was a mere seventeen and she (more than many) knew full well the potential downside of such flings. For in reality, Stirling's cousin and wartime co-conspirator John Craufurd is in fact his half-brother, the result of a very brief and impulsive liaison of Aileen's in the spring of 1925 before she met Alfred. Thus Aileen was very well equipped indeed to know what can happen if you are not very, very careful.

Given the indignities he had suffered at school at the hands of sundry thuggish hearties, it is not surprising that Stirling became a dedicated student of the female sex, and nor is it odd that he takes his male friendships very seriously either, for there are relatively few of them. This, we suspect, is not entirely a function of the fact that many of them are dead.

If school had been that unpleasant then perhaps no one would be surprised if the recipients of such treatment turned their backs on these values and went their own way. For Stirling Moss though, the end of the war, the departure from school and the discovery of what it was he really wanted to do offered a rationalisation opportunity. He has never, until now, even mentioned the problems that he had suffered at school and perhaps his inability to tell Alfred what it had been like mandated a strategy that has suited him very well ever since; he tends to keep things to himself.

Left: Stirling and and his sister Pat with some of their trophies. They were a formidable pair in competition.

Above and facing page: First Alfred, then Stirling kept meticulous scrapbooks of family life, and later of his racing career. Photographs, memorabilia and newspaper clippings are contained within many dozens of volumes. These two pages are taken from Stirling's late teenage years.

2

The Learning Curve

Alfred knew that his son was competitive enough to make a racing driver, and now that it was clear that Stirling would never be a dentist, he started to reassess the options open to his son. Given his own adventures at Brooklands and Indianapolis, not to mention Aileen's exploits in her Marendaz, it would have been unfair of him to rule out motor sport altogether. He went so far as to buy yet another car, a pre-war BMW 328, in which he permitted Stirling to enter some trials, driving tests and rallies. It was very low-key competition, but in March 1947, on his first time out, Stirling won, bringing home the Cullen Cup in a trials tournament actually sponsored by Aileen. These events were not races *per se*; rather they were short distance hill-climbs and off-road mud-plugging. But nonetheless, it was his first event and he won it. Stirling readily confesses that he did not explore the limits of the BMW, but over the course of the year, he entered six events and won another of them.

He might have attempted more, but in return for the loan of the BMW he had taken a job as a trainee manager with Associated British Hotels. Based at the Ecclestone Hotel in Victoria, his training was, by the appalling standards of the day, comprehensive. He learned how to be a barman, a telephonist, a night porter, a *commis* chef. He was uneasy about his name though. He took the view that explaining to everyone he met that he was not named after the currency but a Scottish city was going to be something of a bore, so he decided to call himself Toni. It also gave him some anonymity, even the prospect of a double life if his plans came together.

But he was impatient; the life of a trainee is seldom his own, and his was no exception. There was much Saturday work and while he had found digs at Gunnersbury Avenue near Ealing Common, which cost £2/10 shillings a week, his salary was only 30 shillings a week gross, so he found himself running at a loss. Alfred made up the financial difference, but more critical was the fact that he was forced to work both night shifts and weekends. This would not do at all. He confessed to Alfred that the lack of weekends off was a problem, allowing

Previous page: With a great sigh of relief, Stirling found himself on four wheels instead of four hooves. His sister Pat jumps over the bonnet of his car.

Below and facing page: Silverstone, August 1948. *Équipe* Moss with the 500cc Cooper. Alfred wishes his son luck. Once he had accepted that Stirling's mind was made up about racing, he supported him totally.

his father to ambush him with a deal that was hard to refuse; Stirling would now become a farm labourer, working a minimum of 48 hours a week. Without particular regret, Stirling abandoned the digs in Ealing and moved back home. At least he knew that his mother would spoil him, however hard his father was going to make him work. And he did. This was to be more than a test of Stirling's resolution to race; the worst aspect of it was not the actual length of the working day, but the time he had to get up in the morning. Never an early riser, the pre-dawn start was a shock to his system.

Stirling has been a resolutely urban man ever since; the countryside for him merely represents something you drive through on your way to somewhere else. He still recalls his brief farming days with a shudder. 'Everywhere is a suburb of

London.' Alfred already employed Donatus Müller, a German POW who had opted to stay on after the war, and with Cowan, the three of them constituted Alfred's entire work force. It was only a small enterprise, but even twenty acres took looking after, particularly when there was livestock.

But Stirling was philosophical; provided he worked the required total of hours, Alfred allowed some flexibility – few motor race events started at dawn, so if the basic chores were done, mainly very early in the day, he could still manage to free up his weekends. In 1948, he would need to.

Artfully, Stirling contrived one day to drive the BMW, with Alfred aboard, past the Cooper Car Company headquarters in Surbiton. By happy coincidence, a shiny new Cooper Mark II was parked in the showroom. An enthusiastic Stirling

insisted that it be inspected closely. If Alfred knew he was being ambushed he didn't let on; he was nobody's fool.

Inside the works, he was pleased to see Charlie Cooper; the two men knew each other vaguely from the Brooklands days when Cooper was racing mechanic to Kaye Don during the heyday of the circuit. His participation in this project gave Alfred a measure of confidence which he had certainly lacked in Stirling's previous attempt to get behind the wheel of a racing car.

Cooper explained the basic philosophy behind the project. The little car's chassis was made from the front ends of two pre-war Fiat Topolinos. They were butt-welded together to produce a light chassis with independent suspension at each corner. Power, about 45 bhp, was delivered by a 500cc single-cylinder motorcycle engine which turned a solid rear axle via a chain drive. The engine was run on a volatile brew of methanol and used an hysterical compression ratio; this ordained a rather short productive life. A simple alloy body (there was less of a shortage of aluminium), and a rather basic seat completed the car. They were, Charlie Cooper conceded (he was a very conservative and slightly nervous sponsor of all this) selling like hot cakes.

Alfred was rather impressed by the ingenuity behind the product and after a token wrangle agreed that Stirling could buy one. The usual Moss rules applied, however. Stirling would have to dispose of enough belongings to raise the necessary *valuta*; Alfred would broker its disposal. Any

shortfall could be funded, but had to be worked for. Actually, Alfred never sold anything; he merely went through the motions of driving a hard bargain with his son. He simply stored everything. The strategy was a superficially hard one, but the purpose was simply to focus Stirling's attention and ensure that he was serious. Alfred had spotted very early on that there was an attractive but dangerously impulsive streak in his firstborn.

While the car was being built over the brutal winter of 1947–8, Alfred started to tap some of his patients for assistance. This was not purely penny-pinching on his part, as there were genuine shortages of almost everything and to obtain machinery and material was either a matter of joining a long queue or knowing someone on the inside. Alfred chose the latter route. Oil was not rationed, for example, merely very expensive, but the managing director of Sternol Oils was one of Alfred's patients and he undertook to supply a five-gallon drum of the precious fluid. Stanley Greening a director of J.A. Prestwich was another, and he made sure that the little powerplant that arrived was one of the better ones, selling it at a (small) discount. The engines had been originally built for speedway motorcycling; they were designed to turn over at optimum revs for the entire duration of the race so it was important that they were not down on

Below: Early days with huge starting grids and a great diversity of cars and talent.

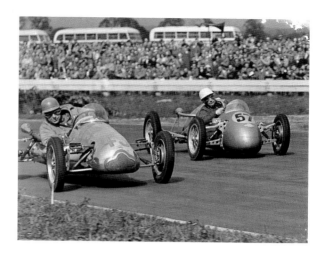

Left: Once the upholstery of the Cooper was modified to give him more support, Stirling's concentration was allowed a freer rein.

Above: The Ray Martin-built Kieft allows Stirling in number 57 the long way round.

Overleaf: The Kieft was constructed around Stirling. Its beautifully fabricated and lightened suspension allowed the power to be put down with confidence. Note the horseshoe with seven holes and the race number 7, which played a role too.

power. Even a few brake horsepower could make a vital difference, as 1 bhp was in effect two per cent of total power, so such small increments were vital. Alfred despite his external reservations started to think that he might actually enjoy this. As for his patients, they were probably well aware that it was not a good idea to upset one's dentist.

The Cooper was the first car Stirling had driven that had been put together purely for the purpose of racing, and modest though it was, it drew on a vast experience of competition, engineering and know-how. Stirling first sat in it on a deserted housing estate that was still under construction at Cippenham. The first thing he noticed was the extraordinary hand-numbing vibration from the solidly mounted single-cylinder engine. It was fed straight through the chassis and up the steering column. Happily, most of the events for which it was to be entered were short. Initially, Stirling drove it by instinct alone. The Cooper was a tiny, bouncy device that needed inspired handling if it was to realise its full potential. At the time of his début with the car, the Moss résumé included probably less than 3000 miles of automotive experience and racing drivers' schools were a thing of the distant future.

Notwithstanding this he entered the prestigious Shelsley

Walsh hill-climb in May 1948. His application was rejected on the grounds that the event was already over-subscribed. This was possibly just as well, as the little car was not even finished. Next up was the Bugatti owners' club meeting on May 9 at Prescott Hill. This time his entry was accepted and *Équipe* Moss marshalled its resources.

They were eccentric to say the least, but quite comprehensive. Alfred was the transport driver, his pre-war Rolls-Royce shooting brake towed a double horsebox (of which there was no shortage *chez* Moss) with its centre partition removed. In the Rolls were Aileen, Stirling, a frequently protesting sister Pat and their mechanic, Donatus Müller. It was Müller's experience as a BMW fitter that had probably led Alfred to buy the 328 in the first place. All the men wore overalls and although Stirling had initially wanted to wear a stylish linen racing helmet, Alfred had put his foot down about safety, acquiring a vast leather dispatch rider's

Above: On the start line at Brands Hatch, 1950.

Facing page: With his armpit clenched over the cockpit coaming, this image of young Stirling complete with unwieldy dispatch rider's helmet, appears in sharp contrast to the previous image.

skid lid that an embarrassed but philosophical Stirling had to wear. It certainly strengthened his neck muscles.

Stirling had never before driven a competition car in a race and he had never seen the sinuous Prescott hill-climb except as an occasional spectator. It was 1100 yards of narrow metalled road and Stirling broke the 500cc class record at

farting angrily, in a series of short point-to-point surges, connected by apparently untidy slides. The press were appreciative and the next event was at the new Stanmer Park course near Brighton. It was a little longer than Prescott, but this time Stirling, who knew as much as the next man about the course (nothing) managed a win.

They were eccentric to say the least
but quite comprehensive...

51.01 seconds. His new record did not stand for long, as more experienced drivers swiftly toppled it. Nevertheless he emerged with a credible fourth place in the process. Heads turned.

One small problem with the little Cooper was that it was engineered for bulkier people than Stirling. The cockpit was relatively wide and the seat unsupportive so he had no choice but to clench the cockpit coaming under his armpit. It made for a lurid spectacle as he powered the little car, its engine

More minor events came. The first circuit race was a month later at an aerodrome track of the Blackburn Aeroplane Company. The statistics spoke for themselves. First in practice, first in heat, fastest lap, first in final. Gradually, this would become a norm, but Stirling's rate of progress is best revealed by his performance back at Prescott on 18 July. His best time, to win fastest time of the day, had dropped to 49.5 seconds, an improvement of 3 per cent.

What had happened in the meantime? The car had

benefited from a few modifications; the chassis had been drilled for lightness, and the standard nuts and bolts had been replaced with self-locking nuts that, if they added little to the performance of the car, did much for Stirling's confidence that the vibration from the engine would not shake the machine apart. Alfred's experiences brought much to bear on this issue; he had raced at Indianapolis with every single nut and bolt welded solid on the instructions of Louis Chevrolet, and the car at least had finished. Mechanically, the valve area of the JAP engine was increased, the combustion chamber bulled to the nines with Duraglit metal polish, the brake drums were finely reamed out, the wheels balanced to within a few grams and an even higher compression piston – courtesy of Greening – was installed. It all combined to make a vital difference. A further tweak was extra seat stuffing at the sides so that Stirling was no longer obliged to lean from side to side as he drifted the car up the hill. This allowed him to relax. The more he relaxed, the quicker he became. He was learning what many already knew, that confidence in the machine and comfort in the cockpit are just as important as pure grunt. Most important, though, was the growth of his confidence in himself.

But for the young Stirling, there were other issues which inspired this confidence. The Moss household was a very superstitious one. This was mainly a function of Aileen's mild obsession with the number seven. Her birth date, 7 July, had much to do with it and it is a trait that Stirling picked up. Accordingly the traditional inverted horseshoe was applied, with seven nail holes.

The amount of effort that Alfred and Müller put into this project reflects a fast evolution of Pa Moss's attitude in terms of what his son might be capable of. Clearly he was enjoying this, just as he had enjoyed the sight of his son taking on boxing opponents before the war, or his horsemanship, but Alfred was to remain reluctant to commit fully (or openly) for some time yet, despite the evident pride that he took in what were extraordinary achievements. The big question in his mind was whether or not Stirling could actually make a living at this. Very few people did, after all, and many had gone broke – or far worse – trying.

As an inaugural season, 1948 accomplished much. Stirling was still keen rather than confident and still very much in the grip of the novelty of it all. Most importantly, he was learning. Not having had the experience of pre-war driving,

Left: Stirling's twin assets – extraordinary peripheral vision and absurd powers of concentration – allow him a brief wave to the photographer at Silverstone. Note the laid-back driving style.

he had less acclimatisation to undergo, a factor that was to handicap the older generation of drivers somewhat. In short, he felt no pressure to unlearn irrelevant or even downright bad habits. He had not crashed either and while he held vestiges of the young driver's belief that a car will overturn rather than slide if you corner too hard, he counted the 1948 season to have been an almost unqualified success.

For 1949, other possibilities opened up, not least of which was an engine twice the size and more. He was to continue campaigning in the 500cc cars until 1954, which caused

overseas event. It was to be the start of a long association with the informed and highly critical Italian fans. The fact that he won the 1100cc class by more than four minutes was startling enough; the fact that in practice he had out-qualified Mario Tadini aboard a V12 Ferrari was on the face of it unbelievable. He came in third overall. The £200 that he won was a very great deal of money to a nineteen-year-old, but as little compared to the instant adulation of the *tifosi*.

Not only was Lake Garda his most important race so far, but he made the acquaintance of childhood hero, Tazio

... and once Fleet Street had Stirling in its sights, it kept him there

eyebrows to be raised, but the 1949 season was to offer him a measure of international recognition as well as a rising reputation on the home front.

These larger-engined Cooper chassis could be entered in Formula B, where they could compete against unsupercharged cars of up to two litres. The tiny weight of the Cooper would allow it to give a good account of itself against larger competition. For those who found the cheap and cheerful 'poor man's racing' offered by the 500 class a little restricting, the lure of the Continent (Italy in particular) was a strong one.

July 1949 saw him at Lake Garda in Italy for his first

Nuvolari. For the awe-struck Stirling it had been a nigh-perfect weekend.

Back home, once Fleet Street had Stirling in its sights, it kept him there. His improbable youth, his evident and very boyish enthusiasm for what he was doing, and the ever-present support of Aileen and Alfred, ensured that there was usually a story somewhere. The cuttings files were opened and indeed have been getting fatter ever since. A particular fan was Kay Petre who wrote for the *Daily Graphic*; her citing of (and agreeing with) the opinion of Raymond Mays, that Stirling was 'the most promising of our young drivers', offered a startling and reassuring endorsement.

As the 1949 season wound down, Stirling made an important connection. At the Reubens hotel in Victoria, the 500 Club's end-of-season dinner dance had been organised by its new assistant secretary, Ken Gregory. Gregory had been working in the competitions department of the RAC in Pall Mall, and while the two men knew each other vaguely, they were not yet close. They shared a table along with another rising star, Peter Collins and as many young women as could possibly be seated around the table.

Gregory had witnessed Stirling winning the Madgwick Cup in September and while he was no expert on motor racing, he saw something in Stirling that interested him. The two men became close friends very quickly. Given that Stirling was living back at Bray with his parents, the fact that Gregory had a tiny flat in Kidderpore Avenue, Hampstead, was a particularly useful bonus, as it offered Stirling an operating base in London.

Above: Stirling confers with Ray Martin (kneeling) at Brands Hatch, 1951. Ken Gregory stands behind.

Facing page: Seven again. The 1950 RAC TT Dundrod victory served to put his career well and truly on the map.

Overleaf: 500 racing also became popular in Europe, as seen here at Zandvoort. It was a chaotic start to the development of an industry in Britain that would dominate the sport within a generation.

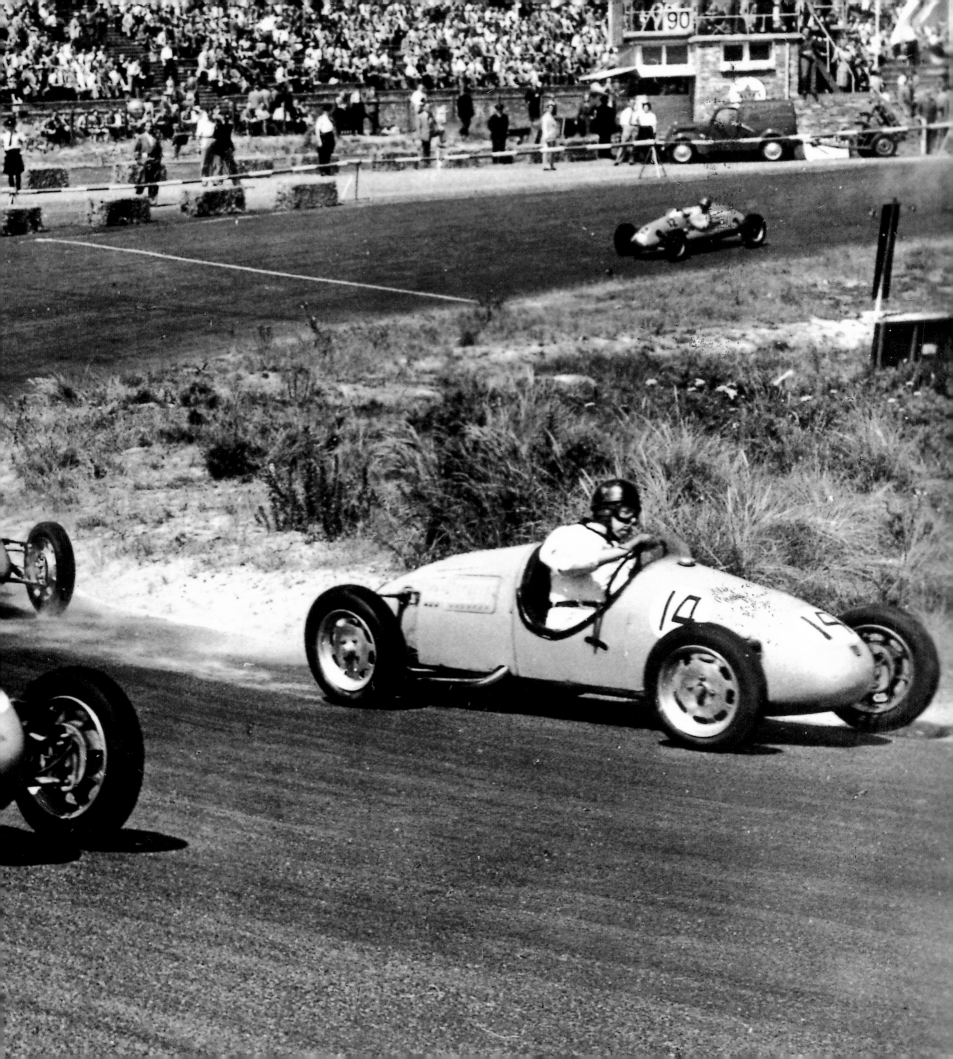

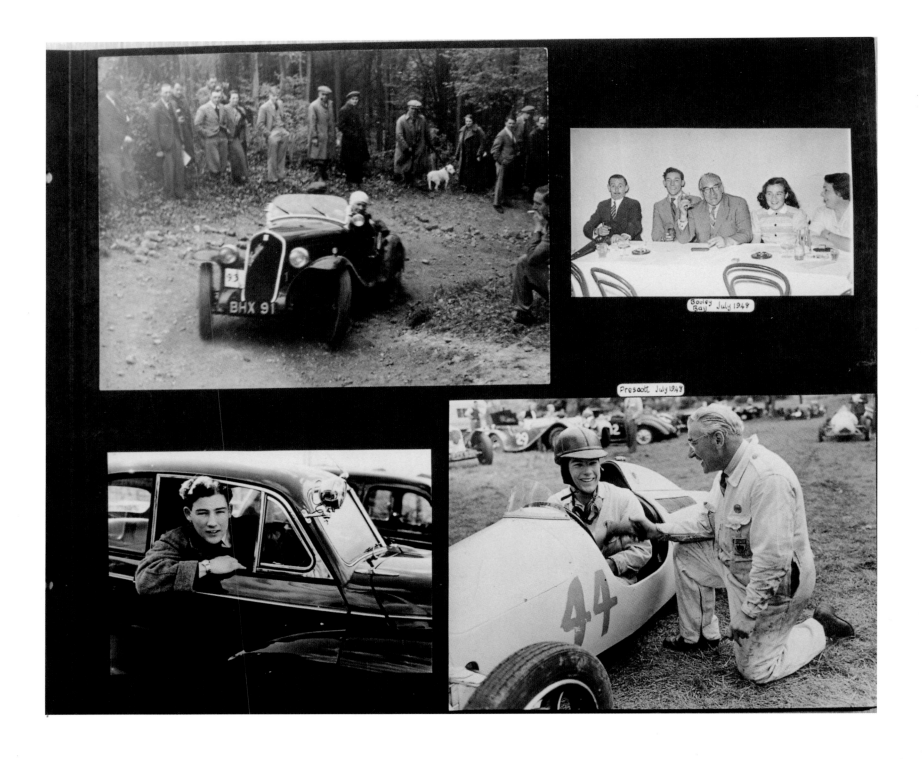

Bouley Bay July 1948

Prescott July 1948

Stirling's scrapbooks offer a unique view of an unparallelled career and soon the
press started paying attention. They never stopped. At this point press clippings
began to join the family snaps and memorabilia.

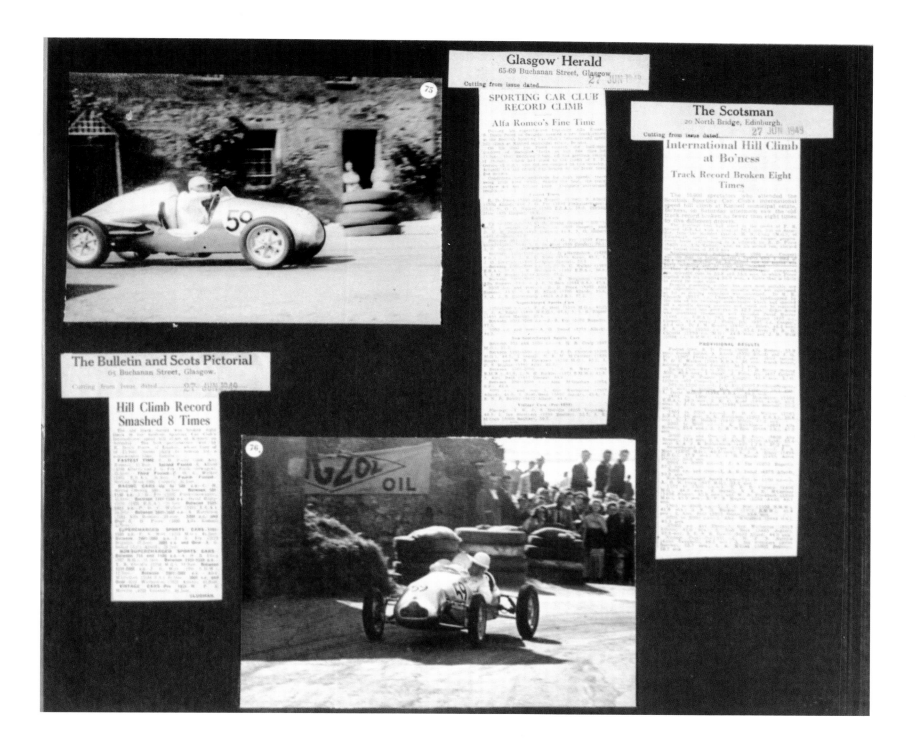

Glasgow Herald
65-69 Buchanan Street, Glasgow.
Cutting from issue dated........... 27 JUN 1949

SPORTING CAR CLUB RECORD CLIMB

Alfa Romeo's Fine Time

The Scotsman
20 North Bridge, Edinburgh.
Cutting from issue dated........... 27 JUN 1949

International Hill Climb at Bo'ness

Track Record Broken Eight Times

The Bulletin and Scots Pictorial
65 Buchanan Street, Glasgow.
Cutting from issue dated........... 27 JUN 1949

Hill Climb Record Smashed 8 Times

3

Recognition

It was the sight of a frenzied Oscar Moore hammering straight a bent valve stem over a rusty anvil in an ill-lit French country garage that made the chief mechanic of HWM decide that he had much to learn about motor racing. It was at Reims, in the high summer of 1949; Alf Francis had been with his employers, a small Surrey-based operation, for just over a year and was attending the Formula 2 race which supported the French *Grand Prix*. Their car came fifth.

While Raymond Mays *et al* were thrashing away at their grandiose BRM project under the eye of a sceptical public, a pair of well-brought-up garage owners in Walton-on-Thames were considering the business of motor racing through the other end of the telescope. They were George Abecassis and John Heath. Abecassis had had a good war; he had finished it as an RAF squadron leader with a DSO. Indeed, he might

have climbed even further had he not been shot down in 1944 and spent the remainder of the conflict as a prisoner of war. John Heath was, in modern parlance, a petrolhead. While Abecassis had been flying perilous missions in lumbering Stirling bombers, Heath had spent his war at Lagonda in Staines, working on sundry military projects that had been the lot of that firm in fulfilling its obligations to the defence of the realm. After that he started a machine shop of his own in Hersham, Surrey, to fulfil subcontracts to Vickers-Armstrong. Vickers occupied the nearby Brooklands site where Abecassis had been a well-known racing driver before the war and where the pair had first met.

In 1945 they bought a redundant building from Vickers in New Zealand Avenue, Walton-on-Thames and established Hersham and Walton Motors (HWM) and after obtaining a

Citroën agency, commenced selling 'proper' motor cars.

Post-war, it was a very good business; cars were scarce and customers were plentiful. Prices spiralled and as a result, the business prospered. By early 1948, Heath and Abecassis had decided to go racing. Their stable was exotic, but mainly pre-war, consisting of a Bugatti type 59, a Maserati 4CL and two newer Altas, one a streamlined sports racer, the other a 1500cc blown *Grand Prix* car. These last were the work of Geoffrey Taylor, whose business was in nearby Tolworth on the outskirts of Kingston upon Thames; almost within earshot was the Cooper Car Company in Surbiton. Abecassis bought one of its cars too. It was nearly to be his undoing.

In April 1948, Heath and Abecassis hired an ex-diesel fitter to work as mechanic for the Alta racing cars. He hailed from Grudziadz, Poland and had spent his war in the Polish Brigade. His given name was Alphons Kovaleski, but he became better known as Alf Francis. It was he who later marvelled at Oscar Moore's pragmatic metal-bashing.

Francis did not initially think that this outfit took what it did very seriously. His first encounter with Duncan Hamilton, who managed the pit at a minor race in Jersey that Francis attended as a taster, left him with the distinct impression that the whole purpose of the exercise was to have a no-holds-barred party afterwards, whatever the result of the race had been. Never a particularly light-hearted man, Francis viewed this introduction to the British sporting gent with some misgivings, but then again, it has to be said that he did not voluntarily leave the sport either.

Francis's main responsibility, the *Grand Prix* Alta car, was an unlucky machine, and Heath and Abecassis decided at the end of 1948 to build their own effort for the 1949 season. Their target was to be Formula 2, as events were springing up all over Europe; the main priority was that it be cheap and reliable, coupled with the possibility of converting the car quickly for road use or sports car events.

The new car, the HW-Alta, debuted on the Easter Monday meeting at Goodwood in 1949. Driven by John Heath, it came fourth in the Lavant Cup. It was, in fact, to have a startlingly good 1949 season, winning the Manx Cup and coming second at the Formula 2 race at Comminges in France. The car had proved itself to be competitive with the best of the European efforts and the process was pleasingly cost-effective. The car had few of the tool-room-built qualities of the BRM, but it was a well-thought out special that worked. It was decided that the HW-Alta could form the basis of a rather more serious effort for 1950.

The first thought after that was to build a trio of cars for Le Mans, as the team had been offered space by the HRG Company and this was the mainspring for production. Le Mans was not to be, in fact, as there was no starting money offered, so the cars were destined for single-seater events. There were five of them; a working 'mule' which was used as a pilot project and four others, three of which would be driven by Abecassis, Heath and another driver for whom they were now searching. The fourth car was sold, usefully lowering the average cost of the others.

Stirling Moss had certainly drawn attention to himself by the time they realised that an extra driver would be needed, but the verdict on him was by no means unanimous. Francis,

Facing page: Scrapbook entry from the early days of an unparalleled career.

Below: 500 racing soon became the official Formula 3.

Previous pages: Keeping his public happy by signing autographs.

who was no driver himself, actually viewed the youngster with some suspicion, refusing to believe that he could keep up the pace that he was setting in his little Cooper with any consistency. The view was echoed elsewhere too; the feeling was that he was driving over his head and once he made a mistake he would come to his senses, slow his pace and sink into obscurity. This was a mark of the polite disbelief with which he was regarded, perhaps overlaid with envy.

Francis was to revise his opinion somewhat at the Manx Cup meeting on 26 May, 1949. The HWM team fielded Abecassis' 1-litre Cooper and was delighted when he set the fastest time of the day in practice, until Stirling beat it. Abecassis recovered his place and as the team started to load the Cooper, Stirling promptly beat it again. Abecassis unwisely rigged a wooden block in the cockpit in order to be able to brace himself properly and set off again. He failed to complete a circuit and smashed into a tree. Perhaps there was more to this Stirling Moss than met the eye.

The approach from HWM came in the winter of 1949 on a freezing dank airfield at Odiham. It did not start well, as Abecassis managed to spin the car even before Stirling climbed in. When he did, he managed to crack the sump on a redundant landing light that he had not expected to come across. 'They were very good about it,' Stirling recalled. He was offered a modest contract for the upcoming season.

Meanwhile, the fourteen-year lease on Long White Cloud had expired. Alfred negotiated to buy a large Edwardian House at Tring, in Hertfordshire, which had a more substantial acreage. It had been the home farm of the nearby Rothschild estate and its facilities suited both Pat and Aileen's interest in horses, and Stirling (and Alfred's) interest in cars. It became the effective headquarters of *Équipe* Moss. Alfred named it the White Cloud Farm.

As the 1950 season got underway, the mini-circus that was HWM started to storm all across Europe. The drivers Moss, Heath and Abecassis travelled about in a company Citroën, the long-suffering mechanics brought up the rear with the cars, spares and tools. Money was always tight, for the mechanics at least, and the attraction of starting money was very often the mainspring of the decision about where to race. As the team achieved more exposure the starting money began to rise and, although Francis was in constant conflict with Heath over cash and expenses (the crew was often compelled to live on credit from comparative strangers), by the end of the 1950 season it was as professional as it could

Left: John Heath in flying jacket, Alf Francis in the beret and Frank Nagel looking at the Formula 2 HWM.

be. There were, however, other frictions at work that often required the emollient skills of Abecassis; he became the peacemaker between Heath, who as an owner demanded obedience, and Francis, who as chief mechanic demanded discretion. It was not always an easy task, but Abecassis was an excellent diplomacist.

George Abecassis played a lesser role in racing the single seaters as the team progressed; there was a business to run at home, after all. He drove for Aston Martin and after sharing a DB2 with Lance Macklin (at Macklin's invitation) in the 1950 Le Mans race, he reciprocated by offering him a job as an HWM Formula 2 driver. John Heath, who at well over six feet tall was less than ideally built for the job, again

form, Farina in the lead, came barging through with a casual disdain for the slower car, but as he passed Stirling, he started to come unstuck, lost his line, and Stirling, displaying an instinct that would become a trademark, took the opportunity to steal his place back. This little episode was certainly not lost on Fangio, who found Farina's evident discomfiture hugely funny and a proper payback for such ungentlemanly conduct.

The HWM also offered Stirling a very chilling acquaintance with danger, as well as a lesson in the risks of ignoring pit signals. The moment came two weeks later in the Naples *Grand Prix*. The HWMs of Moss and Macklin were in the lead, the nimble green cars able to compensate for

As the team achieved more exposure the starting money began to rise

completed the trio of works drivers.

The arrival of Macklin on the scene at Reims in July 1950 was to have an important effect on Stirling. On the face of it the two men had very little in common as Macklin was ten years Stirling's senior, had seen war service in the Navy and was by any standards a sophisticated man, multilingual, well-travelled and an Olympic-class skier. If there was ever an exemplar of the image of the 1950s racing driver, it was probably Lance Macklin.

But quickly the two men (or rather, the man and the boy) identified common ground. They both adored girls, for example, and when Macklin suggested that Stirling might like to meet Miss Italy who was staying, according to Macklin, on the French Riviera, Stirling agreed with alacrity. The only trouble was, Macklin and Moss were miles away at the time, awaiting the Bari *Grand Prix* in southern Italy. That problem was solved by borrowing John Heath's Citroën and covering the distance non-stop. When they arrived to discover that they had missed their target by only a few hours, the pair were philosophical; they simply turned round and drove back to Bari.

It was this Bari race on 9 July, 1950 that revealed a hint of things to come. Stirling, struggling somewhat against Farina and Fangio in their *Alfettas*, was about to be lapped. True to

their relative lack of power by their manoeuvrability and, it must be said, the skill of their drivers. Stirling came up to lap (for the second time) a back marker, Berardo Taraschi, aboard a tiny 750cc device. There had been some talk that the engine of the HWM would need water due to a fault in a sealing ring; the Moss plan was to build up as much space as possible between himself and any challenger so that the water-level could be topped up in comfort. Alf Francis had been frantically signalling him to ease off. Taraschi waved him past, but as Stirling set the HWM up to go by in a four-wheel drift, the Italian lost control of his own car. The tail swung out and collided with Stirling's front wheel, bursting the tyre.

Stirling, committed to his drift, could do nothing; the HWM arrowed off the track and collided with a tree at more than 80 mph. Stirling was stunned, broke a kneecap and his four top front teeth. This did not stop him scrambling, on auto-pilot, out of the car and getting as far from it as he could lest it explode. The records were replete with examples of drivers with relatively minor injuries dying ghastly deaths as their wrecked cars burst into flames; one early hero of Stirling's, Richard Seaman, had perished in just this way and many more would in the future. Lance Macklin won the race, but a dazed Stirling ended up in plaster.

Had the HWM been flimsier, the crash could easily have proved fatal, but these cars were and are amazingly sturdy. That they paid a price against lighter opposition was clear, but one driver at least had every reason to be grateful for the

Facing page: Stirling discusses his tyres with 'Dunlop Mac', the tyre manufacturer's racing representative.

hard work of their makers. Stirling could have done nothing about the incident itself, although the realisation that a puncture or a stub axle failure would have had the same effect must have given him pause for thought, particularly as HWMs started to suffer from such breakages. An alarmed Alfred, alerted by Reuters, flew out to bring his son back to Blighty.

Stirling's attitude to pain was very simple; he put up with it. The cosmetic effect of losing one's front teeth was actually far more distressing to him – he was but twenty years old after all; Alfred ensured that he was not gappy long and took particular care in making an extremely sophisticated 'spoon' denture for his son the very day he returned. It was a very clever piece of engineering and comparatively rare. The knee was in plaster for a fortnight, but healed quickly enough to allow Stirling back into a racing car before the end of August. The accident did not dent his confidence in racing, but the unaccustomed presence of false teeth hardly helped his natural shyness. He was starting to suffer for his art.

Alfred avoided trying to put his son off his chosen career path; he realised it was fruitless. Any doubts that he may have had about Stirling's abilities were fast disappearing anyway, and to take advantage of the Naples crash would

have been grossly unfair of him, so he kept quiet. One can fall off a horse and do more damage, as he himself knew to his cost. The events of the next September were to serve notice to him that further resistance would be futile anyway.

As Macklin started to take Stirling under his wing, the younger man realised that there was much he could learn from him. The finer points of the finer things in life were second nature to Macklin, from where to find a decent tailor or pair of loafers, to which restaurant made the finest zabaglione; he seemed to have a bottomless store of information on all these vital matters. Macklin was also a very fine driver.

The RAC Tourist Trophy race at Dundrod was potentially one of the classiest events on the UK racing calendar and 16 September, 1950 was to mark its post-war revival. Previously, the event had been run at the Ards circuit, but the Ulster Automobile Club felt that perhaps a fresh start was called for. It resolved to create a course using existing roads, which was an unpromising triangle of narrow country lanes with zero facilities and even worse visibility. It was also potentially very dangerous. Given that it was in Northern Ireland, just west of Belfast, no one would be very surprised if it rained either. During the summer and particularly during his

convalescence with the broken knee, Stirling had gone through the entire *Observer's Book of Automobiles* in an attempt to find himself a drive. He was a little indignant to be turned down by every single prospect, even MG. He had, he reasoned, driven in nineteen races and won eleven of them. He had led a minor *Grand Prix* against decent opposition at Naples and on 7 August had set a new class lap record at Brands Hatch, but these virtuoso performances from one so young were perhaps exactly the problem.

His friend Ken Gregory had been lobbying on his behalf too. Gregory, working as he did in the competition department of the RAC, was well placed to put in some useful PR on Stirling's behalf and had spoken at length to Leslie Johnson, the team leader of the Jaguar works effort. To Johnson, Stirling seemed improbably young and therefore

far too inexperienced to handle the new XK120, which had taken the country by storm since its launch (ironically as something of a stopgap) in 1948. Gregory, too, received a dismissive brush-off.

Help was at hand though. The motoring correspondent of the *Daily Herald*, Tommy Wisdom, was a friend of Alfred's. As both a highly successful driver and a prominent journalist he had, for public relations reasons, been allowed to buy a works-prepared XK for his own use. Jaguar had expected him to enter the TT to back up their core works effort, but he took the view that Stirling would stand a better chance than he would himself. He opted to enter in a Jowett Jupiter which he had been offered; a splendid machine, as anyone who owns one will tell you, but hardly competitive. Wisdom offered Stirling a 50:50 split on any winnings and even persuaded William Lyons to lend the boy wonder an ordinary road car for acclimatisation purposes. Lyons assented.

An account of this extraordinary event is unnecessary, save to say that Stirling won it in pouring rain, set a new circuit record and won £140 before handing a delighted Tommy Wisdom his cut. He had driven a virtually perfect race. Alfred had accompanied him as pit crew and in his excitement had urged his son to go faster and faster, which

Facing page: The superb shape of the C-type, penned by Malcolm Sayer, allowed a top speed of 150 mph on a very light throttle. For what was basically a production engine, it was an extraordinary achievement.

Top: At Le Mans 1951, Stirling led in the C-type after 8 hours, when an oil pipe gave out. He broke the lap record three times.

Overleaf: Stirling aboard Gilby Engineering's Frazer-Nash at the British Empire Trophy, Isle of Man, June 1951.

Stirling obligingly did. Leslie Johnson was a humbled but thoughtful seventh. Still a minor until midnight that night, Stirling was approached by William Lyons; would he lead the Jaguar team for 1951? Alfred was present too and this was one contract that he was not about to void on the grounds of his son's minority status. There have been several significant moments in Stirling's career and this was one of them. As Stirling eagerly assented, Alfred saw, probably with some regret, the instant diminution of his role as Stirling's protector. Despite his pride, he probably went to bed that night a very thoughtful man indeed, but his son woke up on the morning of 17 September, 1950 as an acknowledged professional racing driver. It would be his living for the next eleven and a half years. Perhaps in recognition of this fact Lofty England received a rather touching letter dated 20 September which read:

Dear Lofty
I am enclosing a cheque (£25) which I should like you to split up into three £5, one each for the boys, and with the remaining £10 would you buy yourself something to remember the occasion by. I would have bought this gift, but quite honestly I haven't a clue about what you have & haven't. Please thank Mr Heynes and Mr Lyons for allowing me to drive the XK and tell them I am looking forward to the next time! Cheerio.
Stirling

A week later England replied with grave courtesy.

Dear Stirling
Very many thanks indeed for your letter of the 20th September and for your very nice gesture in forwarding a

cheque to me from which I am to give the three mechanics who were in Ireland the sum of £5 each in appreciation of their services during the RAC TT race. This I have done and they are really most apppreciative of your generosity and, in fact, a little overwhelmed since they were already very happy to have been associated with your success.

With regard to your very nice suggestion that with the remaining £10 I should buy myself something, I very much appreciate this but would assure you that I have already received all the reward I require in the knowledge that you were satisfied with the car and of the very satisfactory result which was obtained through your efforts. As there is really nothing I require I trust you will not be offended if I enclose a cheque for you for £10. I think you will have already heard from Mr Heynes that

we would like you to do some driving for us next year and I sincerely trust you will be able to do so since I was most impressed with your general attitude to motor racing, which was something reminiscent of the days gone by when I worked for Seaman and Bira.
My very best regards
E.R.W. England
Service Manager

Because of time pressure, Stirling delayed the formal celebration of his majority until the following afternoon; he flew back, properly elated, to the Brands Hatch 500cc races, to be held the next day and threw a tea dance, of all things,

Below: August 1953; the Goodwood nine-hours race.

for his colleagues. His fellow 500 competitor Stan Coldham had something rather more robust in mind for his young friend than a tea-dance and brought Stirling's twenty-first birthday present to the party. Her name, it transpired (as she gave him a friendly squeeze on the dance floor), was Yvonne.

Yvonne, a member of the *Folies Bergère*, lived in a basement flat which she shared with three other girls at 13 Bolton Street in the West End of London. Her presence in Stirling's life was an agreeable interlude, and served to introduce him to a world of which he had little prior knowledge. With very little hesitation Stirling moved in. This was raffish behaviour (to say the least) in 1950, but then the Moss family had always made its own rules. Stirling had learned to his cost that so did many others. At Dundrod, he had met a charming chancer who lived in the Irish Republic. He had explained to Stirling, who particularly wanted to buy a Nash 'Rambler' so that he could both travel about and

lay down five cars for the next season. These were not the offset two-seaters of the type made so far, but were purpose-built to contest European Formula 2, which was emerging as a lucrative and well-supported class. Not for HWM the agonies of attempting to compete against well-funded Italian works teams and the humiliation that would probably go along with it. From the outset, both Heath and Abecassis had agreed that motor racing should pay its way and so it did.

During the 1951 season Heath's relationship with Francis started to hit new lows. The strain of flogging around Europe was telling on the mechanics and the poor performance of the Alta engine added to their burden. A further problem, which affected the whole team, was Heath's infatuation with a young lady who had very expensive tastes. If money had been tight in 1950, then 1951 was far worse. Reading Francis's memoirs, one gathers that the differences between the two men on a strictly professional level were exacerbated

Stan Coldham had something rather more robust in mind. . .

sleep in it, that despite the unavailability of such imports in England, there was no such shortage south of the border, for cash of course. He knew a bloke. Eagerly, Stirling handed over a hard-earned £1000 so that the chap could acquire this vehicle; Stirling never saw him or his money again. He later reflected: 'I think if you are going to be conned properly, it's really very important that the crook should be charming. He certainly was.'

Despite its unpromising start in 1950, Stirling's relationship with Leslie Johnson actually blossomed – for a while. The older man, like many pre-war drivers who still competed, rather took Stirling under his wing. There were aspects of the sport, particularly financial ones, with which Stirling was less than familiar and about which Alfred knew absolutely nothing; Johnson, a successful businessman in his own right, was quite well informed. What Macklin had done for Stirling in sartorial and social terms, Johnson helped to do in commercial terms.

The Dundrod race was not only the event that brought him to national prominence outside the sport, but it finally assured him (and Alfred) that he could do this for a living.

At the end of the 1950 season the three works HWM cars were sold off; they found ready buyers, one of whom was Oscar Moore (he of the Irish spanner), and work began to

by a feeling on Francis's part that he was just hired help and that his input was required not as contributor but merely as repair man. He was probably correct in this assumption and he left the firm, bearing no grudges, at the end of 1951.

After years of development and a huge racing mileage at circuits no longer remembered, all those who had driven the HWMs knew they handled very well but simply did not have the power to compete with the Continental opposition, or indeed simpler cars like Cooper Bristols. However, they had been developed originally as hybrid sports/single-seaters, and as entrants tired of the unreliability of the Alta engines, it was to this original purpose that the marque started to veer.

For Stirling, the whole HWM experience was a matter of an agreeable lifestyle as much as anything else. He learned a huge amount about cars, of course, but the opportunity to race, coupled with the opportunity to travel, was enriching. Most people simply did not travel in the early 1950s; many who had served in the forces had probably seen enough and the economics of the post-war period rather mitigated against it, unless one was fortunate enough to be wealthy.

The *ad hoc* nature of the circuits, some of which were

Facing page: Stirling at Reims for the French *Grand Prix*, 1953. Note the body belt.

literally set up the night before practice by the simple expedient of laying out straw bales, offered Stirling an unparalleled opportunity to use his own judgement. There were seldom any distance markers, for example, so he used his own judgement about when to brake; later, on more established circuits, onlookers were bemused by the fact that he seemed to pick his own markers rather than using those supplied already; but he knew by then that many of them were not particularly accurate.

One circuit which was not so hastily designed was Monza. Stirling had never raced there before he was entered for the *Grand Prix* on 13 May, 1951. There was also a technical phenomenon which was new to him; the aerodynamic effect of slipstreaming. The simple displacement of air afforded by the progress of one car has the effect of lowering the air resistance for the following car, provided it is close enough. Thus Stirling found that the dumpy little HWM could maintain very high speeds and also spare its engine by simply following the car in front, even though that car might be in an entirely different performance universe. It was a lesson that he would start to apply more and more.

Compared with the previous year, 1951 was to be slightly anti-climactic; it also brought the start of a very difficult relationship with Enzo Ferrari. The initial approach came via a telegram from Modena, routed through the British Racing Drivers' Club, offering Stirling two drives: the non-championship Rouen *Grand Prix* as well as the British *Grand Prix* at Silverstone. Stirling was committed to HWM for Rouen, but he tried to accept the Silverstone ride. This was when he realised that Ferrari did not do business that way – it was either both or neither.

Ferrari issued another offer straight after Rouen and Stirling went to Modena to discuss it. On the face of it, the offer was outstanding. Either a race at Bari on 2 September, or the Italian *Grand Prix* on 16 September, the day before Stirling's twenty-second birthday, or possibly both. All being well, Moss would accompany the team to South America over the winter for the *Temporada* series and then (and this was the prize) there could be a full Formula 1 contract for the 1952 season. The conversation was conducted in a cocktail of languages, mainly French, which in Stirling's case was very much of the schoolboy kind. He accepted, cautiously, because he knew that BRM was also a possibility, albeit a tricky one; he had driven it already and a very strange device it was.

This was a significant development for him. The Ferrari

Left: The ERA G-type. The design would eventually prosper (as a Bristol) but not in Stirling's hands.

works team was, next to the mighty Alfa Romeo, without doubt the premier racing organisation in Italy, which in 1951 meant the entire world. The prospect of a career racing for Ferrari was of much more importance than the measly amount of money offered, for it was well known that Ferrari drivers drove purely for the honour of it, not the financial reward. With Enzo Ferrari holding the purse strings, they had little choice.

Thus, apart from an offer from Alfa Romeo, this was the top of the tree and he was not yet twenty-two. A predictably delighted Alfred accompanied Stirling to Bari at the end of August, hoping that the car on offer, a brand new four-cylinder Tipo 500, designed by Aurelio Lampredi, would be waiting. Stirling did not even get to start the engine. When a mechanic found him trying the cockpit out for size, he was brusquely told to get out and leave the car alone – it was for Piero Taruffi. In later years, Stirling's temper has become a short, sharp thing, which does not last long before equanimity reasserts itself. Not so then. He presumed that he

was being made a fool of and that, for ten years, was that. Ferrari was clearly 'no gentleman'.

This was exactly the point. Enzo Ferrari did not operate like a gentleman and never displayed any pretensions to gentility; neither Alfred nor Stirling fully appreciated this fact. Alfred, schooled in the sport at Indianapolis and Brooklands and himself a very plain dealer under all circumstances, was as taken aback and cross as Stirling was.

Stirling did actually drive a Ferrari at the meeting, albeit only in practice. The car belonged to David Murray, a Scottish amateur who would later found *Ecurie Ecosse*. The car was third-hand, ex-works, ex-Peter Whitehead and now campaigned in by Murray as a Formula 2 machine. Stirling persuaded the Bari Club to increase Murray's starting money (even if he did not drive the car), and set to work.

Critically, Murray's Ferrari had a centre throttle, as many racers (particularly Italian ones) did and Stirling made the classic error, accelerating when he should have braked, and bent the car badly. It was repaired before the engine let go

later in the session. All in all it was an embarrassing end to a fruitless outing, or almost; Stirling managed to obtain some expenses from the organisers for both himself and Murray, £50 or so, but he knew that you could only live for a fortnight on that.

Raymond Mays had also spotted Stirling as a talented driver quite early on; he was one of the few who realised, as he had told Kay Petre that the boy was not overcooking his driving as much as some seemed to think, and Stirling's later performances had not given him any reason to reconsider that view. He had approached Alfred several times in the 1950 season to enquire about Stirling's availability to drive the new BRM, but as Alfred had mandated that 1950 was to be a trial year, after which Stirling's future would be finally decided, his response to Mays had been wary. By the end of 1951, it was clear that Stirling's career path was set. He was also totally free to make up his own mind now that he was no longer a minor, and accordingly Stirling had arranged to try the car out in July 1951, before the Bari episode.

Many people agreed that there was something very, very odd going on at BRM. The sight of Raymond Mays' octogenarian mother haughtily disinfecting a car with a Flit gun after Mrs Peter Berthon had alighted from it was a bemusing one, particularly for those who did not necessarily realise that Berthon himself had already had an affair with the dismissive old lady. Some did suspect that he was conducting an occasional affair with Mays himself. Diverting though all this might have been (and certainly highly amusing for the mechanics), it did little to further an atmosphere of focused creativity. For many who knew the reality of the situation it was always going to be very hard to take BRM seriously, but Stirling was still ignorant of anything untoward as he presented himself at Folkingham airfield in July 1951.

Initially, the BRM car was merely confusing. It was undeniably beautiful and apparently extremely well-made. It was also incredibly powerful, with excellent brakes. It would clearly go and stop, but the vital part in between seemed somehow unfinished.

Stirling undertook to drive it though, and August found him at Monza where the car was being tested under the instructions of the Owen Racing Organisation. While being warmed up, the engine broke a piston. Given that it took several days for the mechanics to strip it down, let alone repair it, there was much leisure time.

Facing page: The Monaco *Grand Prix* was run for sports cars in 1952 and so was the warm-up. Stirling set pole position in the Frazer-Nash, but had to retire.

Above right: As ever, signing autographs.

Overleaf: The crowded start of the 1953 British Empire Trophy Race.

On the face of it, the similarities between the BRM and the current benchmark, the Alfa Romeo 159 *Alfetta*, were extraordinary, but the Alfa was an evolved car (its antecedent had first raced in 1938), whereas the BRM was an attempt to reinvent the best of pre-war engineering. Tony Rudd, who was 'on loan' from Rolls-Royce to BRM (he would actually stay until 1969) was at Monza for that testing. He recalled: 'They [Alfa Romeo] were quite Teutonic, actually, no Italian excitement – they were calm and efficient.'

Mischievously, the chief engineer of Alfa Romeo, Giovanni-Battista Guidotti offered Stirling a test drive in the *Alfetta* which Fangio was testing at the time. It was, in comparison with the BRM, a revelation to him, the first of many in his career. Strong, fast and precise, albeit with relatively poor brakes compared with the BRM's discs, the car made it easy to see how the Alfa marque had exercised such total dominance; the BRM was almost a pastiche of a car alongside it. It made the HWM seem a little workaday as well. It became clear, very quickly, that the whole ethos behind Italian motor racing was radically and fundamentally different from the British sport. This little episode was revealing; Guidotti, who had accompanied Tazio Nuvolari in his victory in the seventh *Mille Miglia* in 1933, usually concealed the *Alfetta* from prying eyes like the school swot; but Nuvolari had already announced at Lake Garda in 1949, to anyone who listened, his opinion of Stirling: 'Watch him – he will be one of the great ones.'

The BRM was ridiculed by a cynical and irritated public, even outside the relatively small circle of motor racing. No-account stand-up comedians laughed at it, the press laughed at it and other builders, no matter how humble their own product, guffawed. The most damaging aspect of the matter, though ignored at the time, was the simply staggering

amount of money which it absorbed.

But 1951 also offered Stirling the chance of being a manufacturer himself, albeit in a very modest way. Cyril Kieft, a South Wales industrialist, had produced a Formula 3 car which was, as a first effort, promising. It was not as well thought out as a machine which Stirling and a team of colleagues were designing. Dean Delamont of the RAC, John A. Cooper, late of BRM but by then the sports editor of *The Autocar*, and Ray Martin, a gifted mechanic, were in the throes of producing a one-off machine that would solve some of the shortcomings of the existing Cooper design. It was a good machine. Ken Gregory, who had driven Kieft's first design in the spring of 1950, completed the team. Kieft rapidly realised that his own product was lacking in sophistication and agreed to incorporate many of the features of the new car in his own product, and better, he would pay for the privilege. Both Stirling and Gregory would become directors of the Kieft company.

Upon returning from Monza and Bari, there was another approach from Ferrari waiting, re-offering him a works drive for 1952. He declined and thus began, professionally at least,

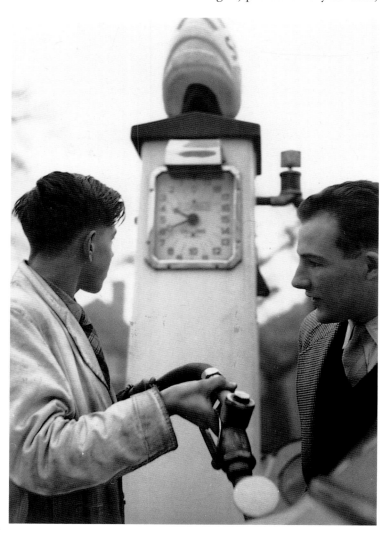

an absolutely dire two years.

But there was rallying. Norman Garrad, head of the modest competition department at Rootes Group, asked Stirling if he would care for a crack at the Monte Carlo Rally in January 1952. Why not? Stirling rounded up John *Autocar* Cooper and Desmond Scannell of the British Racing Drivers' Club (BRDC). A complement of three was, he calculated, well worth the weight penalty in terms of the ability to push the humble Sunbeam-Talbot 90 – a real bank manager's car – out of any ditches in which it found itself. In fact, the trio did pleasingly well. Despite some beginner's mistakes, they managed to place second overall, only four seconds adrift of the very competent Sydney Allard, which made the £50 Stirling was paid seem very good value. Rallying was, by comparison with single-seaters, quite diverting, if only because of the extra disciplines imposed by the rules: it is a matter of correct average speeds rather than outright pace; it is very precise. Many racing drivers despise it, but Stirling does not. It is, after all, competition.

In fact, Stirling was to turn into something of a rally star and his relationship with Rootes was to bear fruit well into the future, particularly because he was able to call upon their good offices for both his own and, much more importantly, another man's benefit.

But in the world of single-seater racing, with the retirement of the Alfa Romeo works team and the apparently abject failure of the BRM project, the FIA pressed the panic button and proper Formula 1 was now effectively cancelled, to be replaced by the current Formula 2 regulations. No one seemed to have a suitable car for the 1952 season.

One who did or claimed he did was Leslie Johnson, who had bought the rump of Mays and Berthon's pre-war company, ERA. Johnson's core business was furniture; he owned a large factory in Walthamstow, so the ERA venture, sited in Bedfordshire, was something of an indulgence. His new car, the G-type, was the work of a designer called David Hodkin. Like the work of his predecessor, Professor Robert Eberan von Eberhorst, who had moved (with relief) to Aston Martin, the chassis was of the 'two bloody great tubes' school, but imaginatively constructed of the wonder metal Elektron. It was certainly very stiff, as well as light, at least on its own, but most of that advantage was lost when the whole car was put together. It was to be powered by a dry-sumped version of the Bristol engine for which Cooper had designed its new chassis. In this form, the engine managed to be eerily (and uncharacteristically) unreliable.

At that stage the ERA car was underdeveloped and ugly with it. It would prosper in time, but only after Johnson decided to cut his losses and sell the entire project to Bristol who then developed the general concept into a successful Le Mans car, albeit a much better-looking one than the ERA. This was a pity for Johnson, who never really had the resources, or perhaps the determination, to develop it. It is likely that he hoped that its driver would make up the shortfalls from which the car clearly suffered.

But those Le Mans days were still ahead as Stirling struggled with the machine; he remembers it as a triumph of Johnson's salesmanship over the quality of his product but it is fair to say that at least the car did not, in Stirling's hands, make a complete fool of itself. On the other hand, he never won a race with it. That he ever expected to do so illustrates well his boyish enthusiasm, which was not yet tempered by the experiences that would make him one of the best development drivers of his generation.

By now, Ken Gregory was Stirling's man of business under Alfred's guidance. It was a good arrangement, for it meant that he now had a companion as well as someone who could concentrate on details, while he concentrated on racing. The pair became inseparable and even shared Stirling's new flat at Challoner Mansions near Baron's Court in west London. Stirling's affair with Yvonne was now a thing of the past. The pair had parted very amicably in the summer of 1951 and remained on friendly terms. The strain of constant separation, coupled with the fact that Yvonne was in the theatrical profession, ensured that it would always have been a difficult relationship to sustain.

But Stirling was seldom single for long. His next serious girlfriend was Sally Weston, another pretty blonde, who was widely assumed to be a member of the family that controlled Associated British Foods. The reality was rather different; she had been christened Jennifer Claire Tollit. She was apparently acquainted with the Weston family and for reasons which seem slightly mysterious now, decided to call herself Weston. Her rationale for this was that her surname sounded too much like a piece of bathroom equipment – she had always been 'toilet' at school. Stirling 'Toni' Moss didn't particularly mind and went happily along with this mild subterfuge. They would stay together until 1955.

Stirling reinvented the idea behind the Nash 'Rambler' in 1952. The £1000 he had lost attempting to acquire one was followed by £800 thrown into a project to build the ultimate caravan. He rationalised that if Ken Gregory was going to accompany him all over Europe, then an estate car would not be enough. It was a luxurious vehicle, laden with every conceivable extra and the pair had high hopes of it. It was

also potentially economical; the money saved on hotel bills (a driver paid his own expenses then) would cover the cost of it in under a year.

It was not to be. Despite the use of a wheeled coupling, the device was quite unstable, particularly at the speeds which Stirling drove the Jaguar that towed it. The end came in Belgium, when Stirling and Gregory found themselves pursued by their new accommodation down a hill after it came adrift. It steered itself into a ditch and was comprehensively wrecked, and what remained of the interior was coated with the remains of three dozen eggs that Aileen had thoughtfully provided. Even without this disaster, 1952 was a difficult year. There were a host of 500cc victories, but given that he had been offered a *Grand Prix* seat in a car which was now steamrollering all before it, Formula 3 was a definite step sideways. These little races were useful, as they were eligible for inclusion in the BRDC Gold Star points system, but only the drives for Jaguar offered him sport at a high level, although the retirements from which Jaguar suffered at Le Mans, in response to the perceived Mercedes-Benz threat, were characteristic of the rest of his season.

Facing page: Stirling was news, even when he was merely buying petrol.

Right: With William Lyons at Silverstone.

Stirling had played a small role in the Le Mans fiasco; he had been so impressed by the sheer speed of the new Mercedes-Benz 300 SL coupés at the *Mille Miglia* that he had sent an impulsive cable to Sir William Lyons: 'MUST HAVE MORE SPEED AT LE MANS.' Having crashed out of that race, he felt that he should at least contribute something. William Lyons took him at his word; a hasty modification was made to the Le Mans C-types whereby they were given longer noses and tails with smaller air intakes and cooling modifications which simply did not match the shape of the revised bodies. All three C-types retired due to overheating and the beautiful but functional 300 SLs glided home in first and second place.

What made things seem even worse for Stirling that season was the arrival on the scene of Mike Hawthorn. He appeared quite suddenly driving a succession of aged Rileys, and in a private 2-litre Cooper Bristol, with which he shone, on occasion leading works 4½-litre Ferraris in *Formule Libre*. It was a remarkable début season in the first rank.

Hawthorn was highly talented, but inconsistent. The main reason for this was that he was not well; he, like Stirling, suffered from a kidney complaint and had done so for most of his life. To the spectators he was the exact opposite of Stirling; tall, blond and raffish with appetites to match. On form, though, he was startlingly quick. Most important for his public, he looked the part. For the media, Hawthorn's sudden arrival was something of a godsend in the middle of a season which was uninspiring from the British point of view. It did not take long for the press to construct a 'rivalry' between the two men, all the easier to accomplish because of the very obvious physical differences between them. The fact that Hawthorn was to join Ferrari for the 1953 season served only to increase Stirling's gloom, as he had not generally broadcast information on the rift with Ferrari, although many insiders knew of it.

If Stirling thought that 1953 could only get better, he was sorely wrong. He had experienced the limitations of the core design of the ERA, particularly its weak engine, but he had seen how Hawthorn had succeeded with the Cooper Bristol. The prospect of following that route was an interesting one, but the thought occurred that perhaps a Cooper chassis powered by an HWM (Alta) engine might offer the best of both worlds. Certainly that was Alf Francis's view; he believed that the Alta engine offered huge potential, partly

Right: Mike Hawthorn, seen here in a Riley, erupted onto the scene in 1952.

Overleaf: 10 May, 1952. Stirling running to the C-type Jaguar at Silverstone.

because of his affection for its maker, Geoffrey Taylor in Tolworth, and partly because of what he had observed Stirling do with the HWMs. As for Stirling himself, he was persuaded that the project was worthwhile after discovering that Maserati was not prepared to sell him an engine.

The first principles established by the Kieft-Norton project, that a sensible design can perhaps be improved with some common sense, were revisited. Alf Francis knew the Alta engine as well as anyone and Cooper undertook to supply all the necessary parts so that the Cooper Bristol chassis could be modified. The car was to be a great disappointment, and a depressing one for Francis. He could not get on with Ray Martin: and after three months of Stakhanovite efforts the new car was eventually finished; Martin sacked him, which is how Francis and his assistant

nimble cornering, but the loss of one was often the price paid for the other. The constant search for the edge had led the little group into the labyrinth from which the European builders had already found a possible exit. It was a learning curve. Clearly very few of these domestic efforts were going to challenge the supremacy of the Continental teams when the new 2½-litre formula arrived for 1954. British cars were dogged by moderate engines and a handling package which, based as it so often was on production car components, could not achieve what Ferrari and others had done already. The huge investments required had been well illustrated by the BRM project, and would be demonstrated again by Mercedes-Benz and Vanwall. Meanwhile, the *garagistas,* as the Emilian Grand Constructors dismissively called them, would have to struggle.

He was unhurt despite his flimsy helmet
. . . which was split in half

Tony Robinson then became Stirling's personal mechanics.

As Stirling would later learn, Francis could be temperamental and volatile, but he was a major asset in those early days of independent racing, even though he occasionally took on projects which were frankly beyond him. What he really wanted to be was a designer, which was perhaps a step too far. Ironically, it was Robinson who would eventually do that with success. But that was much later – the little *équipe* now turned its collective attention to the matter of building a machine that could be the equal of its driver. This Cooper special, which differed from the standard product in many unseen ways, was an ambitious project. It offered little in the way of success and could be said to have been a great leap sideways in terms of the model on which it was loosely based.

But in May 1953 Stirling had another moment which could easily have carried him off. He survived a huge 100 mph roll at Silverstone in the works C-type; baulked by a slower car he failed to ease off and lost the line. Amazingly, he was unhurt, despite his flimsy helmet, which split in half.

The second iteration of the Cooper-Alta, built in just eleven days, was a rather better machine than the first. Running on nitromethane, the engine delivered staggering power (with a commensurately short life) but asked many questions of the chassis which it was somewhat pushed to answer. Clearly, one could have huge straight-line speed, or

Sports cars were a different matter. The extraordinary success of the Jaguar marque had proved that the Italians could be beaten, even if the talents of the engineers were sometimes reigned in by the rigours of tiny budgets. But in Jaguar's case the rationale for success was selling road cars; the cottage industry nature of the British single-seater builders would ensure that it remained a diversified trade, (which would later pay its own dividends) but meanwhile it was a matter of patience. The uniquely tight-knit nature of motor racing today, a British-dominated affair, began here; the complex web of relationships that still exists was evolved through expediency, an unavoidable result of a chronic shortage of money.

Despite the fact that the move back to full Formula 1 under a 2½-litre engine capacity had been well-telegraphed as far back as 1951, most British contenders were far from ready for it. While the development of chassis and underpinnings was well under way, there was a difficulty concerning engines. The Italians, who had been building racing cars for longer than anyone else, had reason to believe that they could triumph (until they clapped eyes on the new Mercedes offering), and Maserati and Ferrari had been busy during the interregnum, breaking in 2-litre engines which could be

Facing page: Stirling pauses while unknotting a drive train from his Cooper, c. 1952.

enlarged minimally to meet the requirements of the new formula. Mercedes and Lancia took a different view and started from scratch. The Germans had enough know-how from the 1930s to design a specific 2½-litre unit and Lancia, never a marque to spend much time on derivative engineering, was working on a new V8 designed by Vittorio Jano, but it would not break cover quite yet.

For someone as competitive as Stirling, the prospects were very muted indeed. 1952 and 1953 had been dreadful jobbing years, leavened only by his success in driving sports cars. The arrival of Mike Hawthorn on the scene, unannounced and charismatically inconsistent, had pushed Stirling out of the limelight. During the Formula 2 years, *Grand Prix* racing had been an Italian affair, particularly dominated by Ferrari, and while the HWM experience had been as enjoyable as the Cooper-Alta experience had been challenging, it was clear that the junior league which they represented was now effectively gone. Further, the performance of the new Mercedes-Benz sports car offerings gave notice that even Jaguar's dominance in that field might be soon displaced. The scale of that displacement when it came was to beggar the belief of all who witnessed it.

Connaught was perhaps another matter. This firm was the motor racing arm of Continental Cars, based at Send in Surrey. It was financed by Kenneth McAlpine, a member of the construction dynasty, who also raced cars from time to time; after leaving the HWM team Stirling drove the chubby type-A Connaught Formula 2 car on occasion. Despite his relative lack of success, he learned much from the experience. One important point was made by Rodney Clarke, the technical head of the firm, who taught Stirling that the absolute power of the machine was secondary to the ability of the chassis and suspension to deliver it to the track where it could be used. He was preaching to the converted, for Stirling's experience with the often uncontrollable BRM V16 had left him with the same impression.

The Connaught marque was probably the best screwed-together machine in the sport (and would remain so until the arrival of the Vanwall), but it would suffer from being underpowered relative to its weight. The unavoidable dependence upon other people's engine designs (Lea-Francis for Formula 2, the Alta for the upcoming Formula 1) was a handicap and although there would be triumph in the hands of Tony Brooks and Archie Scott Brown, the little Surrey firm would never fulfil the potential of its early days.

Facing page: The terrifying roll in the works C-type at Silverstone seems to have had no noticeable effect, except on his helmet.

Right: With Peter Walker, Le Mans, 1953. The pair came second.

The Connaught was a microcosm of the crisis which beset the British motor racing establishment in the early 1950s. All agreed that British cars handled well (with a few exceptions) but there was simply none of the vast experience in engine design and manufacture which could be found on the Continent. The solid experience which resided at Maserati, Lancia and Ferrari, not to mention Mercedes-Benz, had no match in Britain. There were designs which worked well specific to their class, but almost without exception they relied on pre-war thinking and were derived from road car engines. The pure racing engine, designed for the purpose of competition, was basically a foreign concept. Most British manufacturers did not have the resources to build engines except for mass-production; foundries were in the hands of large but specialist companies and the cottage industry that really defined British racing did not really feature on their horizon; those resources existed to service the needs of volume car manufacture. As a result, the lack of a reliable customer engine handicapped the development of the British sport until the application of a little lateral thinking liberated the necessary resources. But that would not happen yet.

So, as far as Stirling Moss was concerned, Formula 1 was only one part of a broader spectrum and the importance of sports car racing probably rivalled that of single-seaters for the whole of his career. There is no doubt that the *Mille Miglia* was as important race as the Monaco *Grand Prix*, for example, or that *Le Vingt-Quatre Heures du Mans* or the *Targa Florio*, even the Monte Carlo Rally, occupied as much space in the awareness of the public as any *Grand Prix* does today. The reason was simple; publicity. The American adage, 'win on Sunday, sell on Monday', certainly applied to the British motor industry and any effort by a UK maker that delivered results was a cause for national pride every bit as fervent as that displayed by the most ardent *tifoso* at Monza.

The economic grip that oil companies had on the sport was not the equal of the tobacco companies' monopoly today, but it was real; they lost no time in trumpeting success in the press. The retainers that they paid drivers were tiny by today's standards but allowed a man to live at least modestly without necessarily having to have a second job. Those who did have other businesses, however, were better equipped than Stirling to survive economically when the income from racing dropped. For him, it was not purely an issue of money; if he had simply desired that, then he could have driven in America and probably have made a great deal. When a driver at Indianapolis could make more by coming tenth in that race than any *Grand Prix* winner could, then the arithmetic is very simple. But, as he puts it now: 'Who the **** is interested in coming tenth?' Stirling Moss was simply not interested in coming anywhere less than first, so the 1953 season, dominated by Formula 3 and the home-grown Cooper-Altas, had been dreadful. His racing season ended early with a very nasty moment at Castle Combe. He out-braked Tony Rolt's Connaught and the resulting collision simply punted his Cooper JAP, somersaulting sending it off the track. His shoulder was very badly broken and would take three months to heal properly.

As he underwent physiotherapy at St. Thomas's Hospital, he reflected; aside from Monza, Enzo Ferrari's cars had won every single *Grand Prix* on the calendar. The only British driver who had scored World Championship points was Mike Hawthorn aboard a Ferrari. Something seemed to be going very, very wrong.

To someone as patriotic as Stirling, there had been an even worse episode. He was caught in the fall-out over questions in the Houses of Parliament concerning National Service; it was all very well these young men careering all over Europe driving foreign-owned racing cars, but what about getting ordered about at Pirbright? The question was actually asked in reference to Hawthorn who, like Stirling, had not been passed fit for National Service. Other drivers, like Peter Collins, were perfectly fit but living in Paris, perhaps to escape the call-up, perhaps because it was an agreeable place – but obviously no one had heard of them. Stirling had applied to join the Royal Air Force even before his National Service call-up was scheduled, but his medical examination concluded that his state of health was actually questionable, on the grounds of the nephritis which had dogged his childhood. He had been defined as of grade 3

Left: Bert Hadley, Leslie Johnson, Stirling and Jack Fairman atop their Jaguar at Monthéry, 12 August, 1952. They had, between them, covered 16,851 miles and averaged over 100 mph.

fitness, so his eager services would thus have been called upon only in the event of an extreme national emergency. It had been quite a humiliating exercise for him.

Alfred, never one to hesitate if his son's honour was impugned, swiftly circulated a copy of Stirling's medical rejection from National Service to the entire complement of MPs. It may well have been, he reasoned, that someone was draft-dodging, but if that were true, it was certainly no son of his. All was settled with no particular fuss, but the issue could not have come at a worse time.

Both Alfred and Ken Gregory viewed Stirling's gloom with some dismay. Clearly, their boy was (at least in their view) anointed with greatness, but equally clearly he was becoming

The obvious (if slightly speculative) first choice for them was Stuttgart, and accordingly Gregory was dispatched there. Rudi Uhlenhaut, the charming Anglo-German technical director of the *Rennabteilung*, was calming though realistic when he arrived for a drink at Gregory's hotel. The factory team had been selected for 1954 and apart from Fangio (a justifiable exception), was to be entirely German. The cars were as yet unfinished, budgets were appallingly tight, and there would, in all probability, be no room for Stirling. Yet he promised an appointment the following morning with vast Alfred Neubauer, head of the *Rennabteilung*. Wishing Gregory, with some irony, the best of British luck, he finished his drink and strolled off.

handicapped by his own plummeting morale. If it seemed absurd that the man who had broken the *Le Mans* lap record three times during the same race simply could not find a decent drive, then it could be explained by two factors: a simple lack of cars and his astonishing youth. Nothing remained but for the pair to attempt to find a works drive for him; neither Alfred nor Gregory were remotely fazed by his statistical lack of Formula 1 experience since they had seen him at work more frequently than anyone. Stirling had asked Ken Gregory to approach Connaught before departing for America, but Gregory consulted Alfred and the pair decided to take the matter into their own hands. Critically, they had a plan B. And, as it turned out, a plan C and D as well. Plan D was very, very expensive.

The next morning at 8.45 sharp, Gregory found himself closeted in Neubauer's office with the Fat Man and his interpreter Frau Bauer and found to his chagrin that the visit was, after all, only a courtesy call. But a prescient one. Nothing much happened in motor racing without Neubauer (or Uhlenhaut, for that matter) knowing about it and while Stirling's résumé was not exactly the hot topic of conversation in Stuttgart, it was at least a matter of polite interest. Tellingly, Neubauer made no reference to even having heard of Stirling when he penned his (*slightly* self-serving) memoirs, preferring to cite the 1954 season as the touchstone of his later interest, but had that been the case, it is most unlikely that he would have said to Gregory what he actually did say. Basically, his view was that Moss did not have the experience to justify bumping anyone out of the Mercedes-Benz works team. In Formula One terms Stirling was something of an unknown quantity, but once he had proved his ability to handle a 300 bhp single-seater, he would certainly merit consideration, perhaps for the 1955 season. He confirmed what Uhlenhaut had already stated, that the hardware was not ready and the 1954 effort would start late. Fangio, the team leader would stay at Maserati until Mercedes were ready for him. If a Maserati was good enough for Fangio…?

Gregory recollected this as a brush-off, but it was not. He and Alfred resolved to try to obtain a works drive for their boy at Modena. Whether it would be Ferrari or Maserati was

Omer Orsi, the son of the owner, knew he had a good product. He also knew that the prospect of the new car, the 250F had tweaked the interest of *Équipe* Moss, because Syd Greene of Gilby Engineering had told him so. Greene had ordered a 250F, to be funded largely by Esso Petroleum, for Roy Salvadori to drive. Stirling, as a driver being paid a retainer by ShellMex-BP, was hardly eligible to be included in anything that Esso was doing (not that this had stopped Gregory and Alfred enquiring).

ShellMex and BP operated a shared marketing strategy in the UK; the combine, ShellMex-BP Ltd, never produced a drop of oil or fuel in its life, but was a promotional joint venture – the sort of organisation which makes Americans

moot; should no offer be forthcoming, well, the answer was simple – they would buy one. They decided not to tell Stirling of their plan; by the time he returned from his American trip, he would either have a works drive or his own car.

But it was late to get a works drive. After a fairly dismal two years of thinly disguised Formula 2, the queue for cars was long, particularly for Italian cars. It had escaped no one's notice that Enzo Ferrari had dominated the class, but Stirling's previous experience at his hands had been confusing and ego-bruising. The safe play was Maserati and Gregory's approach was to lead to a generally wonderful, if occasionally operatic relationship between Moss and 'the other Modena firm'.

It was not an easy start, though. Maserati, in the form of

scream for their anti-trust lawyers. The very fact of its existence is evidence of the priority given to the growth of market share in the UK.

Ken Gregory did not actually get to see Orsi until 7pm on an unpromising December evening. He was cold, tired and

Facing page, far left: Stirling's first event in the reinvented Cooper-Alta at the German *Grand Prix*, August 1953. He came sixth in a car that had been built in eleven days.

Facing page, right: Storming up Prescott Hill in the second Cooper-Alta a month later in September 1953.

Above, left: The 1952 Alpine trial; Stirling cornering the Sunbeam Talbot on the Stelvio. Despite its mundane performane, the Sunbeam made a robust rally car.

Above, right: In the Sunbeam Alpine on the Alpine rally.

hungry and faced with the prospect of spending more money than he had ever seen in his life. His negotiating posture for plan C – a works drive for Stirling – met with polite dismissal. Like Mercedes, Maserati's arrangements for 1954 suited them very well, apart from the prospect of losing Fangio. Moss was, at least by reputation, no Fangio, but there was a car for sale, the eighth of the line. However, it would cost as much money as a Spitfire fighter plane had a scant ten years before.

Gregory, having no choice, agreed to buy it. Orsi gave him a decent dinner (at 1am) and an exhausted Ken Gregory booked a call to Alfred to give him the news. Alfred, who knew that ShellMex-BP was going to pay for at least part of this, assented and went back to sleep after the pair agreed to keep the news from Stirling until Gregory returned to England. Stirling was, at that moment, on his way back from America aboard the *Queen Mary*. He had not raced for two months since the crash at Castle Combe, and was well and truly fed up. The small knot of journalists (artfully tipped off by Gregory) who met the ship at Southampton give him the news; he had had an inkling about the Maserati, but the ship/shore radio had not allowed very much conversation, being both extremely costly and filled with static.

Naturally, he was very happy, but the self-doubt that had started to dog him after two dreadful seasons did not allow him to treat the prospect of the new car with unalloyed glee; so far had his morale plunged that he had even started to have suspicions about his own abilities. 'In motor racing, everything is confidence,' he says now and 1953 was the year he learned that. He was not to know, as he animatedly discussed the prospects offered by the Maserati, that the worst was already over. His career, after two years in the doldrums, was about to take a completely different route.

Perhaps the Maserati purchase was an omen; no sooner was the ink dry on the contract than Stirling won the Sebring 12-hour race in an OSCA, a car designed and built by the original Maserati brothers themselves.

Stirling's inability to leave things as they were mandated that his new Maserati should be modified. As designed, the car invited its driver to adopt a rather perpendicular posture, which he instinctively disliked. There was no particular technical reason to adopt the laid-back style favoured by Farina – it would become a trademark of Stirling's – except

Facing page: Only two Gold Cups for this Alpine Rally were ever awarded, and Stirling has one of them.

Above right: With Lofty England at Le Mans surveying the engine of the C-type.

Overleaf: A rather nasty moment at Castle Combe.

that it looked cool. It telegraphed a state of total relaxation which might have an adverse effect on the competition. Usefully, it prepared him for the advent of the low-slung rear-engined machines which were to come. But that was years ahead as he turned up at the Modena test track on 5 May, 1954 to see what £5500 had bought him.

The issue of the car's central throttle had concerned him, given what had happened to David Murray's Ferrari at Bari, and he wanted it placed in the conventional position, as on a road car. A centre throttle, which allowed the driver latitude to 'heel and toe' when effecting a racing gear change was one of the badges of a competition car in Italy. The general sentiment at the Maserati works was that such interference was tantamount to child-molesting. It became clear that Maserati did not care for their customers messing about with the core design, so when Stirling requested more rake to the seat, which required the repositioning of the bulkheads, the response was a stony silence. There was only one thing for it; Alf Francis sneaked into the workshop and made the

adjustment himself on the eve of the arrival of the coachbuilder, Merdado Fantuzzi. As the bodies were all hand-made, there was no problem with proportions from Fantuzzi's point of view. A further scene was caused by the initial choice of Dunlop tyres over the more advanced Pirellis. Pirelli was the natural choice as far as Maserati was concerned, although the upstart Enzo Ferrari used Englebert rubber. In this case, Maserati was entirely correct and when it later became clear that Pirelli tyres were worth several seconds a lap, Stirling quickly adopted them.

But as Stirling heaved himself out of the cockpit of the customised car, he realised that Neubauer had been exactly right. This car was a single-seater, certainly, but there ended the resemblance to anything he had ever driven before; the Maserati was, like the *Alfetta* had been, a revelation. Its combination of power and handling was something which was quite outside his experience; it was nothing less than an epiphany. He lapped the test track with a best time of 1 minute 4.2 seconds, some 5 seconds quicker than the chief tester and head mechanic Guerino Bertocchi, who was used to being at least as quick as some of his customers. Bertocchi was impressed.

But so was Stirling. The car made few compromises in any particular, but as a customised racer it delivered an extraordinary spread of virtues. The engine, of which Maserati was inordinately proud, was a logical development of the 2-litre A6 power plant designed by Massimino and Bellantani. A six in-line twin-cam device, it was conventional enough, although the hubristic pride evident in its construction was often to let it down. Maserati was, after all, more than a car company; it was, under the Orsi regime, a fully fledged engineering conglomerate. The combination of owning its own foundry as well as a nice line in machine tools allowed some excesses when it came to the engine itself. Such pride (and care) was taken with the machining of the castings that it was considered that the engine needed little in the way of gaskets, for example – precision finishing would do the work of asbestos, copper and cardboard. Well it would, but not without some embarrassing failures.

The 250F presented one or two potential challenges though, quite apart from the obvious ones of being a private car. Not only was the project going through more or less continuous development, Stirling's new car did not have the safety-net of full factory support – it was there but at a price, and that was predictably high. There was huge pride in the

Left: Despite the success of the Ray Martin Kieft, his second effort for Stirling, this Cooper-Alta was an expensive disaster. Here Stirling receives a push from Tony Robinson and Alf Francis (out of sight) as a mechanic whips away the churn.

Maserati effort, but there were also very real commercial considerations.

While Alf Francis would enjoy a good, if volatile relationship with the factory staff, and indeed was accorded the later honour of a workbench of his own in the racing workshop, prudence dictated that the car would have to be treated relatively gently if it was going to last. For racing, the engine rpm was to be kept below 7200, whereas the works cars would rev as high as 7800, as it was a matter of routine to renew the engine's main bearings after every race. Meanwhile, the advice of Rodney Clark from Connaught stayed with him, indeed, has never left him.

The biggest single issue was much more basic than the cost of repairs; Stirling now had a competitive car and it was up to him, within the confines of the technical envelope

to that point (apart from the brief outing in the Alfa 159) seem crude by comparison.

But the issue of the engine's potential concerned him. He was aware that its architecture allowed much higher rpm than he was used to, but also that the factory cars would go higher by a large margin. In getting used to this car, certain vital adjustments would have to be made, and while Francis was clearly up to the task, the process would be both time-consuming and haphazardly empirical. The core of the problem was that in order to preserve the engine, the axle ratio had to be raised. In order to compensate for that, the torque characteristics of the engine had to be adjusted so that maximum torque occurred at lower rpm. It boiled down to a carburation question.

They got it right. Within a month of the car's début at

the Maserati offered Stirling the opportunity to refine his style

imposed, to show how good he was. The immediate sense of relief he had felt after testing the car was one thing; proving himself qualified to pilot the Maserati on a consistent basis was quite another. Any ambitions to graduate up to Mercedes-Benz were firmly put on the back burner as he addressed the matter of his own level of confidence. Obviously, the Mercedes effort was superior on paper at least, but the undignified scramble which would be the flavour of the 1954 (and 1955) seasons – to be the first non-Mercedes home – was to occupy him almost fully. This car was much more than a new toy. If Stirling's relationship with '2508' was not a romance, then it was certainly an intimate dance; if not a tango, then certainly a waltz.

And it was the most amazing fun. As Stirling started to explore both his own limits and those of the car he realised that he had found, potentially, the ideal dancing partner. If he did not step on the Maserati's toes, then it would treat him gently in return, but being Stirling, his first steps were far from tentative ones. He felt that he had time to make up and was not minded to plod. The great thing about the Maserati was that it handled so well, the years of experience that had been fed into the design were evident. Stirling was always happiest in a machine that had evolved, as opposed to one which had been designed from scratch. Simply sitting in the cockpit, he could tell that at least a generation of know-how had gone into it; it made every single-seater he had driven up

Bordeaux on 9 May, Stirling had won his first race with it, and with that first *Formula Libre* victory his morale rapidly started to recover; he really could do this and the mechanical disadvantage could be reduced (but never totally eliminated) by all these little modifications. It was a situation in which he would find himself again and again in his career; the need to update a machine so that it at least approached the level of power with reliability of a full works effort was to suggest to some, wrongly, that he was simply an inveterate fiddler who could not leave well alone.

Such work was necessary and as technology advanced, it would become even more so as the annual increments by which cars improved became greater and greater, as the philosophy of race car manufacture veered away from the immaculate tool-room-built finish of the front runners to machines that were almost disposable.

The Maserati offered Stirling the opportunity to refine his style, although it was initially at the expense of the brakes. He hammered them very hard in those first few races but as

Facing page: Winning the *Daily Telegraph* Trophy at Aintree, 1954.

Overleaf: The 1954 Italian *Grand Prix*. Fangio in 16, who was never at ease in the streamlined Mercedes, sits calmly while Ascari in 34 and Stirling adjust their goggles. Stirling would lead this race until his oil tank split on lap 78. He was given the 'moral victory' by Fangio and a winner's bonus by Pirelli. His showing here would seal his fate for 1955.

soon as this was pointed out, he changed his tactics. His driving became smoother as he learned to exploit the virtues of the car rather than to fight its vices, which were very few. He was not yet the Stirling Moss whom a nation would come to revere, as this was his first Formula 1 season, and he had yet to score any Championship points.

Stirling had yet to formulate his view that the driver was paid to interpret the wishes of the designer and thus add value to the process of driving the car. He would later develop the opinion that the driver was almost an adjustable component of the car, and his experience with the Maserati went a long way towards teaching him that. It would pay dividends, particularly when he arrived at Aston Martin. So,

as a teaching aid, the Maserati was well-nigh perfect, albeit expensive. It allowed him experiences he had never had before: 'It was a very honest car; it was like having a really good teacher at school; one who really gets your attention.'

So the Maserati became a 250 bhp, four-wheeled Sidney Beckwith. Having been built in Modena, it spoke no English, but by virtue of its robust straightforwardness, coupled with its undeniable pedigree, it offered Stirling the chance to refine his craft. He grasped firmly the potential of the car's strengths and just as vitally, its drawbacks. But a weakness in a road car can be a strength in a racer. Whereas a car sitting in a garage under a dustsheet (or even on the grid) is an entirely stable thing of neutral balance, the reality is rather different once it is under way and under load. Stirling began to realise that instability created by small, incremental actions could also be used to place the machine exactly where he wanted it to be:

If you can use that instability to your benefit, whether by braking, accelerating or whatever, you can build an advantage over someone for whom that instability is a minus. If you can keep a car balanced the way you want it

balanced, by creating a situation of being potentially out of control, then that's an enormous advantage. Your actions as a driver in triggering that instability are always going to be quicker than your reactions in sorting something out that the car has already done for itself.

This philosophy is exactly what the builder is seeking when he creates a machine purely for racing. The very best driver is therefore one who can think just like this, who looks beyond

The very best driver looks beyond the
limits of mere technology

the limitations of mere technology and seeks the opportunities offered by Newtonian physics, whether he understands it academically or not. Interestingly, the Moss opinion of two cars designed by men who were in their own right excellent drivers, reveals a clear paradox. Neither Uhlenhaut's Mercedes nor Chapman's Lotus (at least in its early iterations), were cars that Stirling found particularly easy to drive. The Vanwall too, as laid out by Chapman, was 'difficult'. A skilled driver who designs a car will always build in a certain amount of personal preference; an engineer will wrap his device in physics. Moss prefers engineers' cars, like the Maserati. The above statements reflect a theme which is firmly set in Moss's mind and should be clear to anyone who witnesses a motor race. An early realisation for Stirling was that both steering and braking can slow a car down equally; he relegated the steering wheel to a secondary role behind the throttle, which with enough power available, he started to use as the primary means of getting through a corner. Don't try this at home. He says:

The steering wheel is used to present the car to a corner and to some extent to indicate the direction. However, when one is talking about a powerful car, the wheel is often used more to compensate or negate the accelerator. When one is learning the art of handling a vehicle, one is

taught to brake in a straight line and accelerate through a corner. This is OK until one finds that it is possible, even beneficial, to leave one's brakes on, even into the corner. I have found that by holding my brakes on (though usually easing them) I can use their contribution to assist placing the car on the road…to benefit my speed and balance through the corner. Remember also that the effect that brakes have on a car varies a lot, depending upon when and how they are used. If the car is understeering and they are applied, it will probably promote even more understeer. If they are applied when in an oversteer situation, the car could easily spin. To prevent this, a fair degree of opposite lock should reduce this tendency.

But how much lock? How much power?

When turning in, one should have a fair idea (!) of the trajectory one is looking for. Whether one is going to power through on one's present course, or maybe that one needs to run the apex further ahead, thereby affording a bit more distance to adjust the car's attitude on the road for the full power-on exit.
Or, maybe, one is running one corner into another and the second corner is slower. If this is the case, it will probably necessitate allowing the car to slide across the road (thereby scrubbing off some speed) and adding some extra braking and corrective lock as well. All the time one should be able to balance one's forward thrust against the sideways g-force and come out in a smooth, power-on slide, where one's car finishes up alongside the edge of the road just as its cornering force fades away. Remember that, in principle, the earlier one gets the power down, the faster one should be. Remember, too, the more steering one uses, the more drag is the result.

He also learned that concentration is more important than reaction speed:

If you overcorrect a car, it snaps round so fast that however fast your own reactions are you are simply not going to catch it, but if you instigate a problem, you can often control it, because you are ahead of it.

Facing page: Despite his success at the top end of the sport, Stirling would continue to race in Formula 3 as long as he could. He makes a move in his Beart Cooper on redoubtable competitor Don Parker driving a car of his own design.
Previous page: Aileen receives a push in Stirling's Maserati at Aintree, May 1954
Overleaf: The 250F was a revelation: 'It was like having a really good teacher.' Goodwood, 1954.

The experience of the Maserati was to insert itself in Stirling's mind very firmly, as did that offered by the Aston Martin DB3S and DBR series a little later. Again, the key to the Aston Martin (an engineer's car) was handling.

It is not always the case that statistics reveal very much except the very obvious, but Stirling's 1954 season tells us exactly what was happening. Not only did he win his first Formula 1 race, but he scored his first *Grand Epreuve* points and actually led his first World Championship race, which after the unfulfilling experiences of 1952–3 was progress indeed. (A *Grand Epreuve* race is one which counts for the World Driver's Championship. There were many *Grands Prix* and many sponsored Formula 1 events. The *Daily Express* Trophy, for example, was just as important a race as the British *Grand Prix*, and carried a bigger purse, but it

came for the German *Grand Prix* at Nurburgring, his car was as close to factory specification as a private car could be. That 1954 German *Grand Prix* was to be significant for him, but tragic for Maserati. Fangio had departed for Mercedes-Benz, and there was a vacancy in the team. Fangio's protégé, Onofré Marimon (who was thirty-one to Stirling's twenty-four) had expected to be offered the job, and may have been uneasy at the news that Maserati, impressed at Stirling's qualifying the car third on the front row of the grid, had offered Stirling a place in the works effort, albeit in his own car. That he had over-revved the engine and run a bearing was something he and Francis knew, but they did not.

Marimon attempted to raise his game and improve his grid position from a provisional eighth place. When he did not return, there was

He grasped the potential of the car's strengths
...and its drawbacks

was not a *Grand Epreuve*.)

Irritating mechanical failures dogged him though. His fine third place at Spa in June, albeit a lap down, was the only *Grand Epreuve* he actually finished that year. He was persuaded to lend the car back to the works so that Luigi Villoresi could enter the French *Grand Prix*, in exchange for a total overhaul at Modena, complete with the latest evolution of cylinder head, so the car was as well-prepared as it could be for the British *Grand Prix* at Silverstone. Maserati was keen that he should shine at his home *Grand Prix* so an interesting offer was made, via Alf Francis. If Stirling would drive at a factory level of rpm, they would undertake to rebuild the engine, or whatever else, *gratuito*, if he ran into mechanical trouble as a result.

Stirling took Maserati at its word and as a result was lying second to Froilan Gonzales' Ferrari when his transmission failed only ten laps from the end. Honourably, Maserati overhauled the car again, so that when the time

a murmur of unease, which gave way to horror when the news came through that he had been found, clearly dead at Wehrseifen, a dangerous 90° corner.

Obviously a gesture had to be made. Out of respect, Maserati withdrew Villoresi's entry and swiftly Stirling became a private entrant again. Others followed and a subdued race, won by Fangio in the Mercedes-Benz home debut, went ahead. As for Stirling, his damaged bearing let go on the first lap, but the starting money (all his, of course) was some consolation.

Perhaps Stirling's most important effort was not in a race at all, but in practice for the last-ever Swiss *Grand Prix* at Berne. He put the Maserati on pole position in the wet, which startled Mercedes, even if it only impressed

Previous page: A company car. Stirling manoeuvres his green and cream XK120 on the Silver City Airways loading ramp, 1953.

Facing page: The fruits of victory, Oulton Park.

Fangio and Gonzales, who both beat the time in the dry next day. It was this feat, coupled with the fact that he was to lead the Italian *Grand Prix* outright a few weeks later until a lubrication problem put him out, that decided his fate for the next year. Fangio, who won the Italian race, gave Stirling the moral victory and so did most of the spectators.

But no one at Maserati seemed to notice; they were more interested in the fact that they had not won the Italian *Grand Prix* than the fact that one of their cars had led the Silver Arrows. Orsi assumed, without actually asking, that Stirling would stay with the Modena team for 1955. Had he done so, Stirling would have accepted and, having accepted he would have stuck to it. But Orsi did not ask, an omission he would soon regret. The prediction made by Alfred Neubauer was entirely accurate; the telegram flopped onto the mat of Challoner Mansions on 22 November, 1954:

CABLE WHITHER STIRLING MOSS BOUND FOR 1955 STOP OUR ENQUIRY WITHOUT COMMITMENT STOP MERCEDES-BENZ

He was on his way to America to take part in a rally which was to start a week later, and distracted by the prospect of travelling alone, was dismissive of the approach as he left the flat. Gregory was more circumspect, and as soon as Stirling had headed off for the airport, telephoned Alfred for his counsel, which was straightforward – find out the price.

It transpired that it was so huge that there was a serious risk of paying it all to the taxman. Alfred, Ken Gregory and Felix Nabarro, Alfred's lawyer, rapidly came up with a plan which would not only save tax, but would also smooth out a potentially volatile future income stream. If Stirling's fees could be paid to a company – Stirling Moss Limited – and Stirling himself would sign a service agreement to the company, in effect becoming the property of a limited liability firm, then the income from the Mercedes deal could be spread out. It was clever and simple. Alfred and Ken Gregory would be able to vet any approaches, as Stirling would now technically be their employee. But that development would now depend on him; how would he react to the car?

Right: RAC TT, Dundrod 1954. Peter Walker (with cigarette), Stirling's co-driver, attempts to listen to two conversations at once. The grit-blasted Jaguar D-type, oil pressure gone, came 18th after Stirling pushed it over the line.

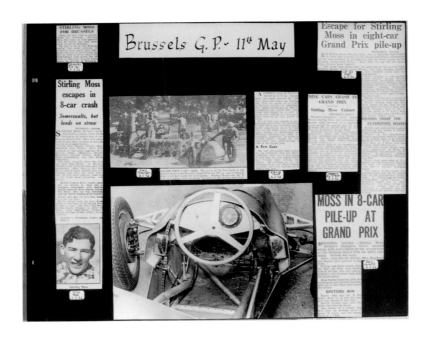

More scrapbook pages. . .the 1954 scrapbook reflects the importance of the
Maserati as a launching pad for a great career. The clippings attest to the fact that
Fleet Street now had him in its sights and Stirling's improbably youth made him even
more attractive to the tabloids.

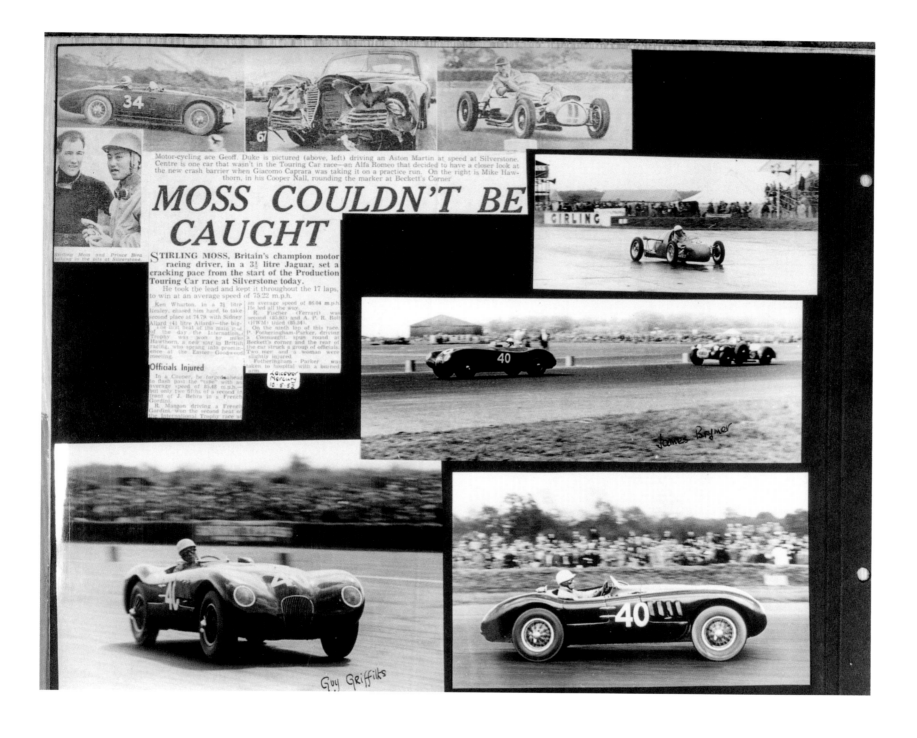

Motor-cycling ace Geoff. Duke is pictured (above, left) driving an Aston Martin at speed at Silverstone. Centre is one car that wasn't in the Touring Car race—an Alfa Romeo that decided to have a closer look at the new crash barrier when Giacomo Caprara was taking it on a practice run. On the right is Mike Hawthorn, in his Cooper Nall, rounding the marker at Beckett's Corner

MOSS COULDN'T BE CAUGHT

STIRLING MOSS, Britain's champion motor racing driver, in a 3½ litre Jaguar, set a cracking pace from the start of the Production Touring Car race at Silverstone today.

He took the lead and kept it throughout the 17 laps, to win at an average speed of 75.22 m.p.h.

Ken Wharton, in a 2½ litre Healey, chased him hard to take second place at 74.79 with Sidney Allard (4 litre Allard)—the big-gest field of the main r of the day the Internation Trophy was won by Mike Hawthorn, a new star in British racing, who sprang into promin-ence at the Easter Goodwood meeting.

Officials Injured

In a Cooper, he forged ahead to flash past the "tape" with an average speed of 85.48 m.p.h. but only two fifths of a second in front of J. Behra in a French Gordini.

R. Manzon driving a French Gordini, won the second heat of the International Trophy race in an average speed of 86.04 m.p.h. He led all the way.

R. Fischer (Ferrari) was second (85.81) and A. P. R. Rolt (HWM) third (85.34).

On the ninth lap of this race, P. Fotheringham-Parker, driving a Connaught, spun round at Beckett's corner and the rear of the car struck a group of officials. Two men and a woman were slightly injured.

Fotheringham - Parker was taken to hospital with a burned arm.

Stirling Moss and Prince Bira talking in the pits at Silverstone

Guy Griffiths

James Brymer

French G.P. & 12 Hour Race - 5th July

Moss No. 2

RHEIMS, Thursday. — Louis Rosier, the French racing ace, clocked the fastest time in today's trials for next Sunday's Grand Prix de Rheims motor race, covering a lap of about five miles at over 110 miles an hour.

Britain's Stirling Moss, in a Cooper-Alta, was next at 105.5 miles an hour.—Reuter.

Daily Express 3-7-53

British cars in Rheims Grand Prix

Eight British cars will compete in the 40th Grand Prix to be held next Sunday over the new course at Rheims.

The drivers are Lance Macklin, Peter Collins and Yves Giraud-Cabantous (France) (H.W.M.'s), Bob Gerard and Ken Wharton (Cooper-Bristols), Stirling Moss (Cooper-Alta), B. Bira and Johnny Claes (Belgium) (Connaughts).

Britain's Mike Hawthorn will be in the strong Italian Ferrari team with Ascari, the world champion, Villoresi, and Farina. The Maserati team consists of Fangio, Gonzales, Marimon and Bonetto.

The race, over 56 laps totalling 504 kilometres, is for formula two cars.

Newcastle Chronicle 30-6-53

MOSS PUTS JAGUAR FIRST AGAIN

RHEIMS, Sunday. — Stirling Moss and Peter Whitehead drove a Jaguar to first place in the 12-hour endurance race and Mike Hawthorn won the Grand Prix at Rheims today.

British cars and drivers took four of the first seven places in the endurance race. A Jaguar — they were placed 1, 2, and 4 in the Le Mans 24-hour race — was fourth, a Bristol fifth, and a Fraser Nash seventh.

TOUGHEST

The winning Jaguar's speed was 105.459 miles an hour. Second was the French Talbot of Rosier and Giraud-Cabantous, and third came America's Briggs Cunningham and Sherwood Johnston in a Cunningham.

Mike Hawthorn drove what he described later as "the toughest race I have ever had" to bring his Ferrari home one second ahead of Fangio's Maserati in the Grand Prix. His speed: 113.635 miles an hour.

Third — only two-fifths of a second behind Fangio — was Gonzales, also in a Maserati. Alberto Ascari, world champion and Hawthorn's team mate, was fourth.

Daily Express 6-7-53

A GREAT BRITISH MOTORING VICTORY IN THE ENDURANCE TEST AT RHEIMS ON JUNE 5 : STIRLING MOSS AND PETER WHITEHEAD. Stirling Moss and Peter Whitehead won the twelve-hours endurance test at Rheims on June 5 in a Jaguar. They covered 1265 miles, averaging 105.416 m.p.h. This victory follows the recent Jaguar triumph in the twenty-four-hour race at Le Mans.

Illustrated London News 18-7-53

MOTOR RACING

RHEIMS, July 5.—Mike Hawthorn, a British member of the Ferrari works team, won the Rheims Grand Prix here today from Maserati driven by the Argentinians J. M. Fangio and Gonzales. Hawthorn covered the 500 kilometres (about 310 miles) in 2hr. 44min. 18.6sec. at an average speed of 182.885 k.p.h. (about 113 m.p.h.). He finished 1sec. ahead of Fangio, with Gonzales another .4sec. behind. The Italians in the Ferrari team—A. Ascari, G. Farina, and L. Villoresi—finished respectively fourth, fifth, and sixth.—Reuter.

ENDURANCE TEST WON BY A JAGUAR

RHEIMS, July 5.—Stirling Moss and Peter Whitehead, two of Britain's outstanding racing motorists, drove a Jaguar car to victory in the 12 hours endurance test which started here at midnight yesterday. They covered 2,036.356 kilometres (1,265 miles), averaging 169.696 k.p.h. (105.416 m.p.h.). A Talbot (L. Rosier and Y. G. Cabantous), of France, was placed second, a Cunningham (Briggs Cunningham and Sherwood Johnson), United States, third. Jaguar (Sir James Scott-Douglas and N. Sanderson), Britain, fourth, and a Bristol (P. Wilson and J. Fairman), Britain, fifth. The Bristol was placed first in the class for cars between 1500 and two litres.—Reuter.

The Times 6-7-53

STIRLING MOSS WINS FRANCE'S 12-HOUR CAR ENDURANCE RACE

BRITAIN won another great motoring victory on the Continent yesterday by taking four of the first seven places in the Rheims 12-hour endurance race.

British-driven Jaguars—which took first, second and fourth places in the Le Mans 24-hour race last month — were first and fourth yesterday.

Stirling Moss and Peter Whitehead drove the winning car, covering 1,264 miles non-stop at an average speed of 105 m.p.h.

A Talbot, driven by the French team of Rosier and Giraud-Cabantous, was second, and an American Cunningham was third.

Fourth and fifth places were all British: Sir James Scott-Douglas and Ninian Sanderson (Jaguar) and P. Wilson and J. Fairman (Bristol).

Italian Ferraris were sixth and the British pair D. A. Clark and Peter S. Russell (Fraser-Nash) seventh.

The Bristol took first place in the 150 c.c. to 2000 c.c. category.

The cars in the first seven places held their positions steadily during most of the race.

In the first six hours a disqualification of the leading Ferrari and a crash by a U.S. Cunningham changed the leadership abruptly.

Moss and Whitehead took up the running and held it until the end. At times their Jaguar, whipping round the 4½-mile circuit, was seven laps ahead of the Talbot which finished second.

Mike Hawthorn, of Britain, driving an Italian Ferrari won the 500 kilometre Grand Prix at Rheims, which followed the 12-hour race. The Argentinians Fangio and Gonzales, in Maseratis, were second and third. Nine British cars started, but were not placed.

Daily Express 6-7-53

Mercedes-Benz

The Mercedes-Benz motor racing effort was uncompromising and therefore very costly. The company had been banned for some time from international competition by the FIA as a result of the political capital Adolf Hitler had wrung out of the successes of the Mercedes-Benz and Auto-Union teams in the 1930s. That ban had been lifted in 1950, but the Stuttgart company was not about to be hurried back into competition. Like Jaguar, its view was that racing was a sport that had a simple objective which was to sell cars. Mercedes was armed with a distinctly soft exchange rate, a first-rate management infrastructure and a well-defined mission. But it was also acutely aware that Marshall Plan aid, the mainspring of the German economic miracle, had stopped in 1952.

The cars were uncompromising and far from easy to drive. Rudi Uhlenhaut, who in his day was as quick as many of his drivers, had comprehensive records that went back to the earliest days of the factory effort. After having been forced to pay a hefty price for the repatriation of their most advanced pre-war car, planning had started in 1952 for an all-out assault on the World Championship. The announcement of the rule changes for the upcoming Formula 1 season had been made as far back as December 1951. Fangio had swept the board in Mercedes' short 1954 season, but it was important for the factory to discover what progress the opposition had made as Mercedes went for the double – dominance in both sports car and *Grand Prix* racing.

Stirling's test session in December, 1954 at the Hockenheimring was impressive to both sides. Aboard a 1954 *Grand Prix* car on a drying circuit, Stirling broke the lap record at 201 kph.

A characteristic of the Mercedes-Benz works effort that rather goes against the received wisdom, is that the factory saw its job as being very straightforward; it would build a team of cars as identical as possible, incorporating any driver's individual preferences, and supported by an awesome array of personnel and material resources. As to winning the race, well, that was really up to the driver. As the starting flag fell, Mercedes-Benz took a step back except to advise the driver of any information which he would not ordinarily know. Alfred Neubauer's role as team manager had therefore more to do with the welfare of the people, rather than the state of the cars or the race. He nursemaided his drivers, mechanics and support staff with a huge level of commitment, but he was not a race strategist. The fact that he was present did as much to reinforce the impression that this was a serious team as anything he actually did. He had been the public face of Stuttgart before the war and he still was; he represented continuity. For Stirling, Neubauer represented a steadying hand, which is a thing he has always needed.

But the sheer attention to detail was a new experience for Stirling. The fact that a mechanic was on hand in the infield of a windswept circuit with a bowl of hot water, soap and flannel (all delivered with a properly deferential heel-click and bow) so that Stirling could wipe the brake dust from his face was as impressive as anything else, because of what it suggested about the philosophy of the team as a whole.

But this was all quite normal; it was not a display for Stirling's benefit and as he was to come to realise, it was the painstaking attention to small items of driver comfort such as this that accounted for the vast level of self-confidence which the team displayed. As Alfred Neubauer took the trouble to attend, mother hen-like, to the smallest concerns of his charges, the drivers were filled with a pleasantly warm glow. All knew that nobody else went racing like this, which offered both a relative and absolute advantage.

Juan Manuel Fangio was definitely the number one driver, but a close inspection was needed to find any outward manifestation of his status, save his slightly flashier company car.

Previous page and above top: The vital Mercedes test session at Hockenheim, December 1954.

Above bottom: The W196 Mercedes was never an easy car to drive, but Stirling won his heat at the January 1955 Buenos Aires City *Grand Prix*. In this *Formule Libre* race, the car used the 3-litre engine destined for the 300 SLR.

Facing page: A relaxed wave after winning the 1955 *Mille Miglia*.

Overleaf: The Moss/Jenkinson 300 SLR approaches the flag at Brescia just before 5.30 pm, 1 May, 1955.

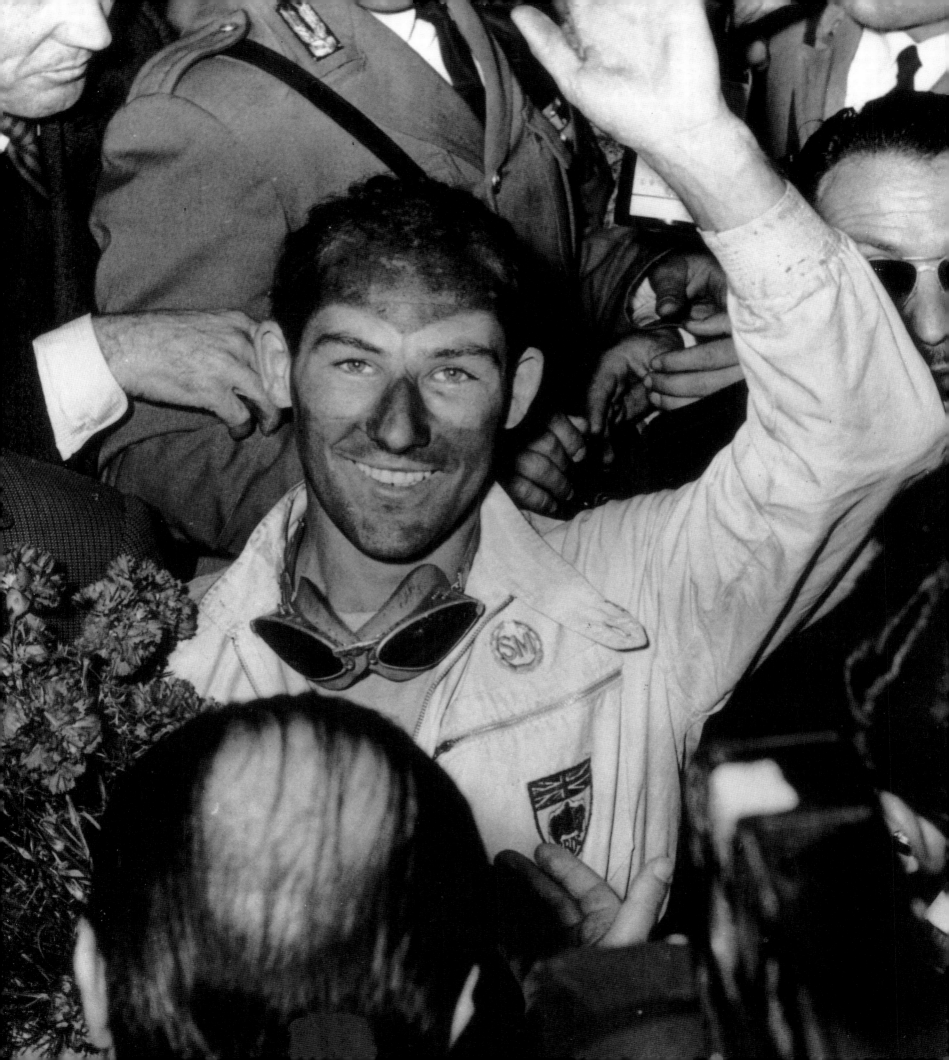

Stirling's own vehicle was a 220A saloon, whereas Fangio's was a more prestigious 300. Whoever you were, the cars had to be kept spotless. An allowance of $1 per day was made for the cars to be washed and polished. Typically, Stirling would attend to this himself and pocket the allowance.

The season started early, in Argentina. There were two events, each in their own way as important as the other. The first was the Argentine *Grand Prix*, the second was the city

but notwithstanding that, his win was an extraordinary effort. (Fangio's little pills were legendary – it seems likely that the stimulant he used was not cocaine, as has often been suggested, but more likely yerba maté. Commonly used in Argentina as a powerful tonic, it was and is quite legal. It takes little imagination to envisage the potential effect of cocaine on a *Grand Prix* driver, particularly behind the wheel.) Whereas other drivers, including Stirling, were

Stirling acquitted himself rather better
the second time around

of Buenos Aires own event, a free-for-all *Formule Libre* race, where Stuttgart was to offer up the 3-litre sports car engine for the first time in competition. These engines were not simply bored-out versions of the *Grand Prix* engine, they were entirely new: alloy castings rather than fabrications, although the unique desmodromic valve gear was almost identical, offering huge rpm, vast, accessible power. (Desmodromic valves are both opened and closed by mechanical means. Whereas a conventional engine valve is closed by means of a spring, and is thus dependent upon the deflection rate of that spring for it to work at high rpm, a 'desmo' system uses the follower to both open and close the valve, theoretically offering a rev limit that is dependent on other more controllable variables.)

But as a 1955 works debut, the Argentine *Grand Prix* was something of a letdown, although the practice had been very promising. Stirling, like Hans Herrmann, was driving a 1954 car, whereas Fangio and Karl Kling had shorter 1955 models. Nonetheless, Stirling managed to qualify on the third row of the grid. Less than two seconds separated the first ten qualifiers, which proved to Stuttgart that the opposition had certainly raised its game somewhat over the winter.

Not only was it Stirling's Mercedes début, it was the first time either he or most of the rest of the Mercedes works effort had experienced the heat and humidity of the *Ottubre 17* circuit and it affected both cars and drivers, except Fangio. The world champion was not above resorting to a little local chemistry to boost his already famous stamina,

obliged to share cars due to a combination of vapour-lock and fatigue, Fangio stormed through to win single-handed.

The second event in Buenos Aires, held a fortnight later, was run in two heats. It carried no Championship points but offered a chance to try out the 3-litre version of the Mercedes engine to be used in the W 196S – the 300 SLR, four of which were still under construction for the sports car season that would soon commence with the terrifying *Mille Miglia*.

Stirling acquitted himself rather better the second time in Buenos Aires having had some time to acclimatise; he came second on aggregate. The total distance run was under 300 miles, so it was hardly a test to destruction, but the straight-eight engine delivered a huge 340 bhp both before and after the race, so it was at least promising. The state of tune of the engine would actually be milder for its sports car application, but not by much.

As Stirling went up to receive his award from Juan Perón, the President noticed that he was wiping his face with a fairly disgusting looking piece of rag and courteously offered him his own handkerchief. By its rather feminine appearance, it might even have been one of the late Evita's, and given that it was now covered in brake dust and sweat, Stirling was rather embarrassed as to what do with it. Perón insisted he keep it, which he did.

The *Mille Miglia* was a race which he knew well but did not much like; not many drivers did. Indeed, it was one of the few events that would cost him sleep the night before. It was a race capable of giving moments of unalloyed pleasure, but it was not one that allowed room for the sort of tactics which can make a difference in a 300-mile *Grand Prix*, or

Facing page: With Fangio, 1955.

Overleaf: Aboard the Union Flag-bedecked Mercedes W196, Monaco, 1955.

even at Le Mans. It was, after all, a single lap in brisk traffic and he had never managed to complete it before, in three separate attempts for Jaguar.

It was therefore important for Stirling to deliver. His chosen navigator, Denis Sargent Jenkinson, was not only apparently totally nerveless but was an influential journalist whose high opinion was a necessary element of any British driver's résumé. Partnering Eric Oliver, 'Jenks' had been three times world sidecar champion, and as a totally committed motor-racing enthusiast never made allowances nor took any

prisoners in his assessment of a driver. With an intensity seldom found in any other sport he spoke as he found and Stirling felt that he had to impress him, if only to offset some of the more chauvinistic elements of the British press who found Stirling's alliance with Mercedes disappointing, rather echoing the view held by Alf Francis, although not quite for the same reason. Jenkinson, on the other hand, despised jingoism, clearly agreeing with Dr. Johnson that it was the

Previous pages: Movement is tranquillity. Stirling in the W196.

Above: Dinner with Jennifer Tollit, also known as Sally Weston.

Facing: A baseball hat is a very modern touch. Note the lack of sponsors' logos.

last refuge of the scoundrel. Stirling recalled:

There I was with an audience; Jenks simply wasn't the sort of man to come up to you after a race and congratulate you, so you knew that if he was impressed, then you'd done a good job. When he was sitting there I could feel that he was fairly impressed with what I was doing and that was very nice.

Because the *Mille Miglia* was an important race on the calendar and contained massive hazards, preparation for it was as thorough as the German works could manage. There were two chief difficulties: first, the local drivers knew the course better than anyone else; and second, being an open race the variance between cars and drivers was wider than at any other event, even Le Mans. From Fiat Topolinos to thinly disguised *Grand Prix* cars, this extraordinary event offered a terminal hazard for every metre of its length. Only two non-Italians had ever won it before: the great Rudolf Caracciola in 1931 aboard a Mercedes; and Huschke von Hanstein in 1940 driving a BMW.

The works effort was geared towards winning, of course, ideally 1-2-3-4, but each car was allowed its own tactics as it was not an unpredictable event that could be run to any pattern. Fangio drove alone, as did Karl Kling, whereas Hans Herrmann was accompanied by a brave volunteer Mercedes mechanic. Fangio never wanted to carry a passenger since the time he had crashed in a marathon South American road race and his navigator had died.

Jenkinson was armed with a set of comprehensive pace notes on a long roll of paper inside an alloy and Perspex case. Given that the two men had not practised the race at maximum speed, it would be interesting to see if the hand signals by which Jenkinson communicated would be understandable. Speech was out of the question; the unsilenced car was deafening at a hundred yards, never mind actually inside the cockpit. They had already experimented with an intercom system but Stirling had been unable to hear anything that Jenkinson had said. The equipment worked perfectly and it was only years later, when discussing the matter with an academic from Cornell University, that the pair discovered that Stirling's own level of concentration blocked out the messages, rather than any technical fault. Denis Jenkinson's response, typically trenchant, was: 'Well, that just goes to show, if these rally drivers were really going on ten-tenths, they couldn't hear the pace notes, could they?'

Even practice was hazardous; they managed to collide with an ammunition-laden military truck as well as an unfortunate sheep. In total, they drove six complete circuits over a period of as many weeks, in between Stirling's other racing commitments. There was no opportunity to practice under race conditions, simply because the roads remained open until race day. This meant that the race strategy itself was the result of something like a jigsaw, as the course had to be explored in separate sections: the race itself was the first time that they attempted the full circuit uninterrupted.

And famously, they won it in a record time, averaging a shade under 100 mph (97.96) for the 992.329 miles. This time would never be beaten. It was a Herculean effort by any measure and it had one very simple effect; it made Stirling a superstar, although not in his own mind. Jenkinson was enchanted by the experience and afterwards Stirling was moved to say: 'I might possibly have finished the *Mille* without Jenks (although I doubt it) but I couldn't possibly have won it.' From then on, Stirling could (almost) do no wrong in Jenkinson's eyes. Jenks's approval was, in its way, almost as important to Stirling as actually winning the race.

In terms of sports car racing the team never actually ran under orders (except once at the Ràbelöv circuit at Kristianstad in Sweden; the sportscar championship could have been at stake) but Stirling, despite his small reservations about the car, was to put in another year of hard learning. There was but one rule which applied in all circumstances; if any Mercedes car was 30 seconds ahead of the field, then positions should be held. Stirling had established to his own satisfaction that in terms of sports car racing he probably had the measure of the Argentinian maestro, but the differences between the Mercedes and the Maserati, given that the Italian machine had afforded him such insights, left him quite content to follow in the master's wheel-tracks, and a very fine academy that was. A concentration that had been completely absent at school suddenly reasserted itself.

One reason why Juan Manuel Fangio was a truly great driver was his simple willingness to have as a team mate a man he thought could actually beat him. The contrast with today is clear. Stirling's view of the situation, however, was that he played the role of keen pupil, in single-seaters at least. So closely did he track Fangio that from some angles the Stuttgart team appeared to have entered an eight-wheeler. This was to cause some concern to Neubauer; he looked upon 'the train', as the formation driving was quickly dubbed, as potentially hazardous. If Fangio made a mistake, it would be simply impossible for Stirling to avoid him; not only was there a risk of losing two drivers, but two cars as well. Stirling's response to this encapsulates the essence of his professional relationship with Fangio: 'Juan Manuel simply did not make mistakes.'

Neubauer was not particularly mollified by this but there was very little he could do about it, as it was team policy that drivers ran their own races; it was basic to the philosophy. While the balletic grace with which the pair raced was supremely elegant, even a beautiful thing to watch, it also rammed home very firmly the fact that Stirling could actually follow in Fangio's wheel-tracks to a centimetre, which was no small thing in itself. He was making a very important point, revisiting the experience of 'getting a tow' that he had first encountered in the HWM. As for Fangio, his

view of Stirling's willingness to put himself in harm's way by such formation driving simply reflected the total trust that Stirling was displaying; a flattering challenge, so to speak. That he was also airily unconcerned by any prospect of his being shunted from behind (the pair were occasionally separated by mere inches) was also reciprocally flattering to Stirling. But quite often, they were the only two even on the same lap. As back markers were encountered, a slight disengagement often took place.

Visually 'the train' was a hugely strong image as the mighty silver cars built up and held vast leads, almost participating in an entirely separate competition from the rest

of the field. It displayed an apparently casual attitude which was to serve the team well, making it clear that providing the cars were reliable, there was little point in anyone else trying seriously to beat them.

But 'the train' was a *Grand Prix* formation; neither driver was sufficiently optimistic to risk it in sports car events where the variability of the opposition (in terms of cars and drivers) was huge – wider than it had ever been. We have to look upon 'the train' as an indulgence which could be afforded, whatever it did to Neubauer's blood pressure.

As the European leg of the *Grand Prix* season got under way at Monaco, followed by Spa-Francorchamps, no one was to know that it would be a severely truncated one, for no one could have foreseen what was to happen at Le Mans. Monaco was an embarrassing and untypical fiasco for Mercedes; both Fangio and then Stirling retired for the same reason – their engines unceremoniously vomited up their oil. Stirling pushed his car over the line to a miserable ninth place, which, given that he had led for 75 laps, was galling. These mishaps left the race to Maurice Trintignant in a Ferrari, but only because Alberto Ascari managed to drop his Lancia into the harbour. He was unhurt, but would die days later in a stupid accident while testing a Ferrari sports car.

His death was to have a complicated effect on Italian racing; indeed, the Lancia works effort started to grind to a halt after his demise. There was a young thruster, Eugenio Castelotti, who would take up the challenge and at times drive the Lancia with a grace and commitment easily the equal of Ascari, but it was a matter of simple economics, brokered and sponsored by Fiat, that would drive the Lancia works effort into the hands of Enzo Ferrari before long.

Anyone who knows anything about automobiles will tell you that Lancia (up to that point at least) had never made a bad car. How exceptional this chubby V8 racer was, nobody was quite sure, as Ascari's driving had perhaps served to obscure its qualities. At Spa though, an energised Castelotti put one firmly on pole position before rain slowed down practice, so Fangio and Stirling, running as 'the train', had

Previous page: Although the Mercedes is prepared for the heat (note the exhaust shield), it rained rather hard in Argentina, 1955.

Above: Rainmaster.

Facing page: 'The train', airbrakes deployed at the Swedish Sports car *Grand Prix*, Ràbelöv.

Overleaf: A very relaxed wave, despite the fact that this was Stirling's first *Grand Epreuve* win, Aintree, 1955.

much to do in order to compensate for the humiliation of Monaco. They managed it with a 1-2 win, and some semblance of the *status quo ante* returned to the world of *Grands Prix*, at least from Stuttgart's point of view. Then, however, came Le Mans...

Stirling had every reason to be delighted at the prospect of sharing a car with Fangio; he knew that he could beat him in sports cars, but this pairing meant that he did not have to; that thought pleased him. His natural sense of justice mandated that it was somehow improper to learn from a man in one school and teach him in another. Everyone else was fair game, of course.

The tragedy that was to unfold started innocuously enough. The serious contenders, Mercedes, Jaguar, Ferrari and Aston Martin, had all made their usual preparations. There was a new member of the Mercedes team, a Frenchman named Pierre Bouillon who raced under the pseudonym of Levegh. He was paired with the American John Fitch. The third SLR was to be driven by Karl Kling and another newcomer, André Simon.

The cars were configured as single-seaters, with single headrests, as no passengers were carried at Le Mans. There was one important modification though; an air brake

mounted on the rear deck was installed in order to enhance the retarding effect of the traditional drum brakes that Mercedes was still using. Up against the disc-braked D-type Jaguars, they might make all the difference. The gearing of the Mercedes offered a maximum speed of 185 mph, so it was vital that the stopping power was up to the mark.

And so it proved, with one fatal exception. There was an unforeseen extra benefit, in effect, a very modern touch – downforce. As the great flap was raised, so the rear (driving) wheels were instantly given more grip. However incongruous the arrangement looked, it worked very well; sufficiently well that by the time the first refuelling stop was permitted, the German team was well in the lead, able to outbrake even the Jaguars, provided the driver thought far ahead enough.

At just before 6.30, Mike Hawthorn arrived in his D-type at the pit straight for his first fuel stop. He was in front of Stirling's old friend Lance Macklin, who was aboard an Austin-Healey 100S. As Hawthorn braked before pulling in, Macklin was forced to both slow and move to the left. This took him straight into the path of Pierre Levegh's 300 SLR which, although not travelling at absolutely top speed, was still moving at 130 mph. Fangio was just behind him.

Levegh simply had no choice and therefore no chance; he

too moved to the left, but had nowhere to go as there was simply not enough room and hardly time to even stab the wheel brakes, let alone deploy the airbrake. The Mercedes slammed into the rear of Macklin's Healey and ran up the sloped boot of the car, becoming instantly airborne. The car floated on to the low retaining earth bank of the spectators' enclosure exactly opposite the pits. It exploded and broke up; the engine, still roaring, together with the front suspension, radiator, brakes and wheels ripped through the tightly packed crowd. Poor Levegh died instantly, brutally catapulted out of the cockpit as the silver car impacted. Mercifully, he was to have no knowledge of the ghastly effect that his accident was to have, not only on the casualties (over 80 were killed) but also on his beloved sport. Macklin was unharmed, at least physically. He immediately blamed Hawthorn, to his face.

Opinions differ as to who was responsible for the accident. The biggest single peril at Le Mans was (and is) the huge variance between the qualities of both cars and drivers. But in 1955 the circuit itself was another danger, since it had not kept pace with the technical developments of the cars that raced on it. At the point of contact, the track was narrow.

Levegh may have assumed that Fangio was going to pass him, which is perhaps why he was placed where he was when Macklin's Healey swung into his path to avoid the braking Jaguar. Fangio was to say later that Levegh actually saved his life by flicking a hasty hand signal; although it is hard to see this on the film of the crash, it is something that Fangio was to believe until the day he died.

Lofty England saw the crash. His analysis of what happened unsurprisingly exonerates Hawthorn and implicates Macklin, whereas Rob Walker recalled a distraught, semi-hysterical Hawthorn blundering through the area behind the pits, blaming himself for not anticipating sufficiently. To be fair, this was almost immediately after he had spoken to Macklin and his sense of guilt, in the light of Macklin's remarks, is perhaps justifiable – he was a decent man, after all, and the experience had been traumatic.

Stirling did not actually witness the crash, but obviously heard it. He has no opinion of the cause, save that it was not particularly the fault of Mercedes-Benz, so the decision to withdraw the team was, in his view, pointless; it suggested guilt and also denied him victory, as the Fangio/Moss Mercedes was to open up a huge lead before the word came from Stuttgart to withdraw the cars at 2 am: 'It struck me as rather empty theatrical gesture, which came close to

Previous pages: Stirling and Fangio after the Aintree win. A proud Pat Moss (in front of policeman) looks on.

Right: 'To some observers, it seemed that Mercedes had entered an eight-wheeler.'

admitting some responsibility for what had happened...I was very frustrated when we were ordered to withdraw.'

The suggestion had actually come from John Fitch, Levegh's co-driver, who was traumatised by the events which unfolded. He had commented that the team should withdraw as a mark of respect but given that other teams did not, the action might well have been misinterpreted; the entire team had headed for home by the time the race was over.

The British *Grand Prix* of 1955 held at Aintree will always (in a small way) be controversial; did Stirling win it, did Fangio let him win it, or was it a policy decision by Stuttgart that he should win it? By his own account, he does not know. Film of the event certainly suggests that he had the edge on the day. But Stirling is very sensitive about Fangio; his total respect for the man gives him a small mental block about discussing, in anything but the vaguest terms, the question of his ability to beat him, in Formula 1 at least:

> *I knew I could beat him in sports cars, I acknowledged that, because I did it. In Formula 1, he was so good and I had such respect for him, that it would have almost been insolent.*

Stirling guards Fangio's place at the top table of sport with an earnest intensity which speaks very well of both men, and all this in spite of the faint whiff of suspicion that Juan Manuel himself, who was as fond of women as Stirling, may

Above: Dundrod, 1955. The torn rear bodywork was the result of a burst tyre.

Left: To the winner, a birthday cake. Stirling and John Fitch chat while Aileen sorts out the catering. 17 September, 1955, Dundrod.

have been less than honourable towards Stirling in his dealings with Sally Weston: 'Well if it was true – rather him, I suppose, than anyone else,' says Stirling.

Despite that possibility, the personal relationship between the two men was unique in the sport. There were drivers who had close friends who were racers – Mike Hawthorn and Peter Collins, for example, or Harry Schell and the Marquis de Portago, but the Moss/Fangio friendship was something else entirely; almost a spiritual thing. It was fraternal and paternal at the same time and was to endure for the rest of Fangio's life.

Others have observed that 1955 also became, perhaps, a 'politically correct' season for Mercedes-Benz in the light of the Le Mans crash, as Piero Taruffi, the Italian guest driver, very nearly dead-heated Fangio in the Italian *Grand Prix*, an event not many pundits would have necessarily forecast. Taruffi was a wonderfully talented driver, but…Perhaps these are unworthy thoughts, though. As we look at Stirling Moss's career we arrive at several conclusions about him which, added together, offer a remarkable spectrum of skills, particularly an eerie consistency over an extraordinary range

of machines which would be unthinkable now and was rare even then.

The Sports Car *Grand Prix* at Ràbelöv, Sweden in August did actually offer an example of the sports car 'train' at work, as the two 300 SLRs, with Fangio leading, romped around to deliver more vital points in the World Sports Car Championship. Team orders applied in this race; the loss of a potentially huge points score at Le Mans mandated that caution was the watchword, not that this stopped Stirling grabbing fastest lap, despite being second overall.

Due to the cancellations in the wake of Le Mans (none of them, interestingly, a sports car race) the 1955 Formula 1 season was a short one; the sport was pulling its horns in a little in the face of a huge amount of organised protest. While the Vatican's *Osservatore Romana* was unable to persuade the Monza AC to cancel the Italian *Grand Prix*, that journal would become a formidable opponent to motor

Previous pages: A rare sight; a denuded W 196 Formula 1 car at Stuttgart.

Above: Maserati 2508 at Aintree, driven by its owner. The car is now battleship grey, with a Union flag design on the nose.

racing, finally achieving at least one of its objectives in 1957 when it lobbied against the staging of another *Mille Miglia*. This position was perhaps slightly at odds with the unbridled celebrations which generally greeted an Italian (particularly a Ferrari) racing victory, involving the sounding of church bells; it is probably fair to say that motor racing was easily as important as God, but God, it was generally held, probably drove a Lancia.

By the time of the last two championship sports car races of 1955, there were some frayed nerves at Stuttgart. The racing programme, comprising as it did both sports cars and Formula 1, had been horrendously expensive, and the Le Mans accident, although the fault of neither Mercedes-Benz nor poor Pierre Levegh, had left its mark. It was the brutal result of unavoidable technical diversity at a time of rapid

chartered (sight unseen), a boat called *The Shrimp* for himself and Sally and was typically reluctant to occupy it on his own. Haynes readily agreed to accompany him.

When they arrived at the mooring, the two men realised that the vessel was aptly named; it was tiny. Haynes, who, as he readily confesses, 'didn't know one end of a boat from another', was quite unconcerned when his new friend produced mask, flippers and an air tank in order to try his hand at sub-aqua diving. Stirling had not actually tried this sport before, but reasoned that it must be fairly straightforward. Off they went. While Stirling was under the surface, the notorious mistral wind suddenly blew in and visibility dropped to almost zero; Haynes was rather more disturbed by this state of affairs. As the weather closed in, he looked in vain for any sign of his shipmate while at the same

To this day, David Haynes remains
Stirling's closest friend

but uneven development. For Neubauer's team, the withdrawal from the race, abandoning it to Jaguar, had left the future of the World Sports Car Championship in serious doubt. Mercedes was third behind Ferrari and Jaguar. Third, in effect, out of three.

On the face of it, the next event on the calendar, the RAC Tourist Trophy, was not a promising event for the Stuttgart team; the Dundrod circuit was both narrow and cramped and the huge variance between the performances of the vehicles present offered similar risks to the Le Mans race. To obviate the potential effect of this, the Ulster Automobile Club ordered that a great ditch be dug between the pit area and the crowd. Famously, the result was a 1-2-3 for Mercedes, but only just. Desmond Tittrington, son of a Belfast flax merchant, was partnering Mike Hawthorn and using his local knowledge tigered around. But for a broken crank, which was fairly fundamental, they would have managed third.

Stirling, rather at a loose end since his affair with Sally Weston ended, had meanwhile made the acquaintance of the man who would soon become his closest friend. To this day David Haynes remains Stirling's closest friend. They met at the house of the well-known TV presenter MacDonald Hobley. On the face of it, the two men had little in common, save that Haynes too had recently parted from his girlfriend, so he was pleased when Stirling invited him to the south of France for a long boys' weekend. Stirling has earlier

time attempting to control the tiny boat as it was buffeted by the sudden and unwelcome wind. Finally, he spotted Stirling at the very periphery of his vision and somehow managed to hold the boat steady while a startled Stirling clambered back aboard. 'He had no idea what was going on at all,' Haynes recalled, 'but for the grace of God, he would have drowned.' David Haynes, unsurprisingly, has been rather protective of his friend ever since. This episode still costs Haynes sleep to this day. Stirling, quite unconcerned by his near-drowning was fretting somewhat at what appeared to be Neubauer's indecision, so when he was told finally that the team would be going to Sicily, he invited David Haynes to accompany him, partly for the fun of it, partly to help him learn the course, which he had never seen before.

The *Targa Florio* in Sicily was a tall order at the end of the season, particularly as a decider. While it was the world's oldest motor race (and the safest, at least statistically), it was also one of the hardest, having elements within it of both race and rally. The punishment meted out to car and driver meant that not only would the vehicles have to be immensely tough, so too would the drivers.

And they were. Given that this was probably the supreme challenge of all road races, an imaginative leavening of experience and simple *cojones* would be the required mix. Moss and Fangio, of course, had both qualities in abundance,

but Stirling had shown throughout the 1955 season that in sports cars he was superior. After Dundrod, Stirling had been asked to give consideration to strengthening the Stuttgart line-up. Two more drivers were needed to replace Wolfgang von Trips and André Simon.

In response to this rather flattering request, Stirling and Ken Gregory produced two men – Peter Collins and Desmond Tittrington. Collins, a works Aston Martin sports car driver, was willingly released; that company was not minded to enter the *Targa Florio*. Collins was occasionally unreliable, if utterly charming. Once Collins was in a racing car, however, he changed totally. Gone was the irresponsible (and irrepressible) public schoolboy; in his place a fierce if insecure buccaneer. He was to prove this several times, but the *Targa Florio* lifted his reputation out of the also-rans and into the first league, where it would stay.

Tittrington, the Ulsterman whose performance at Dundrod that year had so nearly broken the Mercedes monopoly, had impressed deeply, and he was both available and delighted at the chance to drive.

Alfred Neubauer was under great pressure. He had had to work very hard indeed to persuade Competition Director Fritz Nallinger to enter the *Targa Florio* at all. The alternative option, of a non-championship race in Venezuela, for reasons of local marketing in South America, may have sounded convincing to anyone else but Neubauer, but he was acutely aware that while *Grand Prix* racing was not scheduled for 1956, perhaps sports cars might be. Rudi Uhlenhaut was, after all, working on development models. Whatever stresses he was under, Neubauer hid them well, and did not telegraph his anxiety to the reorganised team.

Since its inception in 1906, the *Targa* had become a unique event. It had evolved into a race of almost 600 miles, 13 laps of the *Piccolo Madonie* circuit, which was a reduced version of the giant course over which the event had first been run. There were obvious issues over acclimatisation, which the Mercedes team addressed with its usual thoroughness. Because there were no co-drivers, only shared cars, the method of pace notes used in the *Mille Miglia* was not practical; total immersion with use of practice vehicles was, however, fulfilling the twin objectives of marketing and acclimatisation. It was a clever marketing strategy. The sight of a Fangio or Moss getting to know the circuit at the wheel of a modest production car was a powerful image.

But learning a 45-mile course which has a thousand corners and one five-mile straight is not easy. Locals had an inbuilt advantage, but then so had they on the *Mille Miglia*. By the time the race started on 16 October, the six drivers knew it as well as they were going to. Stirling had Haynes's

assistance. 'Two days before the race,' Haynes recalled, 'we did three laps together in a cooking Mercedes. We went roung quickly but sensibly. He was shouting out what he wanted to remember and I scribbled it down as best I could. It was the most incredible experience of my life, approaching corners at 120 mph with a sheer drop the other side.'

The 300 SLR was a remarkable machine. Weighing less than a Volkswagen Golf, its straight-eight engine produced 300 brake horsepower from just less than 3 litres. It was also an extremely tough car, its space-frame chassis capable of absorbing truly terrible loads. This was to be a significant factor, for it would need every ounce of its strength.

The Moss-Collins plan was for Stirling to start and run a fast four laps to establish a lead before handing the car to Collins, who would run five, and Stirling would complete the race. All went according to plan with the SLR happily cruising along the *Retilineo di Bornofello* straight at 160 mph, but on lap four, when over five minutes ahead of Eugenio Castelotti and Robert Manzon in a Ferrari, Stirling left the road and the car lurched down twelve feet onto a patch of rocky ground. It was not a particularly life-threatening moment and he was hardly short of assistance. Stirling simply mashed it into gear and scrabbled back onto the track with the aid of some spectators. A lesser machine would have been written off, but despite losing much of its coolant, it seemed just about driveable.

Collins then really earned his money. Barely enquiring as to any damage, he hurled the battered silver car around the track, recovering all the lost time and successively broke the lap record. When he handed the car back to Stirling it was in the lead again. Moss, having quite recovered his composure, took over for the final session and proceeded to go faster and faster. The engine near boiling point, he too set successively faster lap records, culminating in a staggering 43 minutes 7.4 seconds – 62.2 mph. At the flag, he was again five minutes in the lead from Fangio and Kling. Castelotti and Manzon had held on in their Ferrari to come third, closely followed by Fitch and Titterington. Mercedes had won the championship, mission accomplished. Sadly, it was the last time the howl of the 300SLR was heard in competition. At a press conference shortly afterward, the news was broken that Mercedes-Benz was pulling out of competition at all levels.

This was uneasy news, particularly on the sports car front; after two seasons in Formula 1, which had proved beyond any doubt that its cars were totally dominant, a withdrawal was unsurprising, but then the cost of operating at this level

Facing page: The racing line; Stirling negotiates the chicane at Monaco, 1955.

was staggering. For example, the Mercedes entourage at Dundrod had numbered no less than 130 assorted people and they all had to be paid, let alone the other costs associated with the sport. The R&D budget was whimpering under the strain and it was time now to reap the benefits.

For Stirling, the year with the Stuttgart team had been an unparalleled experience, but a surprising one. He had learned, for example, that Fangio was more or less indifferent to the way his car was set up; more often than not he would follow Stirling's lead in matters such as axle ratios, tyre pressures and damper settings, then the sleepy-looking maestro simply climbed aboard and drove. All the attention to detail, coupled with a speed of response to problems which bordered on the bemusing, was naturally a huge support, but all the drivers who had experienced the works in action knew that wherever they spent their next season, the organisational overkill which characterised the Mercedes-Benz effort would be absent. They had all, in short, been pampered.

Stirling's relationship with David Haynes, particularly in the light of the dramas at its outset, has remained firm ever since. As Stirling became busier, so did Ken Gregory. Stirling Moss Limited had set up offices near Trafalgar Square in the same building as Alfred's main West End surgery in William IV Street.

David Haynes was later to become close to the entire Moss family. He recalled his amazement at Alfred's simple capacity for hard work when he spent a day with Alfred as he made the rounds of all his numerous dental practices. 'It was almost like a production line,' he recalled, 'Alfred would go from room to room, giving an injection here, a rinse there, pulling a tooth or taking a cast – I wouldn't be surprised if he managed to treat forty or fifty people in a day.' This was obviously an enterprise of some vigour, but as Haynes says now:

I had little or no money; I was starting out in our family business, whereas Stirling was earning a lot of money, but because he was always careful, the huge difference in our income did not affect our friendship at all. I will always appreciate the fact that Ken Gregory, his manager and great buddy, would sometimes even ask me to stand in as Stirling's manager. I would treat it as a holiday, of course, but acting as a manager.

Careful or not, Stirling would never allow the lessons he had learned about financial stringency stand in the way of friendship. Haynes recalled a squabble over an electric razor:

On one of the trips we went on, I had forgotten my razor, so I had to go and borrow his. He lent it to me begrudgingly. A couple of months later, I did the same again, but he said 'Well sod it, tough luck,' and took his razor off to practice so I couldn't use it. So I had to go out to the local barber shop and borrow one. Well, I taxed him with this while we were having dinner with Basil Cardew. We had a fair old argument about it, but four or five days later, I was in my flat when suddenly a package arrived with a very smart razor inside with all the voltage adaptors. There was a little note with it: 'Let's have no more of this nonsense.' It was a very nice thing to have done.

Their relationship has an interesting synergy. For Haynes, whose admiration for Moss knew few bounds after his experience on the *Targa Florio* circuit, it offered both an important friendship as well as immersion in a sport he came to love. For Stirling, whose abiding need for companionship (which almost borders on monophobia) was also coupled with a chronic shyness, Haynes' relaxed confidence was a useful counterbalance to that. Stirling's love of women rather outstripped his ability to approach them in the first place, wheras David Haynes felt no such qualms. So, as Stirling had learned from Macklin, now he learned from his new friend and he studied harder than he ever had at Haileybury. It seems he was a very good pupil.

Above: Stirling in the Porsche Spyder in the Goodwood nine-hours race, 1955.

Facing page: Alfred Neubauer.

SENSATIONS OF SPORT

STIRLING MOSS'S GREATEST WIN

The car was airborne for over 200 ft.

THE morning was already sunny and warm when, at 7.22 a.m. on May 1, 1955, Stirling Moss rolled his Mercedes down the ramp at Brescia for the start of the Mille Miglia. More than 530 cars of various sizes had entered for the event and the first had set off at dawn.

This was Moss's first year as a member of the powerful Mercedes team—and the most successful of his career. He was to finish runner-up in the World Championship and gain his first Grand Prix victory.

But now he was about to drive the greatest race of his career—the Mille Miglia over 1000 miles of Italian roads from Brescia to Rome and back again. On this course, shaped like an hour-glass and fraught with danger from start to finish, he achieved what some experts rate as the most amazing drive of all time.

Starting order was decided by ballot, and the late starters had the advantage of knowing how well their times compared with their rivals. Ahead of Moss were such great drivers as world champion Juan Manuel Fangio, Karl Kling, Peter Collins, and Maglioli. Behind him was the serious challenge of Taruffi, the veteran Italian driver, in a Ferrari.

Passengers were optional, and Moss had elected to take along as his navigator Denis Jenkinson, a bearded, bespectacled motoring correspondent. Jenkinson, a man of ice-cool nerves, was at one time passenger to world sidecar racing champion Eric Oliver.

No men can have ever prepared more thoroughly for a race than did Moss and "Jenks" for the Mille Miglia.

Every difficult twist, turn and rise on the tortuous 1000-mile course was plotted on a roller map devised by Jenkinson.

The British pair had worked out time schedules for the course which set them a target of 2 m.p.h. faster than the official record.

LIKE A ROCKET!

THAT morning Moss roared away like a rocket through the crowds and into the sun.

ENICAR watchword for the Sportsman of the Year!

Says Stirling Moss! "It's reassuring to know you're wearing a watch you can really depend on—like my ENICAR Sherpa." ENICAR watches are up-to-the-minute in appearance too. See the handsome range for men and women at prices from £9.15.0. Post this coupon today for the FREE catalogue.

To: Harman Jewellery & Watch Co. Ltd.,
Minerva House, 26-27 Hatton Garden, E.C.1
Phone and ask for the ENICAR free catalogue.

Name
Address

ENICAR ULTRASONIC

Stirling Moss

By Frank Wright

arily to collect the official stamp. Then he roared off and in a few seconds, had passed Castellotti in the pits. The Italian had stopped for new tyres.

After leaving the streets of Rasenna, where he narrowly missed an archway, Moss drove flat-out along the coastal roads in sight of the blue Adriatic. He took blind hill brows and bridges at 176 m.p.h. On one hump-back bridge he took to the air and made a perfect four-point landing at over two miles a minute.

His car had been airborne for over 200ft.

APPROACHING ROME, soon, on the straight roads to Verona, he was tearing along at 170 m.p.h. and maintaining that speed over blind hill brows which propelled the car into the air.

He roared into the streets of Padova at 150 m.p.h.—a shade too fast. He slid round a right-angle corner at breakneck speed, cannoned off the straw bales, and fighting with the wheel, somehow straightened out safely.

It was an incredible recovery, but it was not made without penalty. As Moss bumped into the bales, a grinning Castellotti, in his most spectacular drive, slipped ahead in his blood-red Ferrari.

For miles, Moss drove in the hazardous wake of Castellotti, who was sending up clouds of blinding dust. At Ravenna control, where Moss stopped only moments

DENSE CROWDS FORCED THE BRITISH PAIR TO SLOW DOWN. SLOWING DOWN, FOR MOSS, MEANT AT LEAST 130 m.p.h.

He stopped in the pits to have the rear wheels changed and learned that he was leading by nearly two minutes—ahead of Taruffi, Hermann, Kling and Fangio.

It was a popular saying that whoever led at Rome would not win at Brescia. Moss was determined to break that tradition. He drove as fiercely as ever and soon he passed a wrecked car which had struck a tree. The driver, who had broken several ribs, was Karl Kling.

But soon it was Moss's turn for trouble. The brakes started to grab and suddenly the car spun round and began to slide into a ditch. Moss slipped the car into bottom gear and pulled away with a dented tail. Precious seconds ticked away as he turned the Mercedes around in the narrow road.

Nearly 700 miles had now passed and still Stirling looked completely relaxed. He screamed through Florence at 120 m.p.h. as vast crowds gaped in wonder at his progress.

The British champion raced on

FANTASTIC TIME

OVER the last 50 miles, there were more terrifying slides on melted tar and it seemed impossible that Moss still had control. But each time he pulled out of danger by quick thinking, and soon he came in sight of the last corner before the finish. He took it at well over 100 m.p.h. believing that every single second counted.

Caked in dust and dirt, oil stained and black faced, the British driver staggered from his car at the finish, turned to his

into the heart of the Appenines, several times going into fearful slides on patches of melted tar and oil. He could have eased up the pace, but he was not to know that Taruffi had retired with a broken oil pump and that Fangio had stopped for repairs to an injection pipe.

After passing Hans Hermann, who had stopped by the roadside, Moss's Mercedes screamed into Bologna at 150 m.p.h.

Well ahead of the record, he raced on at 170 m.p.h.—and maintained such a consistently high speed that he actually overtook two aeroplanes being used to take films of the race. Now he was on the last stage of the Mille Miglia.

small, bearded companion, and asked—"Do you think we've won?" Jenkinson shook his head with uncertainty.

In fact, they had won the 1955 Mille Miglia in the fantastic time of 10 hours 7 minutes 48 seconds—an average speed of almost 98 m.p.h. Moss, the first British driver to win the Mille Miglia, finished half an hour ahead of his nearest rival, world champion Juan Fangio.

Yet this was not the end of the most fantastic day in Moss's racing life. The British champion was so tensed-up after concentrating at the wheel for ten hours that he found it impossible to get a full night's sleep.

He simply could not relax. So, after a short rest at Brescia, he climbed into his grey 220A Mercedes and drove through the night to the motor works at Stuttgart—400 miles away.

Stirling Moss's scrapbooks reflect the importance of the *Mille Miglia* win and the tragedy at Le Mans.

Daily Sketch, Monday, May 2, 1955 7

A dented car sets record

WHIRLWIND MOSS WINS THE CAR RACE OF HIS LIFE

ROME, Sunday.

STIRLING MOSS swept to victory in the greatest race of his career to-day when he out-drove and out-manœuvred the world's best drivers in the 1,000-mile Italian Mille Miglia race to set up a record.

Moss drove his German Mercedes over the twisting route round Italy at an average speed of 97.95 m.p.h. and was the first Briton to win the race.

The old record of 88.3 m.p.h. was set in 1953 by Italy's Giannino Marzotte.

Moss led a powerful Mercedes team with Argentinian world champion Juan Fangio and Hans Hermann. Fangio, who was second, finished 30 minutes behind Moss, who covered the course in 10hr. 7min. 48sec.

A FIGHT

The 253 starters thinned out early and it became a fight between the Ferraris and Mercedes.

Until Mercedes driver Karl Kling skidded and overturned at the half-way mark outside Rome and Hermann retired soon after with petrol trouble, the four Mercedes cars dominated the race.

Shortly before the half-way mark, Moss passed Ferrari's Taruffi, Hermann, Kling and Fangio in that order.

Two Italians, driving a Lancia Aurelia, were badly hurt when their skidding car hit a wall.

SATISFACTION

"After the race Moss said: "This victory has given me the greatest satisfaction of my career. I let myself go."

STIRLING MOSS (seated on right in the car) at the Rome check-point during the Mille Miglia. He led the field at this stage.

The Mercedes already testifies to the hazards of the race—the front is dented as the result of a slight collision.

Spectators crane over the barrier for a good view of Moss, who won the race in record time.

BRILLIANT TRIUMPH BY STIRLING MOSS IN ITALIAN "CLASSIC"

IT was Britain's day yesterday in international car and motor-cycle racing. Britons won the classic Italian Mille Miglia, the senior event of the Spanish Grand Prix, and swept the field in the international motor-cycling races at Mettet, in Belgium.

These reports from the Continent tell of British triumphs:

Brescia (N. Italy) Sunday.

Stirling Moss, 25-year-old British champion, driving a German Mercedes sports car, won the classic 1,000 Miles Italian Mille Miglia Road Race which ended today.

Women plunged into the crowd near Padua injuring 15 people, including 11 children. The driver was unhurt.

Two Italians in a Lancia Aurelia were badly hurt when their car hit a wall.—Reuter.

STIRLING MOSS WINS GREAT ITALIAN MOTOR RACE. STIRLING MOSS THE WELL KNOWN YOUNG BRITISH DRIVER BECAME THE FIRST BRITON EVER TO WIN THE GREAT MILLE MIGLIA, THE MOTOR RACE OF ALMOST 1,000 MILES WHICH COVERS HALF THE LENGTH AND THE WHOLE OF THE BREADTH OF ITALY. DRIVING A GERMAN MERCEDES BENZ MOSS COVERED THE 992 MILES COURSE IN 10 HOURS. 7 MINS. 46 SECS., AVERAGING 97.8. m.p.h. a record for the race.
F.44323. Stirling Moss being assisted in after his victory.

Mesterlige MOSS

Motorsportens engelske kronprins skabte stor højspænding paa Roskilde Ring

BILLED BLADET

KUN 7/10 SEKUND skilte Stirling Moss fra sejren, og han kunne ikke skjule sin skuffelse efter det knaldhaarde slutopgør med Gunnar Carlsson.

DET er en dejlig bane at køre paa, og jeg vil meget gerne komme igen næste sæson.
Saadan sagde den verdensberømte engelske mesterkører Stirling Moss efter successløbene paa Roskil-de Ring, og hans udtalelse vil sikkert vække glæde hos alle motorsportinteresserede. For nok var det svenskeren Gunnar Carlsson, som løb med laurbærkransen og førstepr* mien, men det var Moss, som fik broderparten af bifaldet fra de 40.000

La mort a frôlé notre photographe qui vu l'Austin-Healey tuer ses deux voisins

Sur les cinquante mètres du drame c: spectateurs occupent la place des victimes

5

Vanwall & Many More

Guy Anthony Vandervell was a fat, clever and brutally straightforward old Harrovian who had a very clear idea of what he wanted to do – to construct and enter a winning *Grand Prix* racing car. It would be green, British and better than anything the Italians could offer.

As Britain's foremost manufacturer of engine bearings, he had been a major sponsor of the original BRM project in 1950, but had rapidly tired of the string of excuses from Raymond Mays and Peter Berthon concerning the problems they encountered in the production of the BRM car. He mistrusted both men; all he could see was that they seemed to be making a very decent living at the expense of the hard-pushed sponsors. This didn't stop Vandervell from making an abortive attempt to hijack the whole project, however.

Another magnate who was on the committee that oversaw the affairs of the BRM project was Alfred Owen. Owen was a man so nice that he bordered on the saintly; he was also a very good businessman and was boss of the Rubery Owen empire, which was to motor car chassis what the Thinwall bearing was to their engines. Mays and Berthon realised that if Vandervell

obtained control of the project, they would be out of a job; they appealed to Owen for protection. He assented and Vandervell's *coup* was swiftly dispatched. Shortly afterwards, the project became part of the newly formed Owen Racing Organisation. BRM would prosper as a marque, but not for some time. The Owen organisation did not have to pay much; the cars had a certain curiosity value, but beyond that the whole venture was something of a leap of faith for Owen. Vandervell would never quite understand his patience with BRM.

Apart from Vandervell Products Ltd, Vandervell had close links with Norton, another fine engineering company. He had also drifted into a relationship with Coopers, the starting point of which was a generous offer by him to assist them with the acquisition of Norton engines. In return for this assistance Coopers readily agreed to fabricate a chassis frame for his new

car. It was a straightforward enough task for the Cooper chief engineer Owen Maddock, and the result was a structure not so far removed from the Cooper-Alta specials which Stirling would campaign in 1953.

The process by which the Vanwall was reinvented was more or less serendipitous, and was a function of the close nature of the British motor racing community. One of the small army of staff involved with the Vanwall team was Derek Wootton, who performed a variety of services. He was a friend of Colin

Previous pages: Stirling with Harry Schell and the Marquis de Portago on the Tour de France, 1956.

Below: Stirling sandwiched between Archie Scott Brown driving number 6 and Mike Hawthorn in number 4 at Goodwood for the Glover Trophy, 1956.

Anthony Bruce Chapman, who was then struggling to build up his Lotus car business in a damp, dismal shed in Hornsey, north London. Operating on a shoestring, Chapman had by 1955 accomplished a great deal. He had developed a small line of sports cars built around other people's proprietary parts, which handled superbly and were externally styled by Francis Albert Costin, chief engineer in the aerodynamic flight test department of the de Havilland Aircraft Company. Vandervell knew of Chapman, but little about Costin who shunned the limelight.

Costin and Chapman were retained separately for the Vanwall project, but Costin undertook the design work on the basis that Chapman would do the chassis and vice versa; it was a symbiosis that had worked before and indeed had redefined the genre of the minimally engined road racer.

Meanwhile, Stirling had been keeping a weather eye on the developments at Vanwall, as anything which Vandervell did was likely to be of some interest. He was now the best-qualified

driver in the world; he had learned with his Maserati many of the subtleties of racing, an experience refined in Fangio's wheel-tracks. He had also learned that a race is a series of intimately connected events, not laps but corners or even segments of corners, each of which had to be addressed not only individually, but also as part of a greater whole. Laps were an accounting convention and useful for officials and spectators.

After the exertions of the Mercedes season, he was in some confusion as to what to do; there were three British marques and all had merit. The Connaught was now redesigned as a Formula 1 machine with a reworked engine based on the work

Above: Rivers Fletcher and Raymond Mays look on as Mike Hawthorn and Stirling discuss the 1956 BRM at Goodwood.

Above right: According to one witness, a Connaught mechanic, Scott Brown simply 'buggered off' at the start of the 100-mile-race...until his engine broke down.

of Geoffrey Taylor, a core design architecture that HWM had used. The BRM P25 was a possibility, although Stirling would always have reservations about the firm. And then there was the Vanwall which, although it had been totally redesigned, was still something of an unknown quantity. There was an extraordinary similarity between all the British offerings; all were beautifully built, all used relatively simple four-cylinder twin-cam engines and all had broadly similar underpinnings. The Vanwall differed slightly, in that it employed a transverse leaf-spring suspension layout, *à la* Cooper (this would soon change) but more vitally, they all wanted Stirling to lead their teams.

Such was the esteem in which Stirling was held that it was a simple matter for Ken Gregory to persuade Vanwall, BRM and Connaught to arrive at Silverstone on 22 November, 1955, each with a car for Stirling to test. All knew that there was an open offer from Maserati already on the table, so Connaught, the most financially restricted of the trio, must

have been rather gloomy at the prospect. In fact, Stirling set almost identical times in both the BRM and the Connaught, at 1 minute 50 seconds, the same speed as the fastest lap in the last *Grand Prix* which had been held at Silverstone in 1954. It was a decent enough time but certainly not one outside his experience – he had raced his own Maserati at that speed. But when he tried the new Vanwall, he managed a time three seconds quicker than that, which was very much on the far side of Mercedes territory, at least on that circuit. 'Bloody fast' was his diary opinion, but his experience of testing the old model Vanwall a fortnight before had left some doubts about an obvious flat spot in the power curve of the fuel-injected engine.

He found it hard to make up his mind; his gut instinct was to stick with what he knew, the friendly but slightly chaotic Maserati works team. The Vanwall was obviously a very serious contender, but despite the ministrations of Chapman and Costin,

it was still raw and unrefined. Having just left Mercedes-Benz, the world was his oyster, but he also realised that to commit fully to a British dark horse might be a mistake. He was as keen as ever to see a green car win, but the sheer professionalism of the German factory team had left him gasping with admiration but seeking more flexibility. In short, he had been spoilt.

He decided to seek external advice from an informally convened panel of the great and the good from within the ranks of the Guild of Motoring Writers, who recommended unreservedly that Stirling sign for Maserati.

There was an emotional tug for him, too; he had come to miss his Maserati as well as the sometimes comic-opera business infrastructure that went with it. Maserati was a very laid-back place, in sharp contrast to the Byzantine politics at Ferrari and the anally retentive orderliness at Stuttgart. He had occasionally driven his own car, chassis 2508, in 1955 but had also put other drivers in that cockpit and pleasingly none had outperformed him. Since leaving it behind as his main car, he had learned a vast amount with Fangio as a teacher. He had also delivered the World Sports Car Championship for Stuttgart. He relished the opportunity of going to Maserati in order to concentrate fully on consummating his first serious automobile relationship, perhaps with the World Championship?

It was not an unreasonable hope, and although the sheer excellence of the rebadged Lancias now being run by Enzo Ferrari were an obvious threat to anyone's ambitions, the phone had not rung from that quarter in years and probably would not now that Ferrari had secured the services of Fangio for the season at what, rumour had it, was a suspiciously cheap price. If no British machine could reliably deliver, and reliability was the key, then it would have to be a foreign one and Maserati was more like home than anywhere else. 'After Mercedes, it was like going back to an old friend,' he says now.

With Mercedes absent, the pressure was back on the Italian manufacturers to start winning again. The Maserati personnel – who had switched smoothly from being Stirling's biggest fans in 1954 to a slightly cooler demeanour when in 1955, he had reverted to being a mere customer – were to prove themselves equally adept at dusting off their old enthusiasm for him, and Orsi, Ugolini, Bertocchi and all the rest were to redouble their efforts throughout 1956. They had enjoyed two years of development opportunity while Mercedes had dominated and were philosophical. About the Germans, they had been able to do little; about Ferrari, they might do a lot, particularly with Moss on board again. His decision to return to Maserati was

Left: Stirling gives the one-handed Archie Scott Brown a well-deserved lift back to the pits after his engine broke down. Scott Brown also had difficulty walking. 'He really was an incredible little bloke.'

the cause of some celebration in at least one factory in Modena, while any grumbles at home could be safely dealt with by those who had been instrumental in advising him to do it. The press could always throw a bone to any dissenters; Stirling was to be the Aston Martin team leader for the upcoming year.

To ask the press for its advice is a very clever thing to do; few journalists, particularly motoring journalists, are immune to the flattery implicit in such a request, particularly when it comes from a young man like Stirling. From his point of view, the advice merely confirmed what he already felt, but the endorsement was useful – they could hardly say bad things about him should the season be a let-down. Nor did they.

The first domestic sessions of 1956 were perhaps to make Stirling wonder if he had made the right decision. After an encouraging result in his own Maserati in the New Zealand *Grand Prix* (pole position, first place and lap record) and a disappointing retirement at the Argentine *Grand Prix* driving the works machine, Stirling came up against the British-made

opposition in the spring and early summer of 1956, most famously at Goodwood where he beat Archie Scott Brown in the Connaught B-type, mainly because the Connaught's engine let go. Hawthorn was part of that great dice, but his BRM also broke. The sheer pace of these cars was impressive, although the BRM was certainly not 'right' yet. Hawthorn was to later remark that the machine had tripled his laundry bills.

But at Silverstone, Stirling drove the new Vanwall for the first time in competition. It was the car's début race after Costin and Chapman had reworked it and what had started out as an interesting experiment turned into a full-blooded dice with Hawthorn's BRM, which Stirling managed to win, sharing a new lap record with him. So the Vanwall worked, the BRM (in the right hands) had the legs for it and the Connaught, if driven by a tiger like Brooks or Scott Brown, was also far better than it

Below: An airy wave as Stirling wins the Silverstone International in his first drive aboard the Costin/Chapman-designed Vanwall.

looked. Despite the two years of development time and the huge budgets, perhaps the Maserati 250F was no better than it should be after all. He still liked it though.

Maserati's sports cars were very good indeed. Aside from his Aston Martin commitment, Stirling was free to use the new Maserati 300S which was an inspiring car to drive as well as being utterly beautiful. It had the usual Maserati characteristics; neutral handling spiced with a slight natural oversteer and an F1-derived engine which seemed unburstable. The transmission by Valerio Colotti was well-nigh perfect and it was to be years before it was surpassed, from Stirling's point of view.

But there was unease at the Maserati works. Their intimate connection with Argentina was at the root of it and the

But if Maserati was slightly chaotic in 1956, Aston Martin most certainly was not. The AM racing manager John Wyer was not only vastly experienced but had that vital combination of commitment and discipline which, had it been applied to the Maserati works effort, would have solved at least some of its problems. Wyer knew that preparation was all and that a plan is not simply a polite suggestion; it is holy writ. And Stirling agreed. In his opinion, Wyer was the greatest race strategist of his generation and probably only now surpassed by Ferrari's Ross Brawn. His application went a long way towards overcoming some of the cars' deficiencies, of which, it must be said, there were very few and were mainly age-related.

Importantly, Aston Martin was also a very happy team, and

As the rapidly evolving circus moved around Europe, the practical jokes flew thick and fast

overthrow of President Perón in 1955 set in train a series of events which would hamstring them commercially, resulting in a spell in administrative receivership due to unpaid and repudiated debts. That Argentinian coup would have an impact on Fangio as well, as the new administration took pains to thoroughly investigate the finances of anyone who had been a protégé or a supporter. Fangio certainly fitted into both categories. As a fully paid-up *Peronista* as well as being the most famous protégé the regime had produced (it had financed his first Maserati) he was a natural target for 'investigation'. This did not keep him away from Argentina, as he was far too famous to be at physical risk, but it perhaps put financial pressures on him which Enzo Ferrari had been quick to exploit.

The 1956 *Mille Miglia* saw another Moss/Jenkinson pairing, which nearly did for the two of them when the hastily prepared Maserati locked its brakes and sent the car sliding wildly; it broke through a retaining wall and came to rest against one of a very sparse line of trees which separated the road from a 300-foot drop. Denis Jenkinson was unmoved by the incident; neither the crash itself nor the unidentifiable burning smell which had issued from the engine compartment at over 120 mph bothered him. Much worse for him was the failure of the pair to defend their win of the previous year. He was to ride happily with Stirling the next year in an even more powerful (and even less well-prepared) car.

Wyer's insistence that all matters concerning accommodation and catering were of the highest order available only made it more so. But beneath his rather forbidding exterior and 'death-ray' glare, he was a charming, diffident man, tolerant of the worst of the childish excesses to which his drivers fell prey. Racing drivers of this period, particularly British drivers, could be something of a handful. As the rapidly evolving circus moved around Europe, the practical jokes (which not all the drivers appreciated) flew thick and fast.

Despite his dislike of the taste of alcohol, he was quite able to party and chase women along with everyone else, purely as a result of the adrenalin boost which he enjoyed. Others found such spontaneity harder to generate, but more than one observer seeing Stirling at play, made the mistake of assuming that he was under the influence; in reality, he enjoyed what he was doing so much that he required no stimulants of any kind, save nicotine. He had started endorsing 'Craven A' cigarettes as far back as 1953.

At Le Mans, which was held later than usual due to the Suez crisis, Stirling, partnered by Peter Collins, came second in the

Right: The master. Juan Manuel Fangio in his Lancia-Ferrari on his way to win the 1956 British *Grand Prix* at Aintree.

Overleaf: This famous picture by Patrick Benjafield shows Stirling in the Aston Martin DB3S at Goodwood.

Aston Martin DB3S, a creditable performance as the car was by then anything but competitive, offering a depressing maximum speed of 142 mph. It was an old design, all of three years old, but Stirling remembers it with the same fondness as the Maserati 250. During one of Collins' driving spells, Stirling, with his pilot's vision, spotted a face in the crowd. A girl was standing more or less on the site of the previous year's accident. He waved a pass at her and invited her to the pits. When she arrived, he was deeply smitten. She was Canadian, her name was Katherine Molson, and her presence at Le Mans obviously

Fangio was back at Maserati for what would turn out to be his last full season and although he was driving a car which had been designed three years before, it was now much lighter and equipped with a reliable engine; he was still the obvious contender for the world title. As he would demonstrate later in the year, he was still capable of giving driving lessons to just about anyone else on the grid. For a man who had been born in 1911, it was an extraordinary accomplishment, but Fangio was, by any measure, an extraordinary man.

After a flurry of Maserati-powered activity in Argentina,

His little black address book
was confined to the desk drawer. . .

proved that she was a fan of the sport. She was undeniably very attractive too and it was clear to Stirling after only a brief acquaintance that she was also independent of mind and means.

There were few people who could be more charming when they put their minds to it than Stirling Moss and for him the process of courtship began almost immediately. His little black address book was consigned to the desk drawer – he would not need it for some time. So 1956 was a good year, despite the moment on the *Mille Miglia*. He had driven three of his favourite cars, two Maseratis and an Aston Martin, and again come second in the World Championship behind Fangio. Most importantly, he had fallen in love.

But Vanwall now beckoned. It was clear to him that the Maserati was still a fine car, but that the green offering with some objective science behind it was now a serious prospect. Any misgivings he had felt about it were banished by his assessment of the commitment which supported the project. This time Stirling did not hesitate.

The year 1957 was to be a tantalising season for Stirling.

Cuba and Sebring, Stirling finally engaged with the Vanwall at Syracuse in the non-championship *Grand Prix*. It was a typically mixed result; while he led for 28 laps and successively smashed the lap record, he came in three laps behind Peter Collins and Luigi Musso aboard their Lancia-Ferraris. The Heath-Robinson fuel delivery system of the Vanwall had delivered a broken pipe, the repair of which cost four laps.

A fortnight later, at the scene of his win the previous year at Goodwood's Glover Trophy, a pole position was encouraging, although a broken throttle linkage soon caused trouble, pitting Tony Brooks for five laps (before he broke the lap record) and putting Stirling out of the race. The race was won by a tigering Stuart Lewis-Evans in a Connaught.

The *Mille Miglia* that year offered some overtones of comic opera. While the previous year had been life-threatening, the 1957 event was to point out very firmly that Maserati's

Above: The beautiful, if outdated, DB3S Aston Martin.

Facing page: A smiling Stirling, enjoying the 'Maser'.

standards of preparation and finish were perhaps not quite up to their previous levels.

Only Maserati could come up with this extraordinary vehicle, the 450S. Powered by a thunderous 4½-litre 400 bhp V8 engine and equipped with what was effectively a ten-speed transmission for this race, it would reach 181 mph and accelerate from a standstill to 100 mph in eleven seconds. The reverse of that was another matter, even with its vast drum brakes, but while the rolling acceleration was even more extraordinary (10 to 90 mph in six seconds), there must be some thought that it was rather hurriedly put together. Stirling had already experienced the car at the Buenos Aires 1000 kilometre race in January, when he had shared one with Fangio; he had simply stormed ahead of the field before the distressed transmission gave out, and he had rather marked its card as being an unwieldy handful. Despite a certain justifiable nervousness, he and an eager Jenkinson were very short odds indeed to win the *Mille Miglia* for the second time, which would also give Maserati their first success. The pair's own preparations had been as before, with an updated set of pace notes in the same rolling format. Hopes were high; Maserati were inordinately proud of their new flagship racer.

The expedition lasted seven miles, or about three and a half minutes. Under load, at 130 mph, the brake pedal simply snapped off at the root and only by dint of some fairly brutal gearchanging was Stirling able to slow the car to a speed at which the pair could hop out and physically drag it to a halt.

It took a little longer than three and a half minutes to rumble back to the start line, where the energised and optimistic works mechanics were preparing to pack away their tools and spares. Stirling, pumped up on adrenalin and purple with rage, merely had to see the shock on the faces of the pole-axed men who had prepared the car to realise, with Jenkinson's calming hand on his arm, that further comment was probably unnecessary:

They had lavished so much effort and love on that car, the sure favourite which would at last win the Mille Miglia for Maserati, that they were struck dumb. Some just burst into

Above: The Vanwall in Monaco trim, with its nose cone removed to shorten it and aid cooling.

Right: On his way to a rare error, Stirling in the Vanwall at the 1958 Belgian *Grand Prix*.

tears. Our anger evaporated. We couldn't take it out on them...just one look at their faces was enough.

At that stage, no one could know that this *Mille Miglia*, the 24th, was to be the last ever held, for the disaster which would end it had yet to happen. It took place later that day when the Marquis de Portago's Ferrari left the road and mowed down a group of spectators, nine of whom died, including five children. De Portago and his co-driver Ed Nelson also lost their lives. The Vatican had its way and the race was banned forthwith.

Noting with interest the performance of the Vanwall, Orsi asked Stirling after the Buenos Aires race whether Frank Costin might perhaps be available to design a *coupé* version of the 450S to run at Le Mans, which should, on paper, be even faster than the open spider version. Costin agreed to draw up a design and because the usual Maserati body maker, Fantuzzi, was booked solid with early season work, the job was out-sourced to Zagato of Milan who did not ordinarily build bodies for racing cars to anyone else's design. It rather showed, too.

Frank Costin's speciality was the management of air; he used it to create stability, he removed it from where it did not belong, and he put it where it would be most useful – for engine breathing, cooling and the creation of minimum drag. He was a meticulous man and rapidly calculated that the design that he

had already created for the hugely successful Lotus XI would do very well with the addition of a roof. It was a design theme he would recycle again, in fact, for Brian Lister, but never again with an Italian coachbuilder.

Costin estimated that the scaled-up shape of the roofed-in Lotus would offer the potential of over 200 mph (much more than that and it would, in all probability, take off) but he had reckoned without the 'interpretation' put on his design by both Maserati and more particularly Zagato who between them, managed to produce a grotesque pastiche which totally ignored the theory behind it. It was the same general shape, but in all matters relating to Costin's core philosophy regarding air, it was severely wanting.

What staggered Costin when he visited the Zagato factory was the simply appalling quality of the work. The body panels were crudely hammered out, the oldest artisan starting, the youngest finishing, each with successively smaller hammers, until the dimpled panel was completed, whereupon the whole thing was welded together and smeared with body filler of up to a quarter inch in depth. The Vanwall designer was more used to the elegant rolled alloy which was the favoured method in Britain, and not only because the process was quieter. He was quite traumatised. After all, his name was on this.

But at least poor Costin never had to actually drive it. Fangio

took one look at it and opted to drive an open car with Jean Behra, but Harry Schell was made of sterner (or at least more optimistic) stuff and undertook to partner Stirling in the race. The first thing Stirling realised was that the open cars were actually faster, as a cackling Jean Behra totally outpaced the *coupé* in practice. The second was that the air ducts from the engine vented onto his feet. The third was that the air inlet to the carburettors was wrongly sited, which starved them of air, hence the poor performance. All in all, it was a miserable weekend, although everyone outside the Maserati works effort found it hugely funny. Ultimately, the rear axle failed; the car was lying second at the time, which reflects very well on its drivers at least.

By comparison, Formula 1 was relatively straightforward. Stirling and Tony Brooks were augmented by the addition of the ferociously quick Stuart Lewis-Evans, who was out of a drive after Connaught ran out of money. The 1957 Monaco *Grand Prix* was their last race, and Lewis-Evans's fine fourth place, ahead of all the Lancia-Ferraris, reinforced the impression he had made at the Glover Trophy earlier in the spring. He was signed up for the rest of the season.

Suddenly, Tony Vandervell had an all-British team driving green cars; what he could actually accomplish with this combination would be more a matter of reliability than anything else, for there was little doubt that in Moss, Brooks

Left: Stirling winning the 1957 British *Grand Prix* at Aintree.

Above: A rare picture of Tony Vandervell actually smiling, flanked by Tony Brooks and Stirling. A green car has finally won its home *Grand Prix*.

and Lewis-Evans he now had the three finest drivers in the sport, certainly the finest Britain could offer.

Brooks had erupted on to the scene with Connaught in 1955 when he won the Syracuse *Grand Prix* against the entire works Maserati effort; he had not graduated through the school of Formula 3 500cc racing, whereas Lewis-Evans had become that branch of the sport's senior exponent once Stirling had retired

had crashed at Le Mans the previous month and was barely recovered from his injuries; he had a huge hole in his leg), managed to qualify an extraordinary third on the grid (but only just) to Stirling and Jean Behra. By lap 23, Stirling's engine was misbehaving, and as arranged, the two men swapped cars. Brooks, suffering from his leg injury, was unable to climb out of the car on his own without assistance before Stirling took it

Tony Vandervell had an all-British team
driving green cars...

from it. When he won at Syracuse, Brooks was a dental student who had raced purely for the fun of it, but by the time he signed with Vanwall, he had qualified.

Tony Vandervell was under no illusions about the magnitude of the task he was attempting. His car was innovative in several areas, particularly in its use of fuel injection, but innovation often brings with it irritating gremlins, and the 1957 season certainly proved that. But it also offered genuine victories, and whereas these did not stop Fangio from winning the Driver's Championship again in his last full season, it did prove that the Vanwall concept was a correct one; the simple, powerful engine, which on alcohol fuel had delivered over 300 bhp on the test bed, the tough and reliable disc brakes, and the wind-cheating body all combined to offer the first genuine opportunity for a British car to set the pace, albeit without the user-friendliness of a Maserati.

The British *Grand Prix* of July 1957 was the occasion when the plan gelled. Brooks, despite being totally unfit to drive (he

over. Pleasingly, Stirling brought it home in first place, whereas Brooks's new mount suffered more problems and he was forced to retire on lap 51. Brooks's had been an extraordinary effort.

Now that the Vanwall had made streamlining all the rage again, the MG car company, which had so casually turned down Stirling's laboriously written supplication in 1950, decided that a little record-breaking was in order. MG had always been rather good at this, and the effort at the Utah Salt Flats at Bonneville was intended to raise the previous class F (1101cc–1500cc) record to a mighty 240 mph. MG already held the previous record from before the war; but it was felt that it needed refreshing. The device with which MG intended to do this looked for all the world like a half an avocado on wheels. The dodgiest aspect was that the driver was actually unable to open the cockpit – it was integral with the bonnet and had to be

Above: Stirling is fitted for the MG record car.

Right: With some trepidation, he climbs aboard the MG at Bonneville, August 1957.

opened from outside. The steering wheel, Routemaster bus-style, was more or less horizontal and effectively had to be operated from below, as the driving seat was also almost horizontal.

Behind the unfortunate driver lay a twin-cam 1500cc engine, supercharged to three atmospheres which delivered, running on methanol, a whopping 290 bhp. Phil Hill, who had already driven this device, counselled Stirling that to slow the car he had to hold his breath, switch off the engine, floor the throttle and merely stroke the tiny brake lest the cockpit fill with unburned methanol fumes; it was not an experience for the claustrophobic. The records certainly tumbled; Stirling managed 245 mph for 1 mile, 235.69 mph for 5 miles and 224.7 mph for 10 miles. Two years later, Phil Hill would raise the speed by another 10 mph using a slightly larger engine.

So 1957 could be characterised (professionally, at least) as a full-dress rehearsal with a few tempting targets of opportunity, and wherever these were seen they were attacked. At Vanwall, Lewis-Evans proved to be equal to the promise he had shown, and despite an occasionally frail constitution, he proved himself to be a major asset. He was both gentle on the cars and blindingly quick at the same time. His health and therefore stamina were always to be a threat (he was suffering from ulcers and had been very ill as a child), but he seldom allowed that to beat him.

The biggest social event of the motor racing year, however, was Stirling's marriage to Katie Molson on 7 October, 1957, at St Peter's Church, Eaton Square. All his ushers were drivers and the reception at the Dorchester was extravagent, to say the least. The couple honeymooned in Amsterdam before travelling to Casablanca for the (non-championship) *Grand Prix*. It was important to become familiar with the Ain-Diab circuit, as it would be the venue for the final leg of the 1958 World Championship. A 'flu bug prevented Stirling from actually racing, but he made a decision there that would involve him in perhaps the closest professional relationship of his life. Rob Walker, the private entrant, was faced with the prospect of losing his driver Jack Brabham, to the Cooper works team. He had no replacement, so happily shook hands on a deal which would see Stirling driving his privately entered Cooper. Stirling had

tested one after the Glover Trophy and the two men had agreed to talk further. It was nominally a deal for Formula 2, but as things transpired, it would lead to rather more than that

The newly married Mr and Mrs Moss had agreed that they would attend races as a couple – better for her actually to be at the track rather than sitting at home waiting for the phone to ring. This would be very hard for her, in fact, and was a high price to pay in order to keep an eye on him, not that such precautions were actually necessary; the little black book stayed firmly in the drawer.

Marriage to Katie also served to acquaint Stirling further with the pleasures of Nassau in the Bahamas. Her aunt already lived there and it was not long before the couple decided to build a house of their own there. Typically, Stirling undertook to do as much of the work on it as he could (aided by a truly vast tool chest which had been Ken Gregory's present to him) and work proceeded on Blue Cloud, as they decided to name it. It was an association that would last.

The prosperous community of Nassau had observed the economic effect of motor racing on Sebring in Florida as an invariably large, affluent and international crowd descended on the place for some entertaining racing mixed with winter sunshine. It was mooted, and taken up with great enthusiasm, that perhaps Nassau itself might consider its own festival of racing, a 'Speed Week', which would coincide more or less with Christmas. There was not a vast amount of space available, so the site chosen was Oakes Field Aerodrome. The inaugural meeting was to be in December 1957.

The sheer extravagance of the Maserati 450S concept was revealed at Caracas in the Venezuela *Grand Prix* for sports cars, an event rather hurriedly slipped into the calendar for 3 November. The ever-present worry, particularly for the driver of a car as quick as the 450S, was a slower car simply being in the way. A little AC

This page, top and middle: Stirling and Katie leave the church after their wedding on 7 October, 1957. Unhappily, the marriage would not last. Bottom: Stirling and Katie at Oulton Park, April 1958. He had just won the British Empire Trophy.

Right: The bridesmaids look on at a very public wedding.

'Ace', driven by an American amateur Max Dressler, pulled into Stirling's path as he was about to lap him. It was a Pierre Levegh moment for Stirling as the two cars collided; the elegant little AC was smashed in two by a telegraph pole but given the suddenness of the slower car's manoeuvre, Stirling had little chance to evade him. It was a driver's nightmare – a fast driver in a fast car encountering a slow back marker in a slower machine who may not be paying sufficient attention. As at

seldom offering a serious threat in terms of winning, would always increase the probability that something would go disastrously wrong.

But that Caracas race marked the destruction of more or less the entire Maserati sports car effort, something the beleaguered firm could simply not afford. Apart from Stirling's crash, Jean Behra's car caught fire as it was being refuelled, and two more cars collided and were totally burned out as a result. There was

Naples, Stirling found that as he was committed to a path, his options were depressingly few. It was a close call for him; the wrecked Maserati spun to a standstill but at least he was unhurt, save for a bruised toe, whereas poor Dressler was obviously dead. 'The only way you can carry a trauma like that is to think, Christ, at least I didn't cause it,' said Stirling. Such a sentiment may seem hard, and may even reflect denial, but the rules of the game mandated that each driver had to look after himself and be spatially aware of the other drivers and the rapidly changing nature of his surroundings. For the professionals, from a safety point of view Formula 1 was always to be preferred over sports car racing, as the spectrum of talent was much narrower, with a correspondingly smaller chance that another driver would make a mistake. At the opposite end of the scale, the great endurance races would always attract the enthusiast drivers who, while

perhaps a faint chance that victory could be captured, as the burns which Behra received meant that he could not continue, so Stirling took his place. The problem was that the seat cushion of the car was still on fire, a fact that Stirling only discovered when he sat on it. One could not imagine a more calamitous race and for Maserati it was the last straw; it would be in receivership within months having failed once more to win the Sports Car Championship. This would not stop Maserati from racing – the uniquely Italian interpretation of administrative receivership would protect the firm from its creditors until something turned up – but it would later allow some modest competition at sports car level. The next Maserati-powered car which Stirling would drive was to prove even more terrifying than the 450S, if that was possible.

Stirling's relationship with the Maserati factory had become particularly close, despite the occasional but obvious shortcomings in their preparation. However, in light of their looming financial crisis, this lack of care was starting to oscillate between inattentive and life-threatening, but all the time bordering on high farce. Stirling's patience with Maserati in spite of the evidence stems back to the confidence inspired by the 250F, as well as the fact that it had given him his first serious break in Formula 1. The blind eye he was prepared to turn

an ambush, given that the FIA had previously undertaken to announce material changes to particular formulae, which this clearly was, well in advance. This time they did not do so. The more interesting news that accompanied this announcement was that from now on, there was to be a Constructor's Championship as well as a Driver's Championship. In order to tighten up the competition, it was further announced that no points would be awarded to either car or driver for shared

reflected his optimistic confidence that the situation would improve. In fact, it never did, for while its enthusiasm never left the firm, it was struggling in the face of the enforced departure of key staff and a rigorous regime of financial cutbacks in the light of the situation in Argentina. Maserati managed to conceal this very well, but in reality it was going broke.

The announcement, very late in the 1957 season, that for the 1958 season, Formula 1 was to be run according to tighter regulations governing fuel was met with unease. From then on commercial fuel, as opposed to the exotic brews used before, was mandatory. For most teams this was not a problem, as they used carburettors on their engines, but the Vanwall's engines were fuel injected and recalibrating the one-off machinery with the attendant impact on upper engine architecture was potentially a complicated task. In any case, it was something of

drives. This meant that the cars would all have to be reliable; no longer could a number two be pulled in and ordered to hand his car over to the team leader in the event of a mechanical problem. In effect, it was to ensure large grids, as simple probability arithmetic would favour the multiple entrant, as well as offering more starting money per team.

This change in the rules governing fuel actually allowed Stirling his first crack at the 1958 championship in Walker's Cooper. Vanwall did not enter the Argentine *Grand Prix*, as it was struggling somewhat to adapt its fuel injection system to the now-mandatory Avgas petrol. Stirling and Walker resolved to send the little Cooper to Buenos Aires as much for practice as

Above: From left to right, Fangio (Maserati) Collins (Ferrari) and Stirling (Vanwall) set off at the start of the 1957 Monaco *Grand Prix*.

anything else. They certainly entertained little hope of it against the full works Ferrari effort, to the extent that Walker stayed behind. He was to regret that decision (*see pages 221–23*).

Vanwall was ready for the European opener though, which took place at Monaco on 18 May. The race itself was a disaster. Stuart Lewis-Evans, who had qualified seventh, was the first to retire with steering problems. Tony Brooks, who had managed pole position in practice, retired on lap 22 with a shattered sparking plug of all things and Stirling's engine let go on lap 38 while he was leading. All three Vanwalls were thus out before half distance. It was no consolation that Hawthorn also retired with a broken fuel pump; so the result was basically a Ferrari sandwich with Maurice Trintignant and Jack Brabham first and fourth in their Coopers, and Luigi Musso beating Peter Collins home by 16 seconds. Two *Grands Prix* completed, with two out of two to Cooper, with some advantage to Ferrari.

At Zandvoort a fortnight later, the BRMs put on an astonishing performance in the race, eclipsing the outstanding Vanwall practice effort, which resulted in the team occupying the entire front row of the grid. The impressive performance of the revitalised BRMs did not go unnoticed. While the cars looked similar to the horrendous first iteration of the P25, they were, on closer inspection, rather different. There were Vanwall genes in there, courtesy of consulting work by Colin Chapman, and while the brakes would never inspire great confidence, the engine was clearly as good as, or superior to the Vanwall. As a four-cylinder, it was as rough as that of the Vanwall, but it delivered a reliable 280 bhp on straightforward carburettors.

Tony Brooks's victory at Spa did much to further the race for the Constructor's crown, but Stirling's engine broke a valve on the opening lap; thinking that the gearbox was fully engaged, he pressed the throttle – sadly, the box was still in neutral. The engine buzzed to unheard-of rpms and that was that. He was

Left: Stirling sitting in a Vanwall drinking a cup of tea; even here there must be a saucer and a spoon.

Above: The disastrous Costin-designed, Zagato-built Maserati 450 coupé at Le Mans in 1957.

Above: On his way to win the first time out in the Vanwall at the Silverstone
International, 1956.
Right: Harry Schell inspects the results of Chapman and Costin's handiwork. Schell
had put a vast amount of work into the project but was dismissed to make room for
Moss.

appalled; total, unforgivable driver error. Even though he was team leader, the idea of calling in Lewis-Evans or Brooks was out of the question, so he was forced to sit out that *Grand Prix*.

The separate evolutionary paths of European and American racing offered some interesting parallels. The Indianapolis school of thought, which had created hugely powerful but essentially primitive roadsters invariably powered by an Offenhauser four-cylinder engine, was by 1958 as close to the European benchmark cars as it was going to get at least in terms of general architecture, if not power. An ice cream magnate named Zanetti had requested that Maserati build him a special to enter in the upcoming 'Two Worlds' Trophy to be held at Monza, the only circuit in Europe with a banked section familiar to American drivers. This would be a pastiche of an Indy car using an amalgam of parts that lay around in the depressingly quiet racing department. Eager for the work, they obliged with the 'Eldorado Ice Cream Special', an improbable looking confection powered by a 4.2-litre version of the thunderous V8. This engine

had originally been conceived as an Indianapolis contender; rather warily Stirling agreed to drive it.

When the steering snapped at well over 160 mph it was clear that quality control at Modena had not improved since the episode at the 1957 *Mille Miglia*. The brakes were *de minimis*; all he could do was hastily jab at them and brace himself on the wheel as the huge car slid along the top of the 80° banking, peeling back the guard rail like the lid off a sardine tin. He was (for once) strapped in, which only added to his sense of complete helplessness as the Maserati gradually destroyed itself:

My arms just shot round...the thing was out of control and I had virtually no brakes and I remember going up, hitting the top of the wall [guard rail] and closing my eyes, forcing back on the steering wheel. . .and then there was a whole hoo-hah – I don't exactly know what happened because I had my eyes closed – and the car came to a standstill. I jumped out and there was dust and everything, and I

remember thinking: 'Well, if this is hell, it's not very hot, or if it's heaven why is it so dusty?' I was absolutely convinced I was a goner.

As an intimation of mortality, it was the closest yet, and while he had every reason to fume at the shoddy workmanship in the steering department, he also had reason to be grateful that the chassis was as robust as it was. A racing driver of this period had to have a compartment in his mind in which to place such experiences, as well as the mental discipline to keep them firmly under lock and key. The episode at Monza would not be his last crash and nor would it be his worst, but the evidence that people make mistakes when building racing cars just as they do when driving them, was chilling. If racing drivers seem to be unimaginative but superstitious men, then this is perhaps why.

After the terrors of the Eldorado special, the French *Grand Prix* at Reims offered a depressing second place, 24 seconds behind Hawthorn's Ferrari. Ironically, this would be Hawthorn's

only *Grand Prix* victory of the season, and in fact his last ever. In practice, Stirling's Vanwall engine had dropped a valve (of its own accord this time) and in order to preserve the top end of the engine, the team's axle ratios were raised. This made the power less accessible and put the green cars at a disadvantage against the hugely durable if relatively crude Ferraris, which had qualified first and second. The second place man, Luigi Musso, who had chased Stirling so hard in Argentina, had a dreadful accident in his Ferrari on lap 9 and died as a result.

Peter Collins, meanwhile, was in trouble of a different kind. He had only just avoided demotion to Formula 2 for the Reims meeting, his crime having been to allegedly break the clutch on his *Testa Rossa* Le Mans car the previous month, a point which

Above: Movement is tranquillity; the Vanwall, like the Mercedes, was a 'difficult' car, even when it wore the cherished number 7.

Overleaf: Although the Vanwall naturally under-steered, here Stirling has it by the scruff of the neck in a lurid oversteering slide at Silverstone.

the Ferrari toadies were rather keen to tell head office. The reality was that Hawthorn had broken it, but even with reinstatement, Collins's confidence was shaken. The fact that he stormed through to win the British *Grand Prix* at Aintree may have repaired the damage to his relationship with Enzo Ferrari, but possibly not – he was clearly overdoing it. In that race, Stirling's engine rudely poked a con-rod out of the side of the block, denying him a second win in succession.

The problems that the Vanwalls were to encounter with their engines were vexing, to say the least. There were several penalties to pay for the switch to Avgas, one of which was a huge increase in engine temperatures as well as difficulties with power loss. The carburettors employed by other marques had proved simpler to adjust than the finicky fuel injection by the Vanwall and this was to be critical for Stirling's World Championship ambitions.

At Nurburgring in August, Collins, who may still have considered that his place in the team was under threat – Enzo Ferrari was often casually brutal about these matters – had the last of the few crashes of his career and it killed him. Mike Hawthorn, who saw it happen, was devastated and never really got over the loss. Stirling's magneto packed up on lap three, although Brooks enjoyed a fine, if depressing win. So, although things were going acceptably well for the Vanwall team, for Stirling himself, a combination of own goals and unreliability was starting to dog his season. At the Portuguese *Grand Prix* at Oporto, however, it all came together; Stirling won after bagging pole position and managed to lap Hawthorn's Ferrari. As he was completing the race, though, he saw something that moved him.

He knew, as everyone did, that Hawthorn was miserable about the death of Collins, and when he witnessed the hapless Brit attempting to push start his spun Ferrari uphill, he slowed and shouted at him to manoeuvre it around and use the downhill slope, which Hawthorn duly did. He managed to restart it and complete the lap to claim his second place. Stirling did not know at that point that Hawthorn had bagged yet another fastest lap; he had uncharacteristically misread the Vanwall pit signal. All season Hawthorn had been squirreling away the vital points which the quickest lap merited – this would ultimately prove vital for him. But not as vital as what Stirling did next. The stewards took the view that Hawthorn had, by his actions, disqualified himself. Stirling, ever word-perfect as to rules, did not agree. That evening, there was a stewards' enquiry; Stirling stood up and pointed out that Hawthorn had not been pushing his car actually on the circuit, and therefore he had broken no rules.

In the face of such encyclopaedic knowledge, the stewards backed down, so Stirling ended the day with eight points and Hawthorn with seven – six for the second place and one for the

fastest lap. To those close to him, Stirling's actions were quite typical. To others, what he had done was surely bonkers, but the issue was quite simple to Stirling. He had advised Hawthorn to do what he did and therefore he honourably defended him against a disqualification. Of course, this lengthened the odds for the World Championship, but that was only spice; it was not the core issue. He knew that he could probably beat Hawthorn; it was his performance by his own measure that mattered to him more. Besides which, he really believed that Hawthorn's treatment at the hands of the stewards was shabby.

He may have assumed that he could make up any resultant deficit at Monza. The prospect of beating the Ferraris on their home ground was made even more delicious because of the closeness of the contest. Unhappily, it was not to be, as his gearbox unstitched itself. He was delighted at Tony Brooks's victory, but now the chase for the title came down to the last race of the season at Casablanca. If he could win, capture fastest lap and Hawthorn be no better than second, he would manage it. Even in the event of a points draw, he would still win it because he had won more races.

The car that Stuart Lewis-Evans drove was something of a compromise. It was not quite a 'starting money special' as he clearly merited better than that, but despite the long gap between the last two events of the season, it had a tired engine which had not been rebuilt, regardless of the fact that both the Driver's and Constructor's Championships were at stake. If Vanwall could manage a 1-2, then Stirling would win the former and Vanwall was guaranteed to win the latter.

Lewis-Evans's car was powered by engine V5, which had last been used in July at the French *Grand Prix*, when Brooks retired through gearbox failure. The possibility that Lewis-Evans's car was not as well-prepared as it might have been loomed large. It was fairly unusual in those days to totally rebuild engines unless something had obviously gone wrong with them; a well-serviced unit might be expected to last for more than one race. The fact that Lewis-Evans's engine had not been rebuilt was not an example of tightfistedness – in fact it was normal practice – but in the light of the closeness of the competition, it seems perplexing.

The race would go down in history as an example of teamwork. It was as even as could be, with three Vanwalls and three Ferraris. The teamwork came from Ferrari. Moss and Lewis-Evans shared the front row of the grid with Hawthorn separating them. Brooks was back in seventh place on row three. Stirling set a fierce pace; in fact he was to lead the race from start to finish. He could do little else, for as well as

Facing page: Sebring 12-hour race, 1957. Stirling, who shared this Maserati 300S with Harry Schell, doing his share. The pair came second.

Facing page: Close racing, Monza, 1957. The Vanwalls of Lewis-Evans and Brooks almost neck and neck.

Above: The Vanwall was the most distinctive *Grand Prix* car yet of the post-war era.

winning the race by at least a two-place margin from Hawthorn, he had to set fastest lap as well.

From the flag, Phil Hill harried Stirling mercilessly, but was unable to make any serious inroads into the Vanwall's lead, partly by virtue of the fact that the green cars were all disc-braked; Hill's was the only Ferrari with drums, and the others were wisely pacing themselves. After out-braking himself, Hill spun off, but so far ahead of the bulk of the field were the leading group that he was able to rejoin in fourth behind Hawthorn and Joakim Bonnier in the BRM. Hill passed Bonnier and then Hawthorn let him through so that he could resume the pressure on Moss.

On lap 19, a Vanwall set fastest lap, but it was Tony Brooks driving it. This did not help Stirling immediately, except that the pace caused Olivier Gendebien (standing in for von Trips) to make an uncharacteristic error and crash. Stirling re-set fastest time on lap 21, but Brooks's engine let go five laps later. This left the job of interfering with the two Ferraris to Lewis-Evans, driving in what he knew was a tired car. He speeded up appreciably in an attempt to get among the Ferraris and distract Hill and Hawthorn from catching Stirling, but on lap 41, his engine seized at full revs. The transmission locked up and Lewis-Evans spun off the circuit into a small grove of trees. The impact broke a fuel line and within seconds, the Vanwall was a blazing inferno. He struggled out of the car but because he was instinctively protecting his face he could see nothing and did not observe the appalled (and inexperienced) marshals in pursuit. Tragically, he ran away from them and it took them some minutes to catch him. By the time they did, the damage had been done.

In the pits, Vandervell and the crew could see the ominous column of smoke rising from the wrecked car as the tyres, oil and even the bodywork of his car caught fire, but they were not to know until Lewis-Evans failed to register again on the lap chart that their team had been involved. Stirling held on to his lead until the flag. Phil Hill, obeying the logical team orders, had moved over to allow Hawthorn into the second place that he himself had fought so hard to hold, and while Stirling had won the race, he had lost the Driver's Championship.

It was a personal disaster for him. In the long build-up to this race (he had raced only once in the preceding six weeks, winning the RAC Tourist Trophy at Goodwood again) the strain on him had been immense; as team leader for two seasons the delivery of the double World Championship had been his biggest motivator. It was no particular consolation that he had won more races than Hawthorn, but his sense of failure of letting down his public, was total. Later, he would become more philosophical, but on that hot October Casablanca afternoon, it all felt rather different.

Vandervell, on the other hand, had very mixed feelings. He had captured the prize, but at a huge price. A car he had built had won the Constructor's crown, but another one had failed, and one glance at Lewis-Evans was enough to make him realise that his injuries were massive. Vandervell decided to load his driver into a chartered plane and ship him back to England, accompanied by a nurse. The best burns clinic in Europe was at East Grinstead, Sussex, and it was there that Lewis-Evans was sent. Despite his persistent illnesses he was upsettingly strong, but on 26 October he died, brave and uncomplaining to the last.

Vandervell immediately retired from racing. He offered 'Lofty' England the possibility of taking over the team, but England, who was nursemaiding his friend Mike Hawthorn, still depressed by the death of Collins, declined. He had his own agenda and it did not particularly include Formula 1. As for Hawthorn, he informed England that he would retire as soon as possible. He had a family business to run and was to be married as soon as he had made provision for the little daughter he had already (secretly) fathered. Sadly, that was not to be. On 22 January, 1959, Hawthorn would die in a road accident.

Right: A quick glance behind at the 1958 British *Grand Prix* at Silverstone.

Stirling's international reputation is reflected in the press cuttings which now come
thick and fast. Gradually Stirling slipped into the national consciousness.

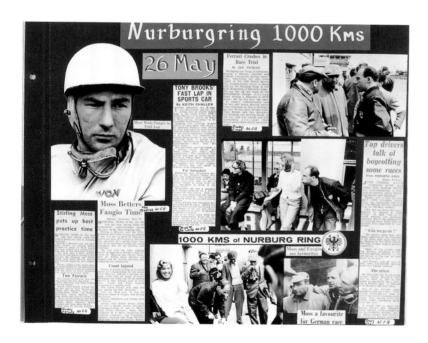

MOSS the magnificent

Motor section CONTINUED

RELAXING AT SPEED—British ace driver Stirling Moss guides his 300 bhp Maserati racing car through a bend on the Albert Park circuit.

Stirling Moss won the Australian Tourist Trophy race yesterday in record time, lapped everyone except his French team mate Jean Behra, and even beat him by almost a minute.

U.K. DRIVER IN ACTION

British racing car driver, Stirling Moss, driving a Holden Special, pictured during an exhibition run at Cumberland Oval, Parramatta, yesterday. Moss will race in Melbourne during the Olympic Games.

BRITISH DRIVER STIRLING MOSS in his Maserati (No. 7) speeding down the track in the Australian Tourist Trophy at Albert Park yesterday. He won the event. BELOW: Stirling Moss gulps down a bottle of drink after his win.

Lower:—Talking tactics between events are (L to r.) Australian driver Reg Hunt, British ace driver and winner of the 100 mile race Stirling Moss, and English hill climb champion Ken Wharton.

RACING "DOWN UNDER"

Stirling Moss Wins Australian Tourist Trophy

From an Australian Correspondent

A grid start was used for the Australian Tourist Trophy. Wharton (Ferrari, left), Moss (Maserati familiarly numbered "7", centre), and Behra (Maserati) occupying the front row.

100,000 See Car Racing Triumph

Watched by close on 100,000 spectators, British motor racing ace Sterling Moss recorded a near-lap win to take the Australian Tourist Trophy at Albert Park yesterday.

Driving brilliantly, Moss hit an average speed of 94.63 m.p.h., covered the 100-mile course in 63 minutes 24 seconds and, with a time of one minute 55.8 seconds, created a lap record.

He took an early lead over Maserati team-mate Jean Behra, who fell back after leading round the first three laps, when a stone flying from under a wheel gashed his lip.

Behra was second, with Britisher Ken Wharton in a Ferrari, third.

Involved in a six-car pile up at Jaguar Corner during an earlier event

MOSS AGAIN

Wins Australian Tourist Trophy by 47 sec.

LEADING from start to finish with ease, Stirling Moss (3-litre Maserati) led team-mate Jean Behra, on a similar machine, over the line by 47 sec., lapping the rest of the field at least once. Wharton (3-litre 750 Monza Ferrari) finished third.

CRASH—IT'S MOSS • CRASH—IT'S COLLINS • CRASH—IT'S HAWTHORN

3 ACES CHEAT DEATH

RACE

THREE ACES CRASH IN BIG RACE

They tangle at 70mph in Monte Grand Prix

From ALAN BRINTON : Monte Carlo, Sunday

BRITAIN'S three top driving aces missed death in a triple 70-mile-an-hour pile-up during the Monte Carlo Grand Prix today. The only injury between them—a bumped nose for Stirling Moss.

Moss, in the lead from the first corner, had brought his Vanwall screaming out of a tunnel on to the quayside on the third lap of the dangerous round-the-houses course. Then his brakes failed.

"I was heading for the chicane (a series of tight corners) at 70 miles an hour," he told me afterwards. "I knew I couldn't get round, so I put my head down and hoped for the best."

He slammed into a safety barrier of sandbags and heavy poles. The poles scattered high in the air like matchsticks.

Right on his tail, Peter Collins ducked as a pole smashed down on to his Ferrari, damaging a wheel and then steering before he hit Moss's car.

Juan Fangio snaked through the tiny gap followed by Britain's Tony Brooks in a Vanwall and Mike Hawthorn.

INTO WATER

Brooks braked momentarily and Hawthorn braked, skidded, and rammed him. A wheel torn off Hawthorn's Ferrari bounded with a great splash into the water below the quay.

Brooks's car was only dented, and roared on to finish second.

Hawthorn's car, right out of control, leapt into the air and landed on top of Collins's car.

The crowd shrieked, but. A few minutes later all three crashed drivers were walking back to the pits.

Later Hawthorn took over another Ferrari, which had been driven by Von Trips. After two laps he had to hand it back again—he found the seat too small for his large frame.

Only six cars finished the punishing course out of 16 starters. First was Fangio, in a Maserati, then Brooks in a Vanwall—only 25 seconds behind, the best result for British cars in a classic grand prix for 30 years. Third was the American Masten Gregory in a Maserati.

COMMANI ON QUAY

of the Queen e Duke of Edin-in Copenhagen row.

experienced and

talented conductor, he listened to the band playing "God Save the Queen," and said he was pleased.

The King, accompanied by Queen Ingrid and their children, Princess Benedikte, aged 13, and Princess Anne-Marie, 16, arrived at five minutes to eight.

On the quay were men of the Life Guards and the

banquet to be changed street. Queen arrange the tions in th and in th hall.

King Fred the bill. C £7,500.

● The Q Duke of Hull in the Britannia or

00 gems

Job and a bit hur hat," said the flat

A new flat

ES PILE-UP

Argentinian, wines. mashes and mechanical ten from the

Fangio was

C. A. S. Brooks, in a Vanwall, Martin Gregory (Maserati), of the U.S., came third. Lewis-Evans (Connaught) was fourth, Trintignant (Ferrari) fifth, Brabham (Cooper) sixth.

PILE-UP . . . Collins leaps from his crashed car

Moss, Hawthorn, Collins in ne-houses ile-up

RDS : Monte Carlo, Sunday
ivers—Stirling Moss, Peter thorn—crashed together in ses Monaco Grand Prix here ured, but their failure gave by Brooks, his big chance.

Only six finish

Fangio, who has won both championship events so far contested—the first was the Argentine Grand Prix—leads with six points. Brooks and Behra have six each.

Brooks started racing only three years ago in a Healey sports car.

He came to Monte Carlo last year to drive a B.R.M. but did not race because the cars were scratched.

In between practice he studied on Monte Carlo beach for his final dental examination, which he has since passed.

Of the 16 cars which started in today's race—ten Italian and six British—only six finished the gruelling event. Three were British.

Danger spot

Stuart Lewis-Evans, 27-year-old driver from Bexleyheath, Kent, finished fourth in a Connaught and Jack Brabham, an Australian, was sixth in a two-litre Cooper—the smallest and lowest-powered car in the race.

The chicane is undoubtedly the danger spot of the Monaco Grand Prix. To emphasise the fact, an Argentine driver, Carlo Menditeguy, was injured in another crash there later in the race.

He fractured his nose and dislocated his jaw.

In the three-car crash Moss's brakes seemed to fail.

"I realised," he said after

CLOSE-UP . . . Collins and wife after the crash.

wards, "that I was going 20 miles an hour too fast to go through the chicane. I must have been doing 70 I suppose.

"Making a split-second decision, I drove smack through the safety barrier of poles and sandbags to the right of the chicane. As I went through I ducked as low as I could in the cockpit. All the same, my nose got a nasty crack. I saw two or three poles go flying into the air."

Continued from Page 1

Watching the race from an hotel window were Moss's fiancée and parents.

Watching from the pits was Collins's 24-year-old actress-bride Louise Cordier.

Moss's fiancée. Miss Katie Molson, from Canada, told me: "I saw it was Stirling's car and my heart turned right over. Then I saw Stirling get out of the car because he bumped his nose and it is swelling all the time."

KATIE MOLSON . . . jumped to her feet with fear as Stirling Moss crashed

Daily Mail 20-5-57

News Chronicle 20-5-57

⑥

Rob Walker & Others

It was clear to anyone who knew him that Rob Walker was a gentleman, and not merely because it said so in his passport. A tall and languid figure, he graced the paddock of many a meeting by virtue of his dry humour and exquisite manners. By any measure Walker was affluent, but he was not Vandervell-rich. Largely as a result of his family's interests in the famous brand of Scotch whisky, he was able to indulge his passion for motor racing from an early age. When he retired from that, he became a team owner, a private entrant. An organisation evolved which operated from the Pippbrook garage on the outskirts of Dorking in Surrey. The Walker team owned and entered a variety of machines, but by the end of 1957 had acquired two outwardly identical Cooper Climaxes as well as the services of Stirling's ex-mechanic Alf Francis to look after them.

Given that the Vanwall effort for 1958 would concentrate only on *Grands Epreuves*, Stirling had been on the lookout for a Formula 2 drive. He was undecided as to whether he should buy a car of his own or drive for his father's new venture, the British Racing Partnership. Alfred was forming this enterprise with Ken Gregory and it would compete in

Formula 2 from the spring of 1958.

There was something rather different about one of Walker's Coopers. It was powered by an enlarged Climax engine, which displaced nearly two litres. Walker had funded this development himself, interested to see whether a lightweight car such as the Cooper could hold its own against full Formula 1 machines. They were more powerful, but critically they were also heavier. Artfully, when Stirling asked to test one of the two cars at Goodwood, Walker and Francis offered him the most powerful one, and the three of them were mightily pleased when Stirling broke the lap record.

To modern eyes, it seems extraordinary that the company that would win the World Formula 1 Constructor's Championship within eighteen months, simply could not afford speculative developments such as this. The Cooper Car Company simply did not have the cash to do it themselves.

Below: With Horace Gould in Buenos Aires. Stirling's eye bandage was removed for the race.

Facing page: Settling into the Walker Cooper, mechanic Tim Wall at his side.

Previous page: That famous wave. Overleaf: Stirling the crowd-pleaser.

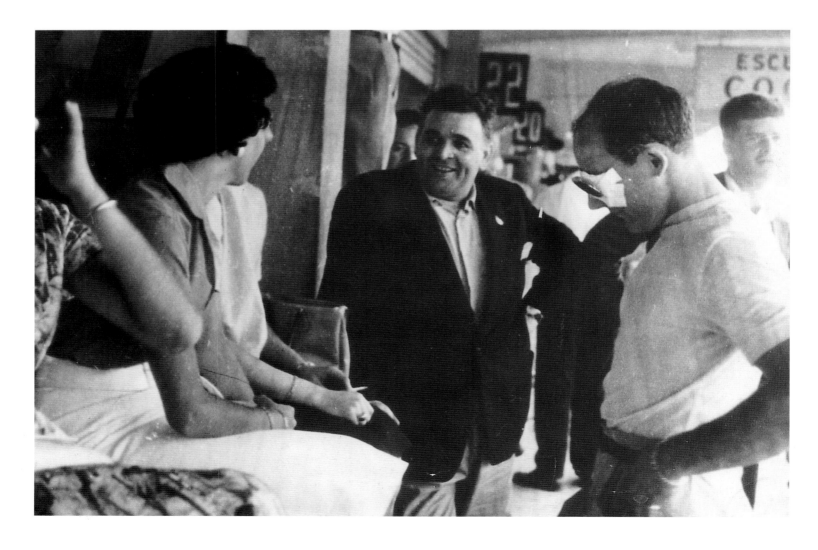

Their first Formula 1 victory was, at the time of Stirling's Goodwood test, only months away; it was this car and driver combination that would delivered the prize.

The Moss/Walker partnership would become a legend of motor racing and last until Stirling's retirement. Tellingly, the handshake they had exchanged in Casablanca in late 1957 was as formal an arrangement as there would ever be; the pair never drew up a contract to confirm it. Walker's view was straightforward, that if a driver did not wish to drive a car then an owner could not possibly make him do so – not with any prospect of success. Everything was a matter of trust.

Meanwhile, Stirling had seen a programme on television which quite appalled him. It concerned the plight of Paul Bates, a national serviceman who, while posted to Malaya in the early 1950s, had contracted polio. As a result, his life was wrecked. He was paralysed from the neck down and his frustration at not being able to travel anywhere, particularly to motor races, rang a bell with Stirling. What particularly

impressed Stirling was that Bates was not complaining, merely observing. By pulling the odd string, Stirling managed to contact Bates. He was startled (and touched) that Bates recognised his voice even before he had announced himself. By pulling a few more strings, he persuaded the Rootes Group to set aside and adapt a van so that this pleasant, almost apologetic young man might have at least part of his life back. The whole project was to be kept entirely secret, but the vehicle would have to be perfect in every way. While Stirling was not in any way qualified to design the van or its fittings, this fact did not stop him 'managing' the project, which he paid for in its entirety. After all, it was novel, it was a gadget, but best of all, it was a worthwhile undertaking.

The van did go a long way towards redefining Bates' life. The two men became genuinely good friends and despite the fact that secrecy was important, Bates was unable to keep silent when it came to telling all on *This is Your Life*, when an embarrassed Stirling was that programme's subject in 1959.

If you are looking for a point when Britian began to dominate motor sport, it must be Buenos Aires on 19 January, 1958. The starting grid was a small one; the little 1.96-litre RRC Walker Cooper Climax was dwarfed by the three new 2.4-litre Ferraris and seven privately entered Maseratis which made up the rest of the field. Stirling had made little progress in practice – a combination of gearbox trouble and a painful scrape on his cornea caused by Katie's thumbnail (quite accidentally) had only allowed him a seventh place. The eye was still sore. The Cooper was very light, which made some amends for its tiny engine, but it suffered from a critical disadvantage; it took ages to change the four-stud wheels. The knock-off hubs of the opposition would give them the equivalent of a lap and a half advantage, so a tyre change was out of the question. The toughest tyres available were made by Continental, the supplier to Mercedes-Benz, and these were accordingly fitted. Petrol consumption was more or less a matter of crossing your fingers and exercising a light foot.

Previous pages: It's never too early to start winning, Easter Monday, 1958 at Goodwood.

Below: Stirling is the first away.

But part of the Moss gamesmanship strategy was the creation of a psychological edge by any moral means possible. At Argentina, his demeanour was so artificially gloomy, his apparent sense of despairing fatalism at the hopeless prospects so eloquently expressed, that his fellow racers simply assumed that he would be forced into a lengthy tyre stop which would negate any advantage his sheer skill might create. Giving away half a litre of engine capacity to the nearest rival would surely handicap him enough, never mind the prospect of any other delays, so it was a confident Ferrari team who took their places on the grid.

Stirling managed to reach fourth place before the clutch broke; because of a locking mechanism that prevented wrong gear selection and that would not permit clutchless gear-changing, the car jammed in second gear. Resigned, he was about to pull into the pits when a tiny stone lodged in the mechanism, jamming it back open and allowing the gears to

work again, albeit without a clutch. Truly, this was *deus ex machina*.

The probable life expectancy of the tyres under normal racing conditions was about 40 laps; the race itself was 80; just under 195 miles. Stirling took the lead on lap 35 and started to watch his tyres very carefully indeed. A sign that they were wearing out would be given by the appearance of the breaker strip which lay under the tread and over the canvas carcass of the tyre. In the pits, Alf Francis and Tim Wall, his assistant, made theatrical preparations to change tyres, in a further attempt to lull the opposition into complacency. The ruse worked, but on lap 65 the tell-tale breaker strip started to appear as the tread was simply smeared off the tyre.

The odds on having a puncture were now very short. The gearbox was holding up, despite the abuse it was receiving, and Stirling began to drive very carefully. He directed the

smoothed and fragile tyres across every piece of grass he could find to ease the friction, while still lapping within a second of Fangio's pole position time. Luigi Musso in the leading Ferrari was urged on as the realisation dawned that this ridiculous little car was going to try to run the race non-stop; Ferrari made their move too late and Stirling sneaked over the line less than three seconds ahead.

was beaten. This was the case partly because Ferrari was always there to be beaten but there is ample evidence to suggest that Stirling was always ready to reach deep and find a little extra in order to rub Ferrari's nose in the dirt.

But it was aboard a Ferrari that he won the Cuban *Grand Prix* in February. The North American Racing Team (NART), managed by Luigi Chinetti, provided a mighty 4.1-litre 335

Stirling sneaked over the line three seconds ahead

What he had accomplished was quite unequalled. Effectively one-eyed, with a broken clutch, a 'crash' gearbox and tyres worn down to the canvas, he had taken on the entire Ferrari works effort and left it floundering. That he did this in what was essentially an obsolete Formula 2 car (and a rear-engined one at that) simply added insult to injury. Even more painful was the fact that he had effectively conned them. The Ferrari team manager Romolo Tavoni was as horrified by the result as he was by the prospect of explaining to Enzo Ferrari what had happened, which was that the sport had just been reinvented – by the British of all people.

There has always been much debate about which of Moss's races was the greatest; the one element many of the races have in common is the fact that it was the Ferrari marque which

sports model, only the third of the make that Stirling had ever driven. It was a slightly controversial race, as the two-day practice was chaotic. First a makeshift bridge collapsed, hurting some spectators and then the evening before the race Juan Manuel Fangio was kidnapped at gunpoint from the lobby of the Lincoln Hotel. It was done on the orders of rebel leader Fidel Castro. It is unlikely that Fangio, despite his distinctly right-wing sympathies, was actually in any danger – his abductors actually allowed him to watch the race on television – but they had wanted Stirling as well. Fangio explained that Stirling was on honeymoon (not true, in fact) and it would be most discourteous to upset his wife. The purpose of the abduction was to draw attention to the conditions into which Cuba had descended by then. 'Battista's brothel', as it had become known, was a fairly apt description. Funded by millions of Mafia dollars, the island had collapsed into a sink of iniquity and, while it was undeniably exotic, many who toured the plentiful night clubs could quite see Castro's point.

The race was as chaotic as the country hosting it. The

Left: The doughty Scott Brown (Lister-Jaguar) has the measure of the Aston through the chicane. As at the 1956 Glover Trophy, Archie's car lets him down and another Stirling victory is the result.

Above right: Like the Maseratis that Stirling enjoyed so much, the Aston Martins were engineers' cars.

Havana street circuit was very slippery indeed and Stirling callously surrendered the lead to a charging Masten Gregory: 'I thought I'd let old Masten find the oil.' Which Masten duly did, but he was still leading when there was a frightful accident. A local driver, Armando Cifuentes, had found rather more oil than Masten Gregory and ploughed into the crowd, killing five spectators. This was enough for the harassed race organiser to order red flags; the race was stopped or so he thought. Stirling, who as he would prove later in the season, knew the rules of racing very well indeed, realised that a red flag is only valid if shown by the clerk of the course at the start/finish line, and the clerk of the course was at the scene of

the crash, and could not be in two places at once. As the two cars slowly approached the line, picking their way through a milling crowd which had assumed that the race was over, Stirling smartly dropped down a gear and nipped past a startled Gregory to take the chequered flag. To say that Gregory was cross would be an understatement:

I was upset, I'd been trying so hard for so many years to beat him. It wasn't an important race, but I wanted it and I went up to Stirling and told him I thought he was stealing it. He said: 'Don't be bloody silly, Gregory, you ought to read the rules, boy, the only place you can get a *red flag is on the line, it doesn't count anywhere else.' He was right, of course, you could always count on Stirling knowing the regs backward and forward, but I wouldn't hold still for it and said: 'I'm going to protest you.' Stirling said: 'Look, Masten, Castro will be in power in another month,' – he was always clued up on all that sort of thing – 'Battista will be out, Castro will be in; if you protest the money will be put in escrow and neither of us will ever see it.' I told him I didn't give a damn, I was going to protest anyway. I said: 'Stirling, I've tried for too many years to beat you.' He said: 'All right, Masten, it's $10,000 first place money and $7000 second, and we'll pool it and split it.' So I said all right, and we sorted it out that way. Some people said that it was the only time anybody came out ahead on a money deal with Moss, but I never did beat him. Never in any of the races we ran together.*

There were many other cars that year with Stirling in the cockpit. The collapse of the Maserati racing programme had already led him back to Aston Martin, which was preparing yet another attempt at the World Sports Car Championship. It was a serious effort, too. His team mates were Roy Salvadori, Carroll Shelby, Tony Brooks and, later in the year, the ill-starred Lewis-Evans. All three Vanwall drivers were involved, indeed Brooks had been a stalwart of the team since 1955, having delivered a splendid win in the Nurburgring 1000 kilometre race in 1957.

The investment that David Brown had made was vast; gone were the aged DB3S cars and in their place was the staggeringly elegant (and beautifully built) DBR1, supported by the even quicker DBR2, powered by a version of the upcoming DB4 road car's engine, but it was ineligible for World Sports Car Championship events where a 3-litre limit was in force. Gone too, was John Wyer; he had moved on to become the company's general manager and was now attempting to act as midwife to the forthcoming new road model. He was not to find this easy, never having dealt with trade unions before. His place was taken by Reg Parnell.

If the new Astons had an Achilles heel, it was in the gearbox department, which was ironic given that the rapidly depleting Brown fortune actually came from gear manufacture. Brown was as obstinate about his transmissions as Vandervell was about his engines; it is perhaps the magnate's weakness. It would be an interesting process for Stirling to compare these new cars with the 1955 300 SLR, let alone the Maseratis from 1957; they were a great improvement, although they were not sufficiently reliable to deliver the championship.

Stirling would deliver wins for Aston Martin at Goodwood's Sussex Trophy, the British Empire Trophy at Oulton Park, the Nurburgring 1000 kilometre and yet again the RAC Tourist Trophy. His appetite whetted, he would stay with the firm for 1959, and while the team would finally win at Le Mans, he would not. In 1958 Stirling's were the only victories that Aston Martin experienced.

Stirling was to make the Nurburgring 1000-kilometre race his own. He had first won it partnered by Jean Behra in 1956, and in 1957, the year Brooks won it, no less than three Maseratis had given up the unequal struggle of bringing him home in fifth place.

The 1958 1000-kilometre race, in which he was partnered by Jack Brabham, was an event which almost certainly qualifies as an example of Moss at his best. He drove 36 of the 44 laps, setting a new lap record in the process. It was an extraordinary bravura performance, which took almost everything he had to give; it would take him a week to recover and the event offered proof, if proof were needed, that the term 'racing driver' is more than a job description.

If the Aston Martin had another potential weakness, apart from the gearbox, it was under the bonnet. The 3-litre engine was as well-developed as it could be, but was sensitive to over-revving. The standard Aston Martin policy was, when in doubt, overgear the car so that the critical rpm limit of 6500 was never seen and thus the (extremely expensive) unit might last longer. Peak power, depending on tune, arrived at around 6500 rpm. To Stirling the limit was, barring accidents such as missing a gear, sacrosanct. He further knew that the main opposition, Ferrari, would have no such difficulties; whatever anyone thought about the relative crudity of the Ferrari's chassis and brakes compared to those of the Aston, the V12

Facing page: Katie contemplates the Aston Martin at the 1958 *Targa Florio*.
Above: Rob Walker and Alf Francis.

engine, like most Ferrari powerplants, was more or less bullet-proof and also comfortably delivered more power.

Stirling's request was that the axle ratio be lowered two increments that would allow him better acceleration, which he would have to use if he was to stand a chance of building a lead. Reg Parnell, the new team manger, was sceptical. He changed the ratio part of the way, to 3.54:1, but when Stirling, tongue-in-cheek, announced that the engine would have to be changed due to its inability to rev faster than 6200, Parnell reluctantly confessed his little deception, startled that Stirling had even noticed; in went the new ratio. (The matter of axle ratios is perhaps worth explaining. A lower ratio allows the driven wheels to turn [in this case] 3.62 times as fast as the crankshaft speed. On a sinuous circuit like Nurburgring or Monaco, the engine needs to be kept in or near peak power, for reasons of responsiveness. At Le Mans, where absolute speed is a requirement, the Aston Martins were geared so that at maximum speed the engines were turning at no more than 5900rpm.) Just to make sure, Stirling went out again. The victory which resulted, along with the new lap record, which was nearly seven seconds under the previous one that he had set with the Maserati 450 in 1957,

was a startling endorsement of the way the car was set up, as well as solid confirmation that a good chassis was to be prized over all things.

The death of poor Mike Hawthorn, barely three months into his Championship year, only served to increase the pressure on Stirling (and Walker) to deliver the world title in 1959. That they both worked very hard to do so is a matter of record, but the inevitable consequences of being a private entrant in what was now a sport with a Constructor's crown as well would present them with a clutch of difficulties which could not be offset by the sheer effort that the team made.

The winter of 1959 found Stirling with Katie in Hong Kong. Despite his enthusiasm for decent tailoring as taught to him by Lance Macklin, he decided to investigate the reputation which tailors in the Crown Colony had long enjoyed. The possibility of acquiring a new wardrobe in twenty-four hours appealed to him just as much as the obvious financial savings involved. Further, he could add his

Above: Driver change at the Nurburgring.

Facing page: Stirling hurling the Aston around the Nurburgring.

Previous pages: Stirling leads the Aston Martin works team home, 1-2-3 at Goodwood, 13 September, 1958.

Left: A favourite number on a favourite car. Melbourne *Grand Prix*, Albert Park, 1958.

Above: A reflective Stirling after the race.

own little touches – a thing that London tailors were loathe to do – but without which he felt he would be compromised in his search for perfection. His only contact in Hong Kong was a man called Peter Garrett who was the Rootes Group manager. Stirling called him and although he failed to reach him, did connect with a Mrs Phyllis Paine, Garrett's personal assistant. Although unique in so many other ways, Hong Kong was no different from other expat communities; the presence of a visitor is usually an occasion for hospitality. He was invited around to the Paine household, where he met Stuart Paine, Phyllis's husband and their two young daughters, Christina and Susan.

He was quite unaware of it then, but this agreeable social encounter was to have a profound effect on his life later on; he became firm friends with the Paine family and usually stayed with them when he had occasion to visit, which was often. He found his tailor too, a Mr Maewo Yang, as well as a shirt-maker, Mr Mi Yee. Over the years, he would keep

fearing that it would be humiliated by Continental opposition. However, the leaps forward in chassis design had offered the opportunity of a simple, robust, 100 bhp/litre unit with 250 bhp as against the 280–300 bhp outputs of the other makers.

The reason for this apparently retrograde step was simply weight. The Cooper did not need as powerful an engine as a front-engined car; everything about it could be smaller and therefore lighter. The lengthy drive train could be discarded, together with all the power losses that it occasioned. The rear-mounted engine also lent support to the chassis itself, which could in turn be lighter, and therefore the brakes could be more modest, the fuel tanks smaller and so on. It all added up to a dry weight saving in the order of 400 pounds against traditional cars. So a reliable engine of easily achievable output would complete the package and basically the racing car was reinvented. The trouble was, the engine was not ready. Given the possibilities offered by the chassis which had done so well in 1958, Walker, Francis and Moss decided to

I met the cutest little girl over there
. . . I gave her a toy giraffe

both men extremely busy, and to some effect as he was soon voted one of Britain's ten best dressed men. Stirling's friend Herb Jones was helping him unpack a case of merchandise acquired in Hong Kong soon after his return from one such trip. 'I met the cutest little girl over there', he said absently, 'She was so lovely I gave her a toy giraffe.' Jones recollected, 'He was obviously very taken with her.' In fact, Susan Paine would become Stirling's third wife many years later.

The year 1959 started well for Stirling, in other ways too. Despite the fact that he had lost the 1958 championship by a single point, he received a consolation prize by being made an OBE in the New Year's Honours List. He had earned it, of course, but it was most welcome; as he would reflect many years later about another, greater honour, it was 'good to be accepted'. He treated the OBE in the spirit of its military nickname; 'Other Buggers' Efforts' and was as pleased for the Vanwall and Aston Martin personnel as he was for himself.

Elsewhere, fingers were drumming in anticipation of the works 2½-litre offering from Coventry Climax, which would be built specifically for use in rear-engined Cooper cars. The Coventry Climax company had been reluctant to deliver its previous full Formula 1 effort, the V8 Godiva engine of 1957,

try out the lusty BRM engine in the back of the Cooper. Happily, Alfred Owen provided one.

Naturally this presented some problems; one was that the transmission would have to be custom-built. There were very few people who could simply produce a gearbox; one person who could was Valerio Colotti, a well-known Maserati chassis engineer and builder of specialist transmissions (Stirling knew his work well). Alf Francis, who had been apprenticed as a clockmaker in his youth and was therefore deeply interested in such matters, swiftly drew up the specifications and went straight to the *Studio Tecnica Meccanica* in Modena where Valerio Colotti had set himself up in business after the collapse of mainstream racing at Maserati had effectively cost him his job.

Sadly, the Cooper BRM would not prosper, and if 1958 had been the season of Ferrari-bashing, then 1959 would be the season of gearbox-breaking as the Walker team was left with no alternative but to use a Colotti gearbox for the Climax engine as well. The Cooper chassis was supplied in completely knocked-down form and Walker could acquire his

Facing page: Right number, wrong chassis. Stirling climbs aboard the BRM P25 with Raymond Mays looking on.

own engines straight from Coventry when the new device was ready. Coopers, sponsored by Esso, were reluctant to supply Walker's BP-sponsored team with their own gearbox, a clever (and proven) adaptation of a front-wheel-drive Citroën design, which Stirling had already used. John Cooper was nervous (he said) that the increased torque of the new Climax engine would overpower a device that had such modest origins. Back to Modena.

Colotti was delighted to help and so Francis prepared a spec sheet for the new device that would be an adaptation of an existing Colotti design, but because of time pressure, the manufacture of the actual gearsets was subcontracted out. They were delivered on time, but it was later revealed that the machining was at best sloppy and the metal used was simply not strong enough. This burlesque of inefficiency (which was totally uncharacteristic of either Francis or Colotti) would cost Stirling the 1959 championship. Today, he is relaxed about it, but not so then.

An unsuspecting Stirling started his season in New Zealand in the 1958 Cooper, now powered by a 2.2-litre version of the old F2 Climax engine and did rather well with it against the bigger opposition. From the back of the grid he took both victory and a new lap record at the Ardmore track in the New Zealand *Grand Prix*, which was unfortunately not a qualifier for the Championship.

The usual flurry of activity continued to Sebring for the 12-hour race, where Stirling would share a Lister-Jaguar with Ivor Bueb. The car had been redesigned by Frank Costin and, while it was clear that the new bodywork was slippery, it was also very large. It rather suggested that this last iteration of the Lotus XI philosophy was a chassis too far.

The race illustrated very well the sort of pressure Katie Moss was under. Ken Purdy was present when Stirling failed to reappear in the fifth hour, having been leading the race:

> *When he didn't come round, someone near the pit loudly expressed the opinion that he'd had a shunt. Some minutes passed, probably only five or six – but that can seem very many – before word came through that he was unhurt and walking back. He came the quickest way, cross-country, and the sun on his white overalls identified him a long way off. Katie Moss went to meet him; behind each of them was a small, growing wedge-shaped mob of the curious. Katie ran the last few steps and they kissed but the sensation must have been something like making love under a spot-light and they walked quickly and soberly back to the pit, their two crowds now massed into one, hustling idiotically along behind them.*

When the 2½-litre Cooper Climax was ready in time for the Glover Trophy it gave little hint of what was to come, as Stirling managed both fastest lap and outright victory. But the Glover was only a 100-miler and the gear box was still brand new; whatever it had been made of it would probably have survived, but Monaco was a different matter.

Stirling put the new car on pole position alongside Jean Behra's Ferrari and Jack Brabham's works Cooper, and although Behra managed to take the lead, Stirling passed him on lap 22 and kept his lead until lap 81, when the transmission broke. It was well known that Monaco was tough on gearboxes – indeed three other cars retired for the same reason – so perhaps it was forgivable, but at Zandvoort, the same thing happened again, at the same stage of the race when it was three-quarters run with Stirling in the lead. The transmission may have been terminally flawed, but it was at least consistent.

Facing page: Stirling, just about to haul Jack Fairman from the cockpit of the Aston Martin at the 1959 Nurburgring 1000-kilometre race.

Above: Stirling with Prince Bira at Monaco.

Maserati, despite their parlous financial state, had not been idle. The 450s, the huge expense of which had hardly helped them, were by now mere curiosities. On a shoestring, but under the benign eye of tolerant receivers, the racing team constructed an extraordinary new car and Stirling arrived in Modena straight after Monaco to inspect it.

It was as different from previous offerings as it could be; and a quick trip around the Modena test track revealed that it was faster (and more agile) than any 250F, despite it tiny 2-litre engine. Stirling found it enchanting, and after marvelling at the ingenuity of its space-frame construction which provided huge strength as well as being light (1300 pounds), asked to see it again later in the season. Because there were limits to the forbearance of even Italian receivers, the factory could not hope to mount a works racing effort with the new car, called the *Tipo 60*, meaning that they would have to find customers for it.

that the chassis was not the one that Stirling had asked for (no scratch) but the engine was strong and the overall level of presentation was very high. Practice was even better – he lapped in 1 minute 40.2 seconds, a ten-second improvement over the last time he had tested the old P25 on the same circuit, so clearly they were doing something right. But on lap five, the brakes totally disappeared. A certain sixth sense had told Stirling that something was wrong, so he eased off and came to a controlled halt. All the old suspicions about BRM came back; while the car had certain Maserati-like qualities so, alas did its preparation.

By the time Walker advised him that the Colotti box was probably terminally ill, he actually had rather few Formula 1 prospects. The fact that the BRMs had done so well at Zandvoort was encouraging, but the idea of a works drive was out of the question (not that Owen lacked the resources for a third car). So Ken Gregory and Alfred started to

A certain sixth sense told Stirling
that something was wrong...

The Cooper Climax was retired for a post-mortem; Walker advised Stirling that it was unlikely to be competitive until the problems were sorted and advised him to look elsewhere. In fact he already had, but purely out of curiosity. With Vanwall a shadow of its former self, Vandervell having retired, there was really only one green alternative. The BRM testing which Stirling had carried out after the Glover Trophy had left him with the impression that the car was transformed in the handling department; he kept an open mind about the brakes, but while the engine was clearly tired in Harry Schell's car, it was very strong in Joakim Bonnier's.

He agreed to drive Schell's chassis – number '7' – fitted with Bonnier's engine in the Silverstone International in May; to make sure his wishes were carried out he scratched a chassis tube so that he would recognise it again and turned his attention to the Cooper BRM which was entered for the Aintree 200-mile race. He had high hopes, having won before, but while in the lead the Colotti gearbox failed (for entirely different reasons than those exhibited later in the season) and he retired. The car was weak in many departments so the lap record he set was a pleasant surprise, but nonetheless the car was sold shortly afterwards.

It was apparent that BRM had made a serious effort in preparing the P25 for the Silverstone race, despite the fact

negotiate for a BRM to be entered and more critically, prepared by their own team, the BRP. Rather like the deal over the engine for Walker's Cooper, this was carried out over the heads of Mays and Berthon, to their intense irritation.

Owen was quite happy with the arrangement; he merely wanted the car to succeed, and was quite aware that if this was the only way he could get Stirling into a BRM cockpit for *Grands Prix*, then so be it. The car was delivered to the headquarters of BRP in Chelsea where it was stripped down and repainted in the BRP house colours – a questionable shade of green – under the supervision of Tony Robinson, chief mechanic of the team. Robinson had worked for Stirling before as Alf Francis's able assistant on the Cooper-Alta special of 1953.

It is fair to say that the BRMs had not done badly so far in 1959; the suspicion in which they were held as a team was probably overdone as the Owen regime had imposed a discipline that had obviously paid some dividends. With Tony Rudd supplanting Peter Berthon as chief engineer the

Right: The remarkable Cooper Borgward – one of the most successful Formula 2 cars of its era.

Overleaf: Stirling in the BRP-BRM at Aintree, 1959. Circuit safety was a thing of the future.

technical aspects of the car were more focused than before, and the success they had enjoyed, although modest, indicated that the curse of unreliability from which they had suffered was slowly being exorcised.

The turnaround had, in fact, happened in the previous year, but the change of state at BRM had been eclipsed by the Vanwall-Ferrari struggle, all the deaths and the retirement of Fangio. In reality, BRM was reinventing itself. The Herculean efforts of Ron Flockhart, Harry Schell, Jean Behra and Joakim Bonnier, not to mention the technical staff, had ensured that the team had that vital element of consistency which had helped Vanwall so much and which Connaught (and BRM, in earlier times), had been denied. It was by now basically a good car.

Except for the brakes. The basic reality, that rear brakes do little of the work in stopping a car, led to the development of an eccentric arrangement whereby a single Lockheed disc was used at the rear, attached to the cheeks of the rear axle. The blaring four-cylinder engine produced a critical vibration, which was fed straight down the propshaft (even longer on the later cars) and built a resonance on the axle which could, in the wrong circumstances, misalign the pads or literally shake out the brake fluid. It was all done in the interests of reducing unsprung weight so that the suspension carried a

lesser load, but in reality it was truly dangerous. It made for an interesting ride, as Stirling had discovered at Silverstone.

Short of redesigning the whole layout there was little that BRP's Tony Robinson could actually do about that problem, even if it had been fully understood. Stirling's view, stubbornly held, was that provided the overall level of preparation was sound (and it was), then he would take his chances. To him, it was all an issue of confidence. The careful preparation which the car received allowed Stirling two outings, in the French and British *Grands Prix*. A huge spin on melting tar capped his ambitions at Reims, but he managed a fine second at Silverstone. He shared fastest lap with Bruce McLaren in a Cooper, so clearly the BRM was at least in the same general universe.

But by the time of the German *Grand Prix*, Walker was of the view that the Cooper Climax was sorted out. The plan had been for Ivor Bueb to drive the BRP-BRM, but he had been fatally injured in a Formula 2 race the previous weekend. The alternative BRP plan, to produce works-BRM veteran Ron Flockhart at the last minute, was thwarted by the organisers who countered for patriotic reasons with Hans Herrmann, Stirling's old team mate from Mercedes days. However pleased Herrmann was to get a ride, he was lucky to survive the ensuing terrifying accident which turned the car

more or less to scrap. As for the Walker Cooper Climax, the gearbox broke again. If anything, this was worse than before, given that it happened on the first lap.

This was turning out to be a dire Formula 1 season, but 1959 would deliver for Stirling, by way of some compensation, possibly his most extraordinary race yet – the Nurburgring 1000-kilometre race. If the 1955 *Mille Miglia* had been classic teamwork and Argentina sheer race-craft, then the 1959 Nurburgring race, with Stirling still aboard the beautiful Aston Martin DBR1, showed what he was really capable of in terms of pure unalloyed artistry. In many ways, this would be Aston Martin's year; the factory would win the World Sports Car Championship (a thing which Jaguar had never done), and also Le Mans, which was David Brown's underlying mission – he probably reasoned that it would be worth at least a knighthood.

David Brown was not quite despairing of winning at Le Mans, but given that 1959 would be the tenth year of trying, he was close to it. After several distinctions and class wins and the expenditure of a great deal of money, the great prize still eluded him. The client base for Aston Martin road cars was essentially Anglo-French, so for the little Middlesex factory the French Classic was now the single priority;

nothing else mattered. There was no plan to contest the Nurburgring 1000-kilometre race, barely a fortnight before Le Mans. Stirling, having won the 1000-kilometre race the year before, was disappointed at what he thought was a slightly defeatist attitude to the season as a whole. Winning Le Mans was one thing, but surely, given the talents of the DBR1, which simply out-handled the competition despite clear deficiencies in the power department, it was worth pushing harder. Stirling undertook to underwrite the cost of an expedition to Nurburgring should he fail to win the race. Aston Martin wasthen, in a win/win situation and Stirling was in effect backing himself. Very fairly, Aston Martin supplied two mechanics at their own expense. All prize money, though, would be Stirling's. 'I think they knew me well enough by then to realise that if I was prepared to underwrite the cost myself, then I really was serious,' he recalled over forty years later.

His partner for Nurburgring was to be Jack Fairman. It would be unfair to say that Fairman was a makeweight; the rules mandated that there had to be a second driver, and they

Above: Stirling, Rob Walker, John Cooper and Jack Brabham.
Overleaf: Stirling in the Aston Martin DBR1 at Goodwood.

stipulated a minimum period during which the co-driver had to be in the cockpit.

Maserati also re-presented the *Tipo 60* for Stirling to compare with the Aston. While the machine caused a sensation, its futuristic design making both the Astons and the Ferraris seem almost horse-drawn by comparison, its engine seized solid before any distance could be covered; Stirling had already made his mind up about it anyway. Despite the unavoidable economic Maserati shortcuts, it was a quite marvellous machine. After the 'difficulties' with Parnell the previous year concerning axle ratios, the same previously proven car was used and in practice Stirling matched the lap record which he had set, although the Ferrari team managed to beat it later by a reasonable margin – six seconds – suggesting that they had not been idle at Modena in the intervening year.

But in the race itself, things were different. Ever conscious of the importance of a good (Le Mans) start, if only for the demoralising effect that it had on others, Stirling sprinted to the Aston, leaped in and was off up the track before any other car had turned a wheel. He gradually extended this lead, breaking his sports car lap record sixteen times in succession before handing over to Fairman after seventeen laps. He had presented his co-driver (who had practiced a full half-minute slower) with the awesome, almost unwelcome responsibility of a six-minute lead, and Fairman, although a doughty driver, was no Moss.

But this was exactly the point; at their respective practice paces, that six minutes would be lost in only twelve laps and this was a forty-four lapper. His intention was that Fairman would drive the minimum number of laps within the terms of the rules, just as Brabham had the previous year. It was another example of Stirling creating his own handicap; as an addicted gambler will often attempt to lengthen the odds, so did Stirling, who was in the grip of something which could almost be termed a clinical addiction.

Then it started to rain. This was good news for Stirling, if not for his co-driver. By half distance, Fairman had managed to hold the lead, but on the twenty-third lap the Aston slid off the road at Brünnchen corner. It lay, quite undamaged, athwart the verge while a frantic Fairman ripped a fence post out of the ground and attempted to lever the 1900-pound car back onto the track. That failed, so he had no choice but to lift the rear of the car and physically heave it back on to the track, leaving an observable buttock-shaped dent in the back as a result. Whatever weaknesses one could observe in Fairman's driving skills, this was an outstanding feat of weightlifting. He managed to restart the hot car (actually no small thing in itself) and headed back to the pits, the six

minute lead having evaporated into a deficit.

Back at the pits, Stirling was ruefully considering what this fiasco was going to cost him. He had assumed, although he had no idea what had happened to Fairman, that the race was over and gloomily started to pack his gear away when his exhausted and muddy co-driver finally arrived in the battered green car.

Innes Ireland, whose *Ecurie Écosse* Jaguar was by now well out of any contention, was commiserating with him:

Stirling and I were walking along the little narrow path at the back of the pits when we saw the Aston coming in. Stirling turned and was off like a flash, back to the Aston pit. Within seconds he had his helmet and gloves on and he yanked Fairman out of the car – practically by the scruff of the neck – and set off after the Ferraris, now in fourth place.

The red cars were by now more than a minute ahead. On lap 29 he reeled them in and handed the car back to Fairman at the end of 33 laps. Predictably, Fairman surrendered the lead (the Ferraris were in the hands of Phil Hill and Jean Behra) before Moss took over again on lap 36. Ireland, meanwhile, had decided to watch the fun:

I drove out to the Flugplatz, a couple of miles from the start. The circuit there goes over a hump, then over a bridge and into an uphill right-hander. Stirling would come hurtling through there with the DBR1 and you could see that he was miles faster than anybody else and really motoring! Every lap he was visibly closer to the Ferraris and the spectators were hanging out of the trees, from sky-hooks, you name it, waving and cheering him on. As he came over the hump the car got terribly light then it banged into the dip and up to the right-hander and Stirling – driving right on the doorhandles and with bags of opposite lock – was waving right back at them! I thought: 'Shit, this is something else!'

Indeed it was. It was another two laps before he recovered the lead again, and he held it to win by 41 seconds from the leading Ferrari. It had been, by any measure, an extraordinary and totally authoritative performance; a thing which, by rights, should not be possible. Even better, the prize money was his, after the usual 10 per cent for the delighted mechanics. Innes Ireland's admiration for what he later called the 'Moss Machine' knew no bounds from that moment.

But there had been a distressing sidebar to this triumph, which offered uncomfortable echoes of Caracas. A Swiss

amateur driver had lost his life after 'swapping paint' with the Moss Aston Martin. There had been no collision as such, merely a touch, but it was clearly enough to cause the other driver to lose control. Yet again, the suggestion emerges that these sports car races were two-tier events:

> *If a slower driver stays where he is, even if he's in the wrong place on the circuit, you can always go round him, but if he moves from there to what is now really the wrong place, when you are already committed on a long bend, there's just nothing you can do; really terrible.*

So there were elements of deflection involved, which a driver who actually navigated a bend, as opposed to drifting his way through it, might not necessarily grasp. It is a chilling realisation. Despite Fairman's moderate (but redeeming) performance at the Nurburgring, Stirling was quite happy to

general use of high pressure hoses, but if it happens just as the engine backfires (a not uncommon event in racing tune) then the results are predictably dreadful. In this case the entire Aston Martin pit was set on fire and Salvadori (among others) received burns to his hands and face.

After an uncharacteristic froth of indecision, which saw a precious four laps go by, the Shelby/Fairman car was pulled in and Stirling took it over. He drove the balance of the race to give Aston Martin the championship which had eluded them for so long. It was not before time for David Brown, whose investment in the racing department had at times bitten deep into his cashflow; with some relief, he could start to wind down the racing department, mission accomplished.

In Formula 1, the development of the full works 2½-litre Climax engine and the evident success which it delivered when mounted in any Cooper apart from Stirling's also offered an opportunity to Colin Chapman. His front-engined

To keep a competition car going for
24 hours is an achievement...

share a car with him at Le Mans two weeks later. Contrary to the received wisdom, Stirling was not tasked with breaking the stamina (or the brakes) of the Ferrari team; he was out purely to win. But Le Mans is not really a race in the same sense as other events are. To keep a competition car going for 24 hours is an achievement in itself, let alone to win with it, but after 3 hours and 20 minutes, the engine let go a valve, and that was that. He did, in fact, damage the prospects for Modena as no less than six Ferrari *Testa Rossa* sports prototypes retired, but that had not been the core objective behind his effort.

The Aston Martin tactics clearly worked though, as the team as a whole managed a 1-2, no less than twenty-four laps ahead of the highest placed Ferrari. While the longed-for objective of winning the French classic was now secured, the victory, when added to Nurburgring, put the British marque in serious contention for the World Sports Car Championship; Ferrari had 18 points, Aston Martin 16 and Porsche 15. The RAC TT race would decide matters.

This time, Stirling was paired with Roy Salvadori and the pairing worked very well; they were three minutes ahead of the nearest competition, the sister car shared by Carroll Shelby and Jack Fairman, but by lap 24 a fuel stop was mandated. Spillages were fairly commonplace before the

Lotus 16 had not been a success, but his plain, boxy Lotus 18 was to change the sport. If Colin Chapman can be regarded as the father of the modern racing car, then this was the vehicle with which he set out his stall.

When it appeared for the 1960 season, it was visually unremarkable. Despite that, the new Lotus contained much of the genetic material which would deliver a totally new species of racing car. It was uncompromisingly light; its handling ensured that the days of the louche, dangerous (but hugely spectacular) four-wheel drift were nearly numbered, to be replaced by a total dependence on the laws of physics. As to whether the structure of the machine itself would survive the loads imposed by those laws, well, that was another matter. The cars were fragile.

The structure of the Moss marriage, sadly, was even more fragile. Katie and Stirling had been sharing a house but little else, since their relationship had developed severe problems at the end of 1958, after barely a year of marriage. They had moved from Stirling's distinctly bachelor pad in Challoner Mansions to a mews house in Shepherd Street, Mayfair and typically Stirling had overseen its refurbishment and decoration. Not unnaturally, Katie had wanted some input in

Facing page: That winning wave again.

Left: Stirling aboard the Walker-Cooper at the New Zealand *Grand Prix*, January 1959.
Overleaf left: Stirling and Alf Francis.
Overleaf right: Katie Moss, Stirling's first wife.

this matter herself, but he flatly denied her the opportunity. This was illustrative of a slightly bleak truth, that while Stirling was always prepared to share many aspects of his life with other people, he was much less willing actively to share in theirs. In Stirling's mind, Katie had never been a accessory or a possession, but it might have felt like that to her at times. To be presented with things, whether it be a mews house in Mayfair or a purpose-built house in Nassau was pleasant, but not necessarily vital – she was wealthy enough in her own right to simply write a cheque for these mere possessions – she had not married Stirling for his money.

He found it hard to give of himself, quite simply because he had never been asked to do so before. A childhood which had veered between the comfortable rituals of a cosy upbringing and the interlude of a hostile boarding school had predictably produced in him a sense of insecurity which no single external influence could apparently balance. In one sense, he had not really grown up at all, but in another, he was now trying to govern his life with what appeared to be almost a poor-boy

need to succeed. He had never been poor, of course, but his penny-wise, pound-foolish attitude, which was the interpretation he had put on Alfred's guidance, and his participation in a profession which was at best risky and at worst life-threatening, had made him cautious in the extreme. He had never had a job, for example, apart from the brief interlude as a trainee hotel manager (which Alfred had subsidised) but just as important, nor had she. In their own ways, both had been spoiled and neither was minded to give way. Katie had brought to the marriage a substantial financial element, but perversely (or perhaps predictably), Stirling would not actually allow her to use it. When he had the temerity to suggest that she should open a shop, her patience started to fail her. As the heiress to a brewing fortune, she had no intention of doing any such thing. It was a ridiculous situation, but despite Stirling's impeccable credentials as a conservative, a slightly puritan attitude towards 'unearned' income was showing through. It was as much a matter of his male pride as anything else, but the issue became a critical

one. After a miserable 1959, the unhappy pair announced their formal separation on 17 March, 1960.

Speculation and much coy comment about Stirling's sex life, which had sold many a tabloid paper over the years since he had become famous, had been fairly muted once he had married, but suddenly he was fair game again for Fleet Street's finest. While the racing press had commendably concentrated on the matter at hand – his racing career – the rest of the fourth estate had revelled in his enviable lifestyle. As his picture on the cover of a magazine would immediately boost its circulation, so a tit-bit about his private life would fill the coffers of certain sections of the national press. No matter that much of the copy was pure fantasy – then, as now, it mattered little. One young lovely, a Danish model, had even gone public in the *Daily Sketch* with her declaration of undying love for him, and off the track, Stirling's reputation as something of a sexual athlete made him an easy target for press speculation, albeit in the rather buttoned-up manner of the time.

Up to that point he had cared little one way or the other about the attentions of non-racing journalists, but as soon as the news broke that he was a bachelor again, there were huge sighs of relief and eagerly propounded theories about what had happened, much of it totally spurious, and all of it quite unwelcome. It was a new departure for him; while he enjoyed a measure of publicity as much as the next person, he was to find that being door-stepped at 2 am with a barrage of impertinent questions was the flip side of a very grubby coin.

Because of the closeness of his relationship with Ken Gregory, certain journalists put two and two together and came up with considerably more than four, assuming that the difficulties in Gregory's own marriage were somehow connected with the break-up of Stirling's. The dire reality of the matter was that an employee of a business in which the pair had an interest had been making free with the company

Above: In Rob Walker's Cooper, Easter Monday 1960, at Goodwood.

Overleaf: Pushing hard in the 1960 Argentine *Grand Prix*, 1960.

cashflow for his own benefit as well as playing fast and loose with Mrs Gregory. In fact Ken and Stirling were to reinvent their bachelor days by sharing a house again while poor Ken went through the embarrassing and painful process of sorting out the resultant mess.

Two days after the public disclosure of what many had privately assumed about the Moss marriage, Stirling became reacquainted with the Porsche marque at Syracuse. Due to the change of regulations for Formula 1 for the 1961 season, when engine sizes would be restricted to 1500cc, any experience of the potential front-runners would be valuable. Porsche was a contender and Huschke von Hanstein, the Porsche racing manager, was delighted to prepare and maintain a Formula 2 car to be entered in the colours of the RRC Walker racing team.

It was at Syracuse that Stirling discovered something about his own level of personal courage. His detachment about the abstraction of courage as a notion was in contrast to his fascination with the rituals of superstition, which had by now

become a habit. What he noticed in that Syracuse race was that he could virtually trick himself into going faster; to avoid the observable phenomenon of a 'shrinking right leg', as he put it shortly afterwards:

It's amazing, when you're going into a corner which you think can be taken flat out, you can find yourself unconsciously easing off a bit as if your leg shrinks, even though you know that the inch you can gain on the inside of the curve can be worth as much as a foot on the outside. In Syracuse there was one corner that I had never taken quite flat out...I was just always easing off. Well, in a racing car, there is a big difference to your time – when I say a big difference, a tenth – between easing off and

Previous pages: Monaco 1960 with spectators watching from the steps.

Above: Victory at Monaco in 1961.

Facing page: Princess Grace and Prince Ranieri of Monaco stand to attention with Stirling as he listens to the British national anthem at Monaco in 1961.

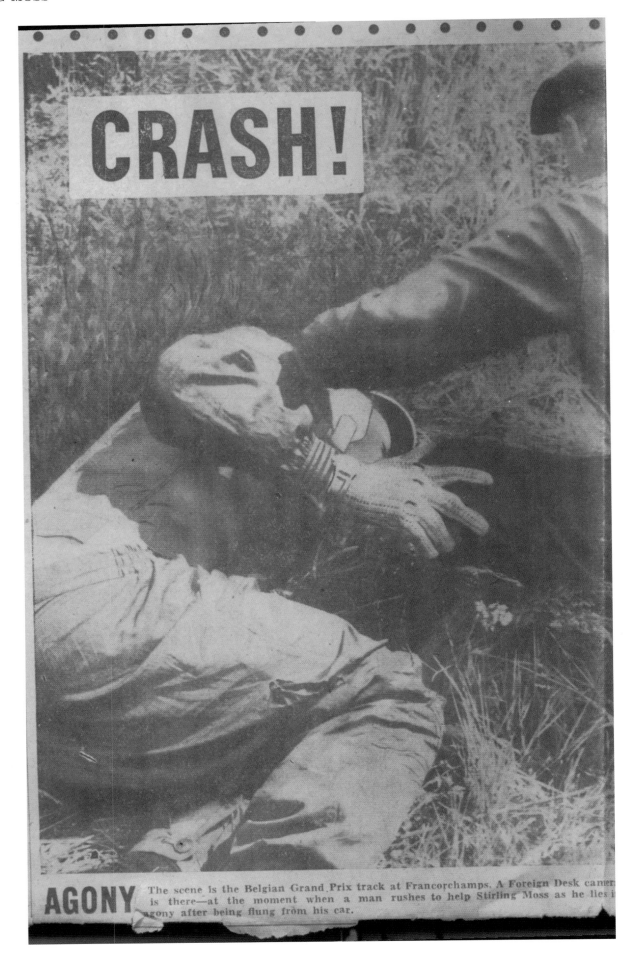

CRASH!

AGONY The scene is the Belgian Grand Prix track at Francorchamps. A Foreign Desk camera is there—at the moment when a man rushes to help Stirling Moss as he lies in agony after being flung from his car.

absolutely flat on the floor, but there's also psychologically a very big difference – in other words, you feel you're really dead safe lifting off, but if you keep your foot down, you're nearly in trouble. And I came into this corner and the only way I could bring myself to take it flat out was by looking at my instruments, not watching the road – you know, setting the car up and looking up when it was too late to lift off.

Given his lowered mental state in the wake of the public collapse of his marriage, this attitude could be interpreted as something much more sinister, but the more likely truth is that freed from the conflicts which his concentration on racing had imposed on his marriage, he was now able to explore further where his limits lay.

Now that Aston Martin had withdrawn from competition having won the World Championship, the sports car calendar offered a chance to try the new iteration of the Maserati

Aside from the indignity of the rather public breakdown of his marriage to Katie, he had to contend with another ignominy in early 1960. For the heinous offence of changing lanes in the Mersey tunnel, his driving licence was taken away. This put him in something of a quandary; without a road licence, he could not hold a competition one; it was in many ways almost a restraint of trade. When this had happened before in 1950, Ken Gregory, who was still working at the RAC, had managed to 'fix' matters, but ten years on, it was rather more serious. Clearly, as he argues, he was unfairly made an example of. The technicalities of licensing mandated that a driver must hold an internation competition licence based on the possession of a national licence. Given that he could not now hold a UK national racing licence, he decided to take out an American one which would allow him to enter both national events in the USA, as well as international events elsewhere. It was a strategy with which the RAC was happy to cooperate, as it was held, and not only by Stirling,

Since I haven't had a licence I've been
driven by a lot of people

sports car, the *Tipo 61* – now known by all and sundry as the 'Birdcage'. Given the firm's still-parlous state, it was unable to field a works entry (although Stirling had won a minor race with a works car at Rouen the previous year), but it was now re-engined, hence the new designation.

Lloyd 'Lucky' Casner, a skilled promoter from Miami, was able to organise a special race series for these cars and even better, he had persuaded the Goodyear Tyre Company to more or less foot the entire bill. His own team, Camoradi (an acronym; CAsner Motor RAcing Division) was to enter Stirling, partnered by Dan Gurney, in a clutch of races, and despite some let-downs the pair managed a fine win in the Nurburgring 1000-kilometre race, which gave Stirling his third successive win there. It would also be his last.

With the irony that dogs motor sport, by the time the Cooper Climax gearbox problems were sorted out, the car as a whole had been made obsolete, which was rather suggested by Innes Ireland's dramatic double win aboard both Formula 1 and Formula 2 Lotus 18s at the Glover Trophy and the Lavant Cup of 1960, after which Walker promptly ordered the Formula 1 version of Chapman's new car. It was not to be ready until a week before Monaco, where straight out of the box Stirling won with it.

that the confiscation of his licence was extremely unjust.

But that was for competition purposes; he could not drive on the road in England. The worst aspect of this for Stirling was being forced to be a passenger. He said in the summer of 1960:

Since I haven't had a licence I've been driven by a lot of people, and I sit in the back sometimes trembling, wishing I'd got my crash-hat on, thinking 'Well, this chap's got his licence and I'm sure I'm safer on the road than this person'. . .What am I to do? I can't do anything about it.

It was a high price to pay for celebrity, and although his fans were both sympathetic and supportive, it was a humiliation. 1960 was to be a year characterised by a series of morale-sapping episodes, of which the formal separation from Katie was only the first, and the loss of his licence merely the second. There were high spots too, however.

In practice for Monaco, Innes Ireland was having trouble even making the cut, as the organisers insisted that only sixteen cars could qualify. Given that Ireland was leading the

Facing page: Stirling moments after the spa crash on 18 June, 1960.

Lotus works team and his team mates Surtees and Stacey had already managed to go quickly enough, this was embarrassing for him, to say the least, particularly after his double defeat of Stirling at Goodwood.

In a gesture reminiscent of Fangio, Stirling simply gave Ireland a driving lesson around the houses; the pair went round in tandem (although not as closely as 'the train' had done) and as a result Ireland qualified well up the grid. The point was also made, mutely, that although Ireland was a works driver and the Walker Lotus was private, a certain gap existed between the ability of the drivers. Ireland already acknowledged that, and although he was bewildered at the

fact that the Walker car was in all ways similar to the factory Lotuses, it was made clear to him by Colin Chapman that the Constructor's crown was the company's primary objective, so he was pleased indeed when Stirling won the race. As other builders had and would discover, a superior driver outside the team with an identical car can act as a very large stick indeed with which to discipline the lads – particularly when it came to paying them. To get paid more, all you had to do was to beat Stirling Moss.

One who would try was Jim Clark, who joined Lotus after Monaco and who made his debut at the Dutch *Grand Prix* a week later at Zandvoort. He retired from that race, but started to climb up the lists very quickly indeed, despite technical problems. Clark would never drive Formula 1 for any other team but Lotus in fact. In that Dutch race, Stirling came fourth, but his pole position as well as a new lap record suggested that the Lotus was a very clever purchase indeed.

But it was also very flimsy; Stirling had not realised that by the end of the Monaco race the front engine bearers had simply snapped off; the roaring Climax motor was only

attached to the car by its water pipes, cables and rear suspension. It would have been quite possible for the whole car to simply come apart around him, to fall in half. It was the first suggestion that the little car was not exactly built to last. But that was exactly the point. To Chapman, if a part broke, it was too light; if it didn't, then it was too heavy. To him, lightness and efficiency were the objectives – safety came a very poor third indeed. As the Lotus marque evolved, time and again vital parts would break, particularly at the cars' physical extremities, as the search for less and less unsprung weight went on. There is no doubt that Chapman was touched by genius, but it came with a price.

The incident at Zandvoort which denied Stirling a better position was not a Lotus engineering failure, but a burst tyre. It took place at over 120 mph:

> *I lost control and shot across the road because I was taking a corner, and there was a big wood there and I thought 'Well, this is my lot.' I managed somehow to regain control in time, or the car came back – anyway, something happened and it was all right. I felt frightened while it was happening but immediately after I didn't get the feeling of fear because I had something else to think about. The tyre was burst, my second position was lost and I had to get back to the pits and so on.*

The irony was not lost on him that his deliberate holding of second place behind Jack Brabham had been a conscious attempt on his part to prove that he could pace himself rather than simply charge around as fast as possible on the basis that it's never to early to start winning. There had been a great deal of adverse comment in the press labelling Stirling as a car breaker, which had been largely as a result of the unreliability of the Colotti transmission. Stirling was rather keen to demonstrate that this was not the case. It was a 25-pound chunk of concrete dislodged from the kerb and thrown up in the air by Brabham's tire that actually caused the puncture. Better, he reflected, to try to lead from the front in future.

With six more *Grands Prix* to go, perhaps the Lotus 18 was the antidote to the disappointments of 1959, flimsiness apart. Not everyone agreed; Alf Francis had been squirreling away as many resources as he could in order to produce his own car, which he had proudly unveiled over the previous winter. It was a Maserati 250 clone in many ways, front-engined with Coventry-Climax power. To his chagrin, he could not persuade even Stirling to sit in it. Whether he

Above: Recovering in St Thomas's after the Spa crash.

Right: Huschke von Hanstein of Porsche with Stirling and Rob Walker.

entertained serious thoughts of the boy wonder actually driving this creation we cannot be sure, but the next Formula 1 event, the Belgian *Grand Prix* a fortnight after Zandvoort, ensured that Francis' car (and much else at Pippbrook) was placed on the back burner.

But before that came a major media event. The BBC had developed a programme format which the public – 14 million of them – found quite gripping. *Face to Face*, as it was called, was presented by the noted journalist and academic John Freeman, who interviewed the *prominenti* of the day. The BBC had been somewhat anxious about bagging Stirling for the series; as a producer's file note suggested, his appearance was a matter of some urgency, as 'He is likely to be killed soon.' It was a prescient remark, given what was to happen the following week. The programme was broadcast live, in the second week of June 1960.

Freeman was of the opinion before him met Stirling, as he later recalled, that Stirling was merely a playboy who had a gift for driving cars and thus he had no particular expectations of the encounter. What he heard was to change his mind. Talking to psychiatrist Anthony Clare in 1988, he recalled:

> *I was astonished to find out what an intensely serious professional he is, and I remember asking him at some point in that interview where fear came into this, and he dismissed the concept of fear completely, saying it wasn't a matter of fear, it was a matter of calculation, had you got the calculation right or not. If you'd got the calculation right, there's nothing to be afraid of. This was a man of cold, precise, clinical engineering judgement, and that surprised me very much indeed…It appealed to me because the notion that a man could live so close to the edge of death and danger, and trust entirely to his own judgement to keep on the right side of that line, I found very stimulating.*

Freeman, who had built up a reputation, entirely deserved, for being a courteous but ruthless interrogator (he was to bring the famously irascible Gilbert Harding to tears later in the year), considered the Moss interview to be the most successful of the whole series. It did no harm to Stirling's reputation either, going a long way to counterbalance the image of him fostered by the gossip columns, which is presumably where Freeman gained his initial impression. The revelation that Stirling was capable of such finely balanced calculation, and that this was effectively his only faith, caught the imagination of many:

FREEMAN: *Is this sport as risky as spectators think it is, or do you calculate it to the point where the risk isn't really all that great?*

MOSS: *It is a calculated risk, but there are unfortunate things you can't calculate for, which are mechanical failures or oil on the track. I am not normally afraid of killing myself. I'm frightened of being killed by something over which I have no control.*

He might as well have been describing what was going to happen a scant week later.

If you are committed at 140 mph to one of the fastest sweeps in *Grand Prix* racing, Burnenville at Spa, and your left rear wheel falls off, there is a very small universe of choice available to you concerning what to do next. In Stirling's case, he managed to steer into the resulting skid, make the car swap ends and when it impacted, he had not only scrubbed off some vital speed, but also ensured that when the little Lotus did make contact with an immovable object (the banking), it did so tail first, which is when he discovered again that Colin Chapman built cars very lightly indeed. The impact threw him out before the car shot back across the road; unsurprisingly, he was very badly hurt. He was also winded, temporarily blinded and in shock.

Wisely, Jack Brabham, who was the first driver to stop, declined to give him artificial respiration lest he had broken ribs, which, judging by the state of the car, he might well have done. A punctured lung would not have helped. His diary entry says it all: '18 June, 1960: Shunt. Back. Legs. Nose. Bruises. Bugger.'

But this was just the practice for the race. The Lotus works

team of Innes Ireland, Jim Clark and Alan Stacey immediately halted their session and their own cars were rapidly checked. Only Clark's car was sound; the other two had cracked hubs. Chapman claimed that the hubs were faulty; they may well have been but as Ireland himself admitted later, the design was always going to be tested hardest by Stirling, simply because he went so much faster than anyone else. His would always be the first diagnosis. Suddenly, it was realised that Michael Taylor, a privateer driving an ex-works Lotus, had also gone missing. After a lengthy search he was discovered trapped in the car, badly hurt. Later on it transpired that his steering column had snapped, which certainly gave Ireland some pause for thought; he had been driving that very car only weeks before.

While this was going on, poor Alfred at race control was going berserk with worry, as no one seemed to know what had happened to his son. An ambulance eventually arrived where Brabham was still patiently waiting and Stirling was taken to hospital at Malmèdy; after undergoing X-rays, he was encased in plaster. The race itself the next day was even more calamitous than the practice had been; Alan Stacey and Christopher Bristow both lost their lives; Stacey was hit by a bird, and Bristow crashed at the same place that Stirling had. British sport reeled under the shock.

Stirling was unaware of this and the next day he was flown back to St. Thomas's Hospital, Westminster, where to his surprise the chief orthopaedic surgeon, M. Urquhart, ordered the plaster casts removed. Stirling's spine was not broken, but he had three compacted vertebrae. Urquhart reasoned that he could probably stand, demonstrating this by placing Stirling's feet upon his own and leading him around the surgery in a bizarre two-step. If he could stand, then the strength of his own muscles would be as good a splint for his legs as anything artificial; it could also hasten the recovery time, but it would hurt like hell, he warned.

Stirling, although initially startled by the novelty of Urquhart's approach, engaged fully in the spirit of this enterprise. Time was money after all, and time spent in hospital was fruitless, boring and, worst of all, depressing. Because of Urquhart's enthusiasm for exercise, he was also quite willing to permit a persuasive Stirling to leave the hospital at night, which allowed him the chance for some gentle dancing at the Colony Club. By 12 July, he was doing just that.

His injuries would force him to miss the next two *Grands*

Left: This photographer clearly interprets 'track pass' to mean what it says as he snaps another favourite car wearing a favourite number.

Prix, which more or less assured that the Championship would not be his in 1960, but when he did return, on 7 August, he did so on top form. The race, the *Kannonloppet* at Karlskoga, Sweden, marked his debut as a sports car driver for the Yeoman Credit-sponsored BRP team. When he actually won it in a Lotus 19, Fleet Street knew that their boy was back. There were even some rumours, fuelled by the fact that he was seen out dancing, that the Moss PR machine rather overstated his injuries at the time, hence the quick recovery, but the simple fact of the matter was that his extraordinary constitution, coupled with Urquhart's quite revolutionary regimen, accomplished the job inside six weeks.

He was less concerned about the injuries than whether Katie might actually put in an appearance. She did not and while he regards that as a perfectly sensible attitude now, he did not feel it then. Stubbornly, he held on to the fervent hope that she might return to him in light of what had happened to him.

He missed the French and British *Grands Prix*, but had every reason to be optimistic about Portugal, having won it twice in succession. Ironically, he was disqualified from the race for doing the very thing which had nearly undone Mike Hawthorn in 1958 – pushing his car the wrong way to restart it. Alas, there was no one prepared to stand up for him and

the stewards clearly felt that his defence of Hawthorn two years before had not established any case law on the subject.

The British teams all boycotted Monza in 1960 on safety grounds, which left the event to Ferrari, but any advantage they may have gained was effectively cancelled out by the scarlet cars' non-attendance at the final event of the year, the United States *Grand Prix* at Riverside Raceway, outside Los Angeles. It offered a pleasing Lotus 1-2 win, with Stirling from pole position leading Innes Ireland home. As the winner, it was Stirling's honour to cut the celebratory cake which was produced in the shape of a racing car. Solemnly, he sliced off the left rear wheel and handed it to Colin Chapman, who was less than amused.

Stirling's first visit to South Africa for the Formula 2 *Grand Prix* at East London offered him his first encounter with apartheid. His sense of natural justice was offended by the sight of racially segregated enclosures and the observable differences between the facilities in them, so his suggestion to the other drivers, that they should wave to the crowd only when passing non-white spectators, was not an act of overt political activism, it was rather Stirling Moss, the Haileybury agitator at work. Of course, the fact that he was the only driver who actually bothered to wave to a crowd in the first place was quite another matter, but it made a small point and went some way toward counterbalancing any sense of guilt about participating. These gestures became something of a *Grand Prix* trend, in fact, maintained as a little tradition even when the race was later transferred to Kyalami.

So 1960 had been a perilous and depressing season. His marriage had fallen apart, the new Lotus had nearly done the same thing at Monaco, Zandvoort had offered yet another glance over the edge and Spa had nearly been terminal.

A pleasing and welcome novelty, however, was the delicious Ferrari 250 GT which Walker ran that year. It was a short chassis version of the Classic Ferrari 250 coupé which had, in various versions, become a benchmark for both speed and toughness since its introduction five years before. It was a relatively simple device, but a good example of what happens when a series of designs of quite modest pretensions simply gel properly. A simple tube chassis, suspended by crude cart springs but propelled by the marvellous 3-litre V12 motor,

(and very pretty) little car designed by Carlo Chiti. He was to enjoy a virtual whitewash in the 1961 season, but with two notable and embarrassing exceptions, both delivered by Stirling aboard Walker's car.

The problems that Walker's team encountered in the early stages of 1961 were to prove vexing. The carburation of the 1500cc engine was deficient for the simple reason that a change in machining practice at the Weber carburettor factory had led to some crucial oversights. The result was that the engine was starved of fuel, which is why the team had such a difficult first quarter in 1961. Denis Jenkinson, who revered Stirling, assumed the worst and accused the Walker team in print of fielding 'starting money specials'. Jenkinson really could not help himself, but it was an unfair accusation, and Walker promptly sued for libel. 'Jenks' was unapologetic; he was so used to seeing Stirling win that he felt that the support which he merited was simply not there, and was silly enough

He was the only driver who bothered to wave to the crowd

this car was a paragon of reliability, compared to certain other marques.

He had already driven Ferraris in competition since the Bari episode in 1951, and by and large he had liked them, but the 250 was a car in which a driver could do almost anything without eliciting any protest from the machine. Again, it was a good example of a logically evolved car with generations of experience behind it.

The changes to Formula 1 for 1961 were inevitably seen as retrograde by the bulk of the sport, as effectively it reverted to being Formula 2, as it had in 1952. Unsurprisingly, the British were caught out by it again. Since the advent of rear-engined architecture, all the British constructors, with the exception of BRM, were reliant upon Coventry Climax as a source of power, as they would come to rely on Cosworth a few years later. This time, even BRM was unready (Mays, nervous of the budgets required, had vigorously protested the change) and a queue formed to acquire the old Formula 2 engines at the Climax factory gate. For the Walker team, things were no different, and they prepared to campaign the Lotus 18 again. Enzo Ferrari was to emerge as the victor in the engine department, as he had already prepared for the new formula by developing a V6 Formula 2 engine in 1960 in a brilliant

to say so. *Motor Sport* magazine, which was contractually bound to publish Jenks' copy in its entirety, whatever it own misgivings, settled for £1000 out of court. Rob Walker, predictably, gave the resulting cheque to charity.

Some diligent homework by Alf Francis, in conjunction with Webers, had ensured that the critical problem was solved in time for the first event of the 'proper' racing season, the Monaco *Grand Prix*. Stirling's mount, the 1960 Lotus 18, still produced perhaps 40 bhp less than the three Ferraris entered. Nevertheless, he plonked the ageing Lotus firmly on pole position alongside Ritchie Ginther's Ferrari and Jim Clark's Lotus. Innes Ireland, unhappily, was unable to start.

The dreadful karma that was to hound Innes Ireland all season started here. In practice, unused to the new ZF gearbox of his new Lotus 21, he picked the wrong gear while barrelling through the Monaco tunnel. The rear wheels locked up and poor Ireland was ejected like a cork from a bottle from the gyrating car. As he put it to me many years later: 'Ah, yes. '61; that was the year when I came out of the ******* tunnel without the ******* car.'

His injuries were superficially quite modest but full of

Left: In the boxy little Lotus 18.

Left: Stirling in the Walker-Cooper alongside Innes Ireland who is dring the new

Lotus 18. Walker bought a Lotus as soon as he was able.

adrenalin and slightly confused, he failed to notice that he was bleeding heavily from a large gash in his shin. Quite calmly, he picked himself up, unaware that a skidding Lucien Bianchi had nearly run him over as he tumbled along the tarmac, then lay down on the harbour side of the track and proceeded to start bleeding to death. A nurse stationed nearby, as luck would have it, whipped a tourniquet around the gashed artery just as an alarmed Stirling drew up; he liked Ireland. Innes recalled: 'He was very good, I remember. He took charge, obtained a cigarette for me from one of the crowd and tried to make me comfortable.'

Ireland's accident put paid to the practice session as he had deposited the entire contents of his oil tank inside the tunnel, which had been the cause of Bianchi's difficulties.

This race is another which has gone down in motor racing lore as one of Stirling Moss's finest. It was the kind of situation he had come to relish, as he had at the Nurburgring 1000-kilometre race and in Argentina – he alone against the entire works Ferrari effort. The fact that he was driving an obsolete car simply added spice to the situation.

There was another chilling omen of Lotus build quality though, when he noticed what appeared to be a crack in a chassis tube while the car was already on the grid awaiting the off. He summoned the faithful Francis to inspect it. The car was fully laden with 30 gallons of fuel, but Francis calmly wrapped wet towels around the tanks and the offending part

and simply welded it with an oxyacetaline torch. It was a remarkably effective way of clearing the crowds, even if it rather challenged the imagination of the driver. To help keep him cool during the race, the lower side body panels were removed and Stirling doused himself in water – he admitted later that he simply thought that wet overalls were rather becoming. But it was a further reminder that the Lotus was not an ounce heavier than it needed to be – which makes what happened next even more remarkable.

The superior acceleration of the Ferrari allowed Ginther to lead from the grid, and Stirling, breaking away from the little cluster of cars which followed, pressed him for 13 laps before passing, whereupon he held the lead for the balance of the race. The repeated efforts of Ginther, Phil Hill and Wolfgang von Trips to dislodge him ultimately proved fruitless. Lap after lap, the three Ferrari drivers changed places with each other to harry the little dark-blue car while Moss drove on, apparently in a state of complete serenity.

His habit of waving to the crowds only served to further emphasise his total authority; it was another technique straight from the pages of Stephen Potter, and while he probably drove harder than he ever had before, flat out by his own measure (and probably at eleven-tenths by anyone else's),

Below left and right: Stirling held off the entire Ferrari works team around the sinuous Monaco circuit, 1961.

he made it look ridiculously easy and came home ahead of the three Ferraris, which were spread out in an exhausted and embarrassed line behind him. Walker was enchanted. He realised that the Ferrari team effort was at full-stretch when an appalled Romolo Tavoni, the Ferrari team manager, hung out a signal for his leading driver that read: 'GINTHER, GIVE ALL'. This unsubtle message was probably as depressing for Ginther as being airily thanked by Stirling as he was

being passed on lap 13, but in adversity, it must be said, Ferrari was never a particularly subtle team.

The well-informed onlookers were staggered; Moss had, in the opening event of the *Grand Prix* season, driven a year-old, hastily repaired car and comprehensively thrashed the entire Ferrari works team in a straight fight. They had witnessed the impossible or so they thought. When the times were analysed, it was revealed that Stirling had run the entire race at an average which was less than half a second a lap slower than his pole position time. Even for a slow circuit like Monaco, his achievement was unique.

Of course, Monaco is a sinuous little circuit – a driver's circuit, as the cliché goes – on which it

is very hard to overtake. The faint possibility of a fluke emerged as the Ferrari team crushed all before them for the next four races, with Stirling scoring barely a single point, until the German *Grand Prix* at the Nurburgring. It was a race which would propel him into a direct comparison with the great Tazio Nuvolari who a quarter of a century before had trounced the factory teams of both Mercedes-Benz and Auto-Union, aboard an ageing (and apparently uncompetitive) Alfa Romeo. So confident were the organisers of that race of a German victory that they had neglected to equip themselves with a recording of the Italian national anthem. Legend has it that Nuvolari had brought his own '78' record with him, which he had been pleased to produce for them to use.

Lotus, on the instructions of its fuel sponsor, was not permitted to sell its new car to anyone and particularly not to Rob Walker. While Colin Chapman himself was fairly relaxed about the matter, as ever concentrating on progress in the Constructor's Championship, Reg Tanner, the competitions manager at Esso Petroleum, was not. The RRC Walker Racing Team was a BP-backed organisation and the opportunities offered by fuel and oil sales was the mainspring of oil company participation. Esso was quite adamant.

Tyre companies were not involved in this sport for any reason other than the sales potential, so when Stirling started to experiment at the Nurburgring practice session with Dunlop 'green spot' rain tyres with huge grip, the Dunlop rep Vic Barlow, would have nothing to do with it. Without rain, he feared the tyres would overheat and break up, with potentially embarrassing consequences. Stirling's response was to paint out the green spots which identified the tyre type and run the race on them start to finish. There were echoes of Argentina 1958 in

Above left: Monaco, 1961.

Facing page above: At the 1961 German *Grand Prix*, Stirling ran his Lotus on grippy wet-weather tyres; the risk paid off and the race delivered his 16th and last *Grand Epreuve* win.

Facing page, below: Not only did Stirling deliver the first post-war rear-engined Grand Prix win, he drove this Ferguson FWD car to victory at the Oulton Park Gold Cup.

this strategy, but the reality was that while the Nürburgring was a twisty circuit upon which a driver could demonstrate a clear edge over a machine, the sheer grunt of the Ferraris would surely tell, even if their Englebert tyres were not equal to the Dunlops, particularly if it rained. In practice, the mechanical superiority of the Italian cars was hammered home very firmly, as Phil Hill put his car on pole with the first ever sub nine-minute lap at the Nürburgring. It boiled down to a gamble on the weather. Light showers were forecast.

The Walker Lotus looked a little different by now. Chapman had agreed to sell some Lotus 21 suspension parts and body panels to Walker, so the previously boxy shape was

now smoother. The car had become a Lotus 18/21 hybrid, albeit a cosmetic one, whereas the Cooper driven by Jack Brabham actually had the new V8 Coventry Climax engine; indeed, he had qualified on the front row with it. An accident on the opening lap would prevent a head-to-head Climax – Ferrari contest, as Brabham was forced to retire.

This time, the Ferraris were unable to outdrag Stirling and he held a tenuous lead; his tyre temperatures headed for the sort of levels which had concerned Barlow so much. On lap two, the weather forecast proved correct and it started to rain. Immediately, Stirling opened up a wider lead. The rain did not last, and while Hill responded with the fastest time of the race on the tenth lap, Stirling came in to win, waving as ever, 20.4 seconds ahead of a rueful von Trips and Hill as well as an impressed crowd of 300,000.

The death of von Trips and fourteen spectators on the opening lap at Monza, the next *Grand Prix*, cast a dismal pall over a season which had afforded Enzo Ferrari his first Constructor's Championship. The demise of the affable German toff, together with the spectators, was to cause Jim Clark, who had collided with him, a raft of grief for several years as Italian jurisprudence mandated that in the case of a violent death, someone has to be held responsible.

It was possibly Innes Ireland's suggestion that the works Lotus 21 be lent to the Walker team at Monza which terminated his career as a works driver. Chapman, as ever keen to see a Lotus well-driven, assented quite happily to the idea without consulting Esso; Ireland swapped cars with Stirling, experiencing for the first time the huge compromises with which Moss had been contending all season. When the tired Lotus 18/21 chassis cracked on the fifth lap Ireland retired, marvelling at the talents of the man who drove this ageing machine. It was a sporting gesture quite typical of Ireland and Stirling relished the opportunity. With two races to go, there was still a chance at the Championship.

If anything, the hastily repainted Lotus 21 was even twitchier to drive than the hybrid 18/21; Stirling qualified a poor 11th on the grid but was going well until a wheel bearing overheated and seized. A depressed Phil Hill won both the race and the Championship. With only one race to go, Ferrari could afford to forgo the US *Grand Prix*; with the death of von Trips (a posthumous second in the Championship) and the Constructor's cup assured, there was no reason and every excuse to withdraw.

Esso was not at all pleased at Ireland's gesture, although he was, in the final round of the season, to give Chapman's works team its first World Championship win in the US *Grand Prix* at Watkins Glen. He was unceremoniously fired shortly afterwards, not initially by Chapman, but by hints given by Reg Tanner's successor at Esso, Geoffrey Murdoch. Chapman, totally in thrall to the oil company, had not the heart to lower the boom. Just as weasel words had failed him when talking to Tony Vandervell in 1955, so they did again. It was one of his characteristics that he simply could not address matters which were in any way 'unwelcome', and as a result this could make him appear very tricky indeed. The whole episode was a precursor of the gyrations that team managers would experience years later at the whim of their sponsors.

Facing page: A soaking start to the 1961 New Zealand *Grand Prix*.

Above: But Stirling wins it, first time out in the Lotus 21.

It had been just over ten years since Stirling's last personal encounter with Enzo Ferrari and a very humiliating process that had been. But Stirling had marvelled at the performance of the little 1½-litre cars; he could afford to since he was the only driver to beat them. Particularly impressive was that as late as 1959, Enzo Ferrari had sworn that building a racing car with its engine in the back would be tantamount to putting the cart before the horse and his hasty *volte-face* on the subject had produced an extraordinary result. If he could change his mind on that, then perhaps there were other matters about which he might perhaps be flexible. From Enzo Ferrari's point of view, despite his success in 1961, his team was fraying at the edges. The death of von Trips had been a huge blow and while the loyalty of Phil Hill was assured, Ritchie Ginther was another matter. Being paid peanuts for his efforts did not persuade him to stay and he decamped to BRM to participate in what might well be their last push before abandoning any ambitions in Formula 1. Alfred Owen was finding it harder and harder to hold the line in terms of what the Owen Racing Organisation was expected to spend.

The only person to have beaten the Ferrari team in 1961 was Stirling Moss *ergo* Ferrari needed him; the involvement of the Walker team with Ferrari sports cars had opened up an avenue of communication. Ferrari suggested a visit.

Enzo Ferrari's casual rudeness was legendary; from film stars and royalty, to the insecure newly rich, visitors to the works were routinely kept waiting for hours, just for the privilege of handing over a large draft in exchange for a car in a noisome little shed. Few were ever invited to tour the works. Observers of Stirling's reception could have been forgiven for assuming that either the Pope or the ghost of Nuvolari had arrived. All bluster put aside, Ferrari saw him immediately and after bussing him on both cheeks like a long-lost relative, stated his case. The conversation, witnessed by George de Carvalho of *Time* magazine and cited by Ken Purdy, was certainly not an apology for his previous conduct, which was not even mentioned:

I need you; tell me what kind of car you want and I will make it for you in six months. Put your ideas on paper for me. If you drive for me, you will tell me on Monday what you did not like about the car on Sunday and by Friday it will have been changed to your taste. If you drive for me, I will have no team, just you and a reserve driver. With Moss, I would need no team.

Stirling had spoken to his mentor Fangio before the meeting.

The Argentinian had counselled, after his experiences in 1956, 'By all means drive the cars, but never, ever, sign for Ferrari.' Not a problem, as it transpired. Swiftly, a deal was arranged. Ferrari would build a Formula 1 car, which would be lent to and entered by Rob Walker and thus painted the dark blue of the RRC Walker team. It was, in essence, the same arrangement that had worked for Moss and Walker with Porsche and for the BRP with the ill-fated BRM. For the Walker team it meant access to an up-to-date car; for Ferrari, it was a useful stick with which to beat his existing drivers. With Moss as a benchmark, there would be no excuses for them. Enzo Ferrari cared very little about which driver won the Driver's Championship, only who was the Champion constructor; he sold beautiful and expensive road cars on the back of his racing efforts, ploughing back a good proportion of the profits into the racing operation. To him, any Ferrari

would do, and it mattered nothing to him who actually entered the car, but it did matter who drove it. Points were points, after all, and a measure of control was well worth forgoing, particularly as Stirling seemed to have made up his own mind already. Usefully, there would be an element of deniability on both sides should something untoward happen, like losing. Ferrari probably reasoned that each would blame the other.

It was a good deal, too; one which would ensure that Walker's team not only had the best car, at least by 1961 standards, but that Enzo Ferrari also had access to the best driver without having to actually pay him. Of course, neither man could really confer any extra status on the other; the relationship would essentially be a symbiotic one with a degree of deniability on both sides. They would work in parallel. Suddenly, everyone was happy. It was also eminently sensible. Despite his disdain for the new school of racing car design, Ferrari had proved that when the factory concentrated hard, developed its cars logically and organically (or better, had the assistance of FIAT, as with the Lancia Ferraris) it could triumph. And, despite his oft-voiced opinion, Stirling was a huge admirer of the difficult Emilian tyrant, which had made the initial humiliation hard to stomach and even harder to forgive: 'I respected what he meant to the sport, and what he'd done for it', he recalled. 'To my knowledge, no driver had ever died as a result of something breaking on a Ferrari.'

After the experiences of the 1957 *Mille Miglia*, and the huge moment at Monza in Signor Zanetti's grotesque Maserati special, not to mention the near disaster at Spa, who could blame him? For Walker, the exercise was simply an extension of the racing programme of the 250 SWB *berlinetta*

which had offered so much success.

But this was Enzo Ferrari; a deal was not a deal until it had been consummated, as Stirling had discovered at Bari. Thus, it was decided to keep the project a secret. It was not a matter of face, just practicality. The Walker team was now showing its hand in terms of what it proposed to accomplish – nothing less than an all-out assault on the World Championship – and for a private entrant to do this was commitment indeed. To have the co-operation of a figure such as Ferrari was a tremendous endorsement, but also a gauntlet to lay before the British *garagistas* upon whom, if the Ferrari deal were to fall through, the team would have to depend.

They would certainly not be depending on BRM; the firm was finally facing up to the reality of commercial life. As Stirling was talking to Enzo Ferrari, Alfred Owen was pointing out to Raymond Mays, very firmly, that 1962 would be a make-or-break season. The budgets for the new formula were demanding in the extreme, and he was going to find the justification for the project very hard to sell to his board and directors unless there were some serious results. Of particular concern was the cost of the new 1.5-litre engine. Some of this he had said before, but, successful businessman though he was, he was as capable as any of throwing good money after bad. This time, though, he meant it.

Facing page: Stirling in the overalls he designed for Dunlop.
Following four pages: These images are taken from Stirling's scrapebook and give a flavour of the interest which Stirling's life and career generated amongst the British press and public. Note the clipings covering Hawthorn's death and Stirling's own brushes with disaster.

Stirling on the Celebration Circuit at Monte Carlo

STIRLING AND SHIRLEE—HE'S AN EXPERT DANCER

HE'S just won the Grand Prix of Monte Carlo. For the third time. By three seconds. So it's time for Stirling Moss to celebrate. With him is Shirlee Adams, his young American friend. And what does it matter if Stirling, only 5ft. 4in. tall, is an inch or two shorter than Shirlee in her high heels? For he's an expert dancer. He once confessed he would have liked to be Gene Kelly—if he wasn't Stirling Moss.

Daily Express 16.5.61

WITH THE GRAND PRIX TROPHY THAT STIRLING WON

GLIMPSE INTO FUTURE

Moss is superstitious; wears a lucky charm; races as number seven if he possibly can. So naturally he made a bee-line for gipsy fortune-teller Delyane.

TELL ME, GIPSY . . .

Von Trips and 11 spectators die in 140 mph crash
PRIX CROWD DISASTER

Sunday at Monza—and death in the sun. Von Trips is sprawled with his head on the track as another driver dodges his battered Ferrari. On the verge stands the Lotus; behind it lies Clark. And the spectators, whom tragedy struck so swiftly, look on. Stunned

DRIVERS' CHAMPIONSHIP
(Best Five Results)

	Pts.
1. Phil Hill (Ferrari)	34
2. Wolfgang von Trips (Ferrari)	33
3. Stirling Moss (Lotus)	21
4. Richie Ginther (Ferrari)	16
5. Dan Gurney (Porsche)	15
6. Jim Clark (Lotus)	11
7. Giancarlo Baghetti (Ferrari)	9
8. Bruce McLaren (Cooper-Climax)	8
9. Jack Brabham (Cooper-Climax)	4
John Surtees (Cooper-Climax)	4
11. Olivier Gendebien (Ferrari)	3
Jack Lewis (Cooper-Climax)	3
Innes Ireland (Lotus)	3
14. Jo Bonnier (Porsche)	2
Roy Salvadori (Cooper-Climax)	2
Tony Brooks (B.R.M.)	2
17. Graham Hill (B.R.M.)	1

British driver tells of wheel-touch escape

From DENIS HOLMES,
Monza, Italy, Sunday

RACING idol Wolfgang von Trips and 11 spectators were killed today when his Ferrari crashed at 140 m.p.h.

The car rocketed into the crowd and bounced back on to the track. At least 25 people were injured, some seriously.

BEFORE THE RACE—Von Trips of Germany with Britain's Jim Clark and Stirling Moss

Ace von Trips dies as car kills 11 fans
RACE CROWD MOWN DOWN
SPEED ACE RAMS RACE CROWD AT 130 MPH

Disaster at Goodwood

By the start of 1962, Stirling was at the very apex of his form. The prospect of the Walker-entered Ferraris, at both sports car and *Grand Prix* levels, was the culmination of more than ten years of anticipation. The little shark-nosed car, which had captured both the Constructor's and Driver's Championships in 1961, had proved so dominant in the previous year that Stirling knew that the combination of the Walker team resources and a car that was actually this year's model, rather than the demi-obsolete Formula 1 cars that RRC Walker *Équipe* had been used to, offered at least the prospect of an entertaining season. The news that Stirling was to drive a privately entered Ferrari Formula 1 car was not yet public; the fact that it was not ready was a little frustrating, but Stirling knew that Modena deadlines were an approximate thing even if the car was paid for; the experience of the Maserati had taught him that.

In reality, given the manifold talents of the new offerings from BRM and Lotus, the Ferrari was not destined to be a particularly competitive car after all. The advantage which the firm had enjoyed in the first year of the 1500cc formula had, by the start

of the 1962 season, been rapidly eroded. The new generation of British engines, tough and basically simple, coupled with some revolutionary chassis work, would put the British constructors' offerings firmly ahead, but as the sport looked forward to the opening of the 1962 season that discovery had yet to take place.

In anticipation of the arrival of the Ferrari, as well as a heavy Formula 2 commitment, the Walker decks were cleared; the Lotus 18/21, now with a Coventry Climax V8 shoehorned into the back, was handed over to the British Racing Partnership, to be managed and entered by them in their unmistakable green livery. It was a compromise of a car and illustrated well the lengths to which a private entrant was forced to go in order to

Previous page: Goodwood, 23 April, 1962. The Goodwood races marked the beginning of the season proper in Europe.

Above: On the grid, from top to bottom, Stirling Moss, Jim Clark, Graham Hill and John Surtees.

Facing page: The last race; Stirling drove the Walker Lotus 18/21 bearing the lucky number 7 and started in pole position.

stay in the game. The necessary surgery to the car had, in the opinion of Colin Chapman, radically weakened it. Chapman did not know that the Lotus cars which Walker entered were, since Spa, routinely modified with tougher drive shafts and sundry strengthening. It was something of a lash-up though, and first time out with the new engine at Brussels it had not prospered (although Stirling had managed fastest lap) and a fortnight later at Snetterton it suffered a badly sticking throttle.

Had the Ferrari been ready for the opening races of the season, history would have been very different; the fact that it was late did suggest that the car, when it arrived, would at least be a 1962 model, so the Walker team merely waited with as much patience as they could muster.

The 100-mile Glover Trophy, an event Stirling had won only once since his epic duel with Archie Scott Brown in 1956, was a race which had, on every occasion since, offered him pole position, fastest lap or even both. He loved Goodwood anyway, and not merely because it had been the scene of his inaugural circuit victory. The Goodwood races marked the start of the season proper in Europe, and served to warm up cars, spectators and drivers alike.

The car was the Walker Lotus 18/21 hybrid which had been so troublesome at Snetterton. As before, it was entered by the UDT Laystall team and presented in their colours. It seemed in fine fettle when Stirling put it on pole position, wearing number 7. Alongside, but two whole seconds slower, was Graham Hill's BRM. All went well until a gear selector problem forced Stirling to pit and he lost two laps as Hill forged ahead.

A favourite Moss expression, 'There's always the lap record to go for', eight words which sum up his attitude to the sport, governed his decision to set off in pursuit. There was very little reason to hope he could catch Hill, but it was a BRM that Hill

was driving, so there was a chance that it might let Hill down. Stirling knew more than many about mechanical failures, and although the pace he set was not a new record, it certainly set the joint fastest lap of the race (with John Surtees) at 1 minutes 22 seconds – over 105 mph. Then total and utter disaster.

The first thing the crowd knew of any drama was an announcement over the tannoy that Stirling had left the road at St Mary's; James Tilling, the race commentator, opined that the brakes had failed, but then commentators have to say something. Ken Gregory, keeping lap charts with Alfred in the pits, tensed along with the rest of the crowd. Whatever the sport's critics say, a bad crash sickens the entire motor racing community.

The brief few ciné frames that we have of the crash have all the visual impact of the Zapruder footage of the John F. Kennedy assassination although they tell us very little, concentrating on the impact itself as opposed to its cause, but even at this distance they make us wince. What has never been entirely clear is what caused the accident. Theories abound – stuck throttle, engine failure, car jumping out of gear, brake failure and worst of all, driver error.

The received version of events is that Stirling, coming up behind Hill in an attempt to un-lap himself, may have misinterpreted a hand signal which Hill gave to a marshal in response to a blue flag signal warning of Stirling's presence. Stirling is supposed to have assumed that this was an invitation to overtake and taken his line into the corner. Hill, discounting the possibility of overtaking at that point, took his own line and

Above: A gear selector problem forced Stirling to pit and he lost two laps as Graham Hill forged ahead.

Pages 286–89: Stirling managed to secure joint fastest lap of the race (with John Surtees) at over 105 mph.

Stirling ran out of space, left the track, lost control and crashed into the grassy bank.

But Stirling remembers absolutely nothing of this disaster; he is sometimes prone to be suggestible about things he does not recall, and worthy attempts have been made in the intervening years to explain what happened. The actual cause, however, remains a mystery, as there has never before been any corroborative evidence of the chain of events.

Reliable eyewitness accounts of what happened on that unhappy St George's Day are extremely rare (there is no obvious vantage point at St Mary's; it is a remote part of the circuit) and most have been lost to us. There is one account though, written five days after the event from an angry and clearly anguished spectator. It was in the form of a letter sent to Alfred at home (as opposed to the offices of Stirling Moss Limited) on 28 April. Alfred (as he generally did) copied all his correspondence, but because it was part of his archive rather than Stirling's own, it has never been published before. It is written by a Mr. E. Hampton, of 14 Ridge Crest, Enfield, Middlesex, who had seen the accident. I reproduce it in its unedited entirety, for reasons which will become clear:

Dear Sir,

I trust that you will forgive me the intrusion during this most tense period of anxiety, to express my deep and sincere sympathy for this very grievous accident to Stirling. I trust and pray that he may fully recover both physically and mentally from his injuries; the latest bulletins published and broadcast are indeed encouraging. May God speed his return to normal health.

I know full well that primarily Stirling's well-being is your chief concern; however I have read the news reports regarding the cause of the accident and unhesitatingly support the view that Stirling deliberately ran out of road to avoid shunting Graham Hill. From where I was watching the race from a mound at least ten feet high at the extreme western end of the blue enclosure, there was no doubt in my mind, nor that of my immediate fellow spectators, for the reason for Stirling's spectacular exit. From this unobscured point of vantage, Hill and Stirling were seen to approach in close company from Madgwick. They passed by, the distance between them closing rapidly. The marshal at Fordwater made a feeble motion of giving the blue flag to Hill, who closed over to the right of the track. At this stage the angle of sight was getting very fine so that the cars appeared almost dead ahead. In spite of this it was clear that Stirling was about to take Hill. The climax came with dreadful speed. Now Hill went over to the left of the track taking a line further over than formerly for St Mary's and in direct

collision with Stirling. There was a spontaneous gasp of apprehension from those around me for it was so very obvious that a collision was imminent. Stirling had no option but to take to the grass and as he did so, a plume of flames shot from above and from the rear of the car. The angle of the flame to the car may have been some 30–35° and was like a burst from a flame gun. This was brief. From the grass verge to the bank the car ran on unswervingly; during this short run, my son, who has very keen sight, thought that Stirling was trying to lift himself out of the seat, but has admitted on enquiry that it may have been the bumpy ride that gave this impression.

The spectators' immediate reaction was that Hill had crowded him off the road. Some expressions were extremely basic and many thought that Hill would retire forthwith by stopping at the scene of the accident to give assistance, at least. I do not wish to imply that Graham Hill would even contemplate such a wilful and dangerous manoeuvre, nor that the Marshal's timorous wave of the blue flag (implied) negligence, but had the marshal made a more vigorous and commanding wave Graham Hill might have realised very forcibly that he was really going to be taken. He was reported to have made two significant statements. That he was surprised that anyone would overtake him there and 2. He saw flames from number 7's (Stirling's car) exhaust pipes.

No one but Stirling the artist could have overtaken there maybe, but it also means that he had not realised the significance of the blue flag at Fordwater, nor had he consulted his mirror. And how did he observe the flames from the exhaust pipes? I feel myself that Graham Hill was concentrating far too much on the road and his own line to even realise how close Stirling was.

I had the misfortune to see poor Dunfee's Bentley go over the top at Brooklands in a tragedy of somewhat similar circumstances, i.e. a faster overtaking driver being baulked. I fully realise that the man in front has the right to the line for the corner but I would be happier at race meetings if some urgent signal could be devised to warn a driver or drivers of this situation. This may present difficulties but something should be done to eliminate the possibility of the repetition of this incident. It is sad, too, because in my humble opinion Stirling was, pardon, is, too great an artist and sportsman to place any other driver in such a predicament.

Yours faithfully,
E. Hampton

After digesting the key points in this, Alfred wrote back on 2 May. His letter in full reads:

THAT BEND WHERE STIRLING CRASHED

MYSTERY CAUSE
OF MOSS CRASH

THEN

MOSS

Moment of impact

CRASHES

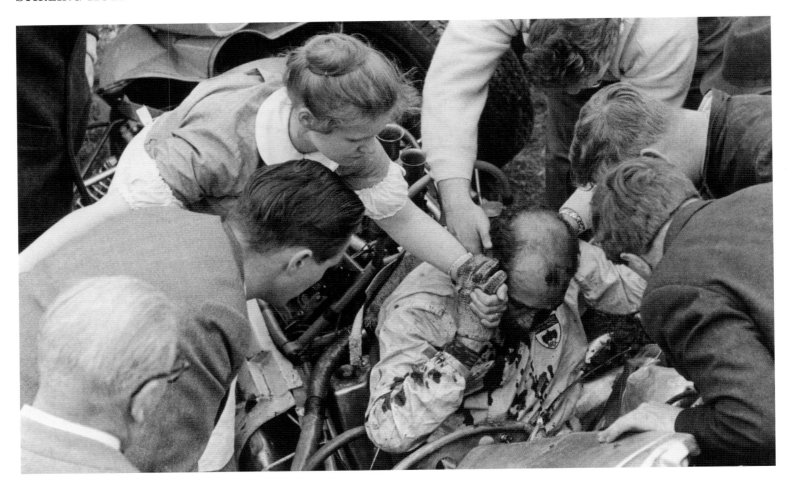

Dear Mr. Hampton,
I hasten to answer your very kind letter sent to my Farm. It has relieved my mind greatly as there have been so many conflicting rumours going around as to what actually happened and I have not previously had any communication from anyone who actually saw the occurrence; I feel sure that your explanation is entirely accurate and accounts for everything. There is no doubt in my mind that Stirling was of the opinion that Hill was giving way to him and when he realised that Graham was drifting towards the perimeter, he deliberately took to the verge to save collision, as you pointed out.

I understand that unfortunately there was a lump of hidden concrete just where he ran off and no doubt hitting this caused the distributor head to jump off and this would account for the flares from the exhaust and for him being thrown upwards out of his seat thus losing contact with the controls.

Knowing Graham Hill as I do I am quite sure that if he had known that Stirling was catching him up at the rate that he was and being so far ahead he would have realised that Stirling was after the lap record and would have given way to him, therefore I agree that the flag marshal, who must

have seen the speed at which Stirling was overtaking, should have given a more definite signal.

I would greatly appreciate it if you would let me know whether the flares from the exhaust took place when the car hit the grass or before it left the course; if it was the former, it would further confirm your assumption.

Stirling is still making progress but I am afraid it is going to be quite a while before he has fully recovered and having been unconscious for so long it is doubtful whether he will remember exactly what happened and you will appreciate that if he thinks his driving was at fault it would upset him greatly. I might mention that the car was in fourth gear and Stirling is quite capable of taking this part of the track flat out in this gear.

Again, thanking you for the explicit details you have so kindly given.

Yours sincerely,
Alfred E Moss

Mr. Hampton, no doubt somewhat energised by this, wrote back the very next day:

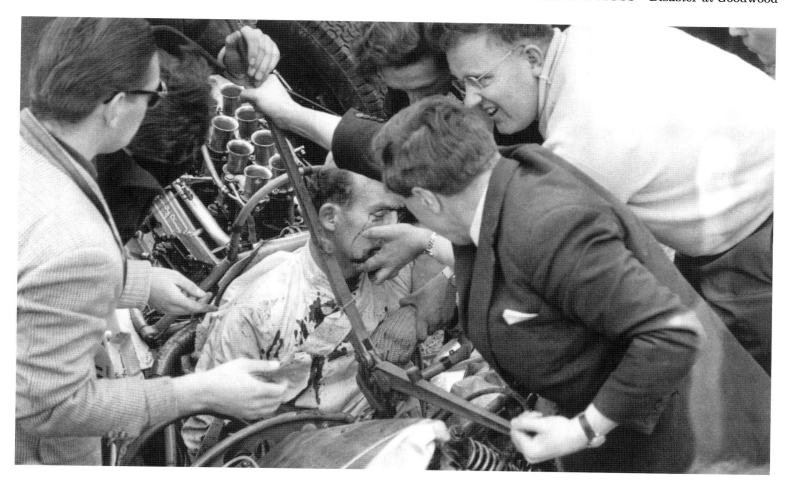

Dear Mr Moss,

I am very happy to know that my eyewitness account of your son's accident has been of some assistance and indeed some assurance to you. I would not normally have had the temerity to write, but I suspected from the various news columns that there was a groping for the facts as well as the reason for this most untoward occurrence.

And now for the subject for confirmation – when did the flames appear from the exhaust pipe? I felt that I had to have corroboration on this point so I cross-examined my son without telling him the reason why, as if I was turning the event over in my mind. His version was that as Stirling left the track and was on the grass so the car bucked violently and the flames came from the exhaust. This confirms my original version – Stirling had no option but to take to the grass, and as he did so, so a plume of flame etcetera! Taking into account the speed of the action, the angle of sight and the intervening distance, the passage on the grass verge before the bump and the flames may have been 2–3 yards. But it is sheer guesswork. However, quite succinctly, he was on the grass and not on the track when the flame appeared.

I am extremely pleased to hear that Stirling is still making progress. My son, with all the youthful assurance and

optimism of his fourteen years, is quite convinced that he will be completely restored to normal health and would be delighted to have these good wishes conveyed to the patient, in which I most fervently join. And if he should need assurance, we are both convinced that his skill did not desert him, but the fickle Jade called Luck.

Yours sincerely,
E. Hampton

Sentiment and period prose aside, these letters reveal much. According to this witness, who was not, of course, qualified but clearly an experienced observer of motor racing (Dunfee's

Pages 290–91: Disaster strikes and the Lotus bucks violently as it leaves the track near St Mary's corner.

Pages 292–93: These images taken from the brief ciné footage show the lead up to the crash and moment of impact.

Pages 294–95: The immediate aftermath of the accident – rescuers, officials and St John's Ambulance members attempt to remove Stirling from the wrecked Lotus.

Facing page above: Annie Strudwick holds Stirling's hand as the car is cut up around him.

Above: Carefully the chassis is cut apart so that Stirling can be removed.

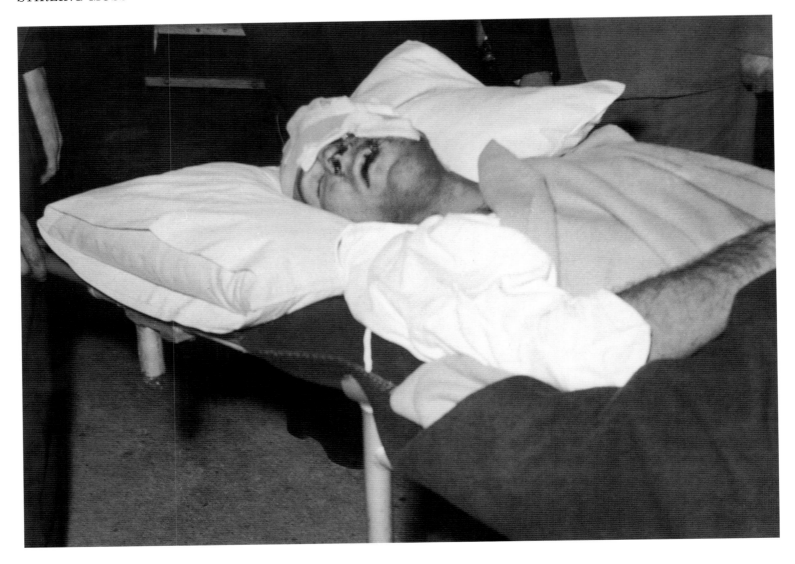

accident had occured in 1932), Stirling was apparently forced off the track, which, while that statement does not discount a mechanical failure as well, goes a long way to consigning it to the possibles rather than probables file. The fact that the car's throttle had stuck at Snetterton gave rise to the theory that it had happened again, but this also discounts the fact that Tony Robinson, one of the best mechanics in the business, was looking after it. There had been gear-selector problems, but apparently those had been repaired, which had cost the distance by which Stirling trailed the field. The issue of the jet of flame from the exhaust suggests strongly, but does not confirm, that the distributor cap was dislodged by the impact with a lump of concrete, causing the car to backfire. It does not take a very large lump to have this effect at 120 mph. On the other hand, lifting off from high rpm can have a similar effect. Either way, this is not observable on the footage of the crash, which is shot from the right of the path of the cars and may only have been visible from where the Hamptons were placed. The observation that Stirling was bounced off the seat of the car is clear, so there he

was, hanging on to the wheel, unable to reach the pedals, with a dead engine, but still accelerating (grass has this effect) doing 120 mph across a patch of corrugated ground with no harness to save him. No wonder he has forgotten it.

But there is no mention in the Hampton letter of any hand signal by Graham Hill, an aspect of the crash that seems to have crept into the folklore, as if it is recovered memory; what it does suggest is that Hill may not have seen the marshal's signal. But he also says that Hill's driving line was more extreme than previously used and that this put him right into the path of a charging Stirling. Given that a blue flag means 'Give way' when merely displayed, or 'Give way or you will be penalised' when waved, then the lack of obvious reaction by Hill is perplexing, but perhaps the fact that he was on his way to his own first Formula 1 victory might just have a bearing. The issue of any

Above: An unconscious Stirling about to be loaded on to an ambulance which will take him to the Atkinson Morley hospital.

Facing page: Stirling's parents leave the Atkinson Morley.

hand signal may be a simple omission (not that it was the point – under the rules the flag was – is – all) but the account is very detailed in all other particulars. Having said that, it is true that from Mr Hampton's position it would have been difficult to see what Graham Hill was doing, as the cars were going directly away from him by the time the crash happened.

The issue of whether Hill should have stopped is much more a matter of manners, but Michael Cooper, the photographer, stated later that Hill did slow down on his next lap in order to ask if he could help; he was told that he could not and drove off to win.

But if Hill stated that he saw the flames from the back of Stirling's car, then he can only have done so in his rear-view mirror as Stirling was leaving the track. Just as possible, though, is that he had been told of the flames by another driver who was behind Stirling and contributed this to his interview through having nothing else to say which might account for the incident. He did apologise, most forcefully, to Aileen Moss after the race, though. She never wrote down the exact form of words which he used, which is perhaps a pity.

Stirling himself famously remembers nothing of the crash, indeed little of the whole day and many of his assumptions about it have been placed there by helpful suggestions from others, including possibly, the speculation about Hill's hand signal. He cannot even be sure whether his memory of helping his friend Paul Bates to find a vantage point took place on the day of the race or even the day before. One thing he does know is that he damaged his Lotus Élite in the car park of the Fleece Inn, which vexed him. Apart from that there is nothing; his mind is a blank.

There is an eerie similarity between Stirling's account of the Caracas crash which killed Max Dressler and Mr Hampton's account of the Goodwood crash. If Hampton is right and Stirling was forced on to the grass in order to avoid an untidy (or obstructive) Graham Hill, then one can hardly be surprised at his action. Despite the fact that Caracas was not his fault, the memory of it had not, indeed has never, left him. In 1962, a racing car gave little protection to its driver should it leave the road, but a collision was potentially even worse.

From this distance of elapsed time, does any of this matter? Well, this writer thinks so and for one very important reason. As Alfred says in his reply to Mr. Hampton's letter: 'if he thinks his driving was at fault, it would upset him greatly'. Just so. Stirling Moss has had wheels fall off, gearboxes break, brakes fail – a host of letdowns, but one has to look very hard indeed to find any example of driver error on his part; it is a record of which he is intensely proud and for that reason alone it is surely worth attempting to sort out the confused and contradictory evidence of that day. The Hampton letter is certainly helpful, but not conclusive; it suggests nothing more than a racing accident.

Naturally, this does not constitute any sort of stewards'

enquiry; it is too late and would be inappropriate anyway. The fact that there was not one at the time is perplexing, given that Hill had run through a blue flag (however timidly waved) but not as perplexing as the veil of confusion which has covered the crash in the years since it happened. One reason was surely that the nation and the sport were all far too concerned about the state of Stirling's health to bother with the reasons for its condition. The press was busy preparing obituaries (*Time* magazine actually had a cover feature on him prepared, just in case), and the simple fact of the matter was that so few people actually saw what happened that the matter rested there.

To our minds, Stirling's reluctance to release this correspondence until now is perhaps odd but is also completely typical of his determined modesty. In an age when racing drivers routinely use their cars as weapons, going so far as to club the opposition off the track with them, perhaps some of the niceties of 1960s driving have been forgotten. Also, it is important to bear in mind that Stirling Moss does not criticise others, only himself. He is not a blamer.

His injuries though, were quite dreadful, far worse than at

Spa. The most visually horrid was the shattered left eye socket, but there were far worse matters. After establishing that he was alive, unconscious, but choking on a piece of chewing gum, the small crowd set about trying to extract him from the car. Annie Strudwick, a young St John's ambulance nurse, held his hand while the chassis of the wrecked Lotus was carefully cut up around him. Photographers were everywhere.

It took three quarters of an hour to release him and he was carefully stretchered off to Chichester hospital. At 1.20 am his condition was considered serious enough to warrant the risk of transferring him sixty miles to the Atkinson Morley hospital in Wimbledon, where the consultant neurosurgeon, Wylie McKissock, was waiting. An X-ray revealed that the impact of the crash had, through deceleration (120 mph to nought in perhaps three seconds) physically detached the right side of his brain from his skull, which accounted for his deep coma. The other injuries, the double fracture of the left leg, the broken left arm, the crushed left eye socket and cheekbone, were, in medical terms (however grisly they were to look at), relatively trivial by comparison. There was even a potential problem in terms of blood supplies: Stirling's blood group is B negative.

Rob Walker was not present at Goodwood; he was at Pau in France supervising Maurice Trintignant in a Formula 2 car. He

was totally unaware that anything had happened until 'Jabby' Crombac, a French journalist, made a concerned enquiry about Stirling's state of health. Walker immediately called Ken Gregory, who was calming though concerned. Immediately, Rob and Betty Walker drove back to England, their car radio tuned to the Home Service which was issuing hourly updates on Stirling's state of health, and on arrival Rob went straight to the Atkinson Morley. He questioned McKissock who was justifiably nervous.

Both Rob and Betty Walker were and are devout Christian Scientists; in the face of the overall gloom about Stirling's prospects, they agreed that the most rational thing they could do was pray, which they and as many fellow Christian Scientists as they could contact, promptly did. The literature of the movement was rich in examples of healing by prayer and so a giant collective appeal to Christ was the result. Initially, nothing much happened; Stirling remained resolutely unconscious, but gradually he began to have moments of lucidity. They did not last long, at least not at first. He would not wake up properly for

Above: Stirling on the biggest date of his life as he takes all of his nurses out for the evening.

Above right: A chairbound Stirling calls in at the Walker workshop near Dorking (from left to right) Malcolm Simpson, Tony Cleverly and John Chisman.

thirty-eight days. It was a slow, groggy process, and he does not remember it well, but vast amounts of flowers feature strongly in what little he does recall. His inability to speak was confusing, although the physical injuries were more familiar. At least his back was undamaged this time, and so, critically, was the Old Boy, by which of course he did not mean Alfred.

initially revealed to him. He assumed that he could not move because he was injured, rather than because his brain would simply not allow it. His friend David Haynes finally revealed the truth; although it depressed Stirling, it also caused him to fight his condition harder, initially to little avail.

Meanwhile, the Ferrari 156 turned up. It was a 1961 model,

He would not wake up properly
for thirty-eight days...

He did not immediately notice that he was effectively paralysed. The physical damage to the left side of his body was made worse by the fact that he could not move it. His instinctive response to injury had previously resulted in a merciless regime of exercise, as taught to him by Urquhart, which went some way towards explaining his previous remarkable recovery speed. This was not an option this time, however, as the massive bruising his brain had received had to heal first. This would be frustrating, to say the least, particularly since the extent of his injuries were not

in fact, and a surprised crowd gathered at Silverstone on 12 May to witness the fully works-supported Ferrari being unloaded from its transporter. Confusingly, it was painted factory red, but with a light green BRP stripe down the bonnet. Innes Ireland drove it to fourth place. Ireland states categorically in his famous memoir *All Arms and Elbows* that it was a one-off drive, and he had absolutely no idea why he had been asked to do it, implying that he also had no idea of any impending deal involving any Formula 1 car for either Walker or BRP. As requested, he wrote

an assessment of the car and thought no more about it.

Given the closeness of the Walker team with BRP, was it possible that Ferrari was entertaining the idea of reinventing his deal with BRP instead of Walker? Most unlikely; it was Moss they wanted and Ireland was merely standing in. Many at the time averred that the car was there as a tribute to Stirling; this would have been an untypically quixotic gesture by Enzo Ferrari. It is more likely that the car had already been entered and it would be interesting to see how it stacked up against the domestic offerings.

Naturally, Stirling's presence in the Atkinson Morley caused something of a sensation inside and outside the hospital. Initially, the switchboard was jammed with shocked enquiries (Frank Sinatra was a particularly persistent caller). As the news filtered down from the top floor where McKissock ruled the neurology department, and it became clear that he would need further help, a frisson of anticipation rustled the starched uniforms. There was a natural nervousness too; this was Stirling Moss, after all, by now the best-known man in the country. Sarah Hobson had recently qualified as an occupational therapist at the Atkinson Morley. She reported:

> He was actually a lovely patient; the occupational therapy department was basically in a little hut in the garden and as he started to recover, he began to spend more and more time outside, entertaining his friends. We had a pianola (player piano) and he particular liked entertaining us – he really worked the pedals hard. We didn't know very much about motor racing, of course, but none of us really thought he would ever drive again – he had been so very badly hurt, but he tried so hard.

Very slowly, he started to recover some motor function, and as the bruised brain gradually repaired itself, he was more and more able to push himself physically, even within the confines of a wheelchair, as Urquhart had taught him. The summer went by, he was apparently recovering strongly, and McKissock who had, as a result of his ministrations become something of a media star himself, was in a quandary as to how to deal with his extraordinary patient. As the physical injuries started to heal and the papers became full of optimistic stories concerning Stirling's

Moss leaves for Nassau

Facing page: A very shaky Stirling leaves the Atkinson Morley in July 1962.

Right: Stirling negotiating the aircraft steps as he prepares to depart for Nassau in order to recuperate in the sun.

imminent return to racing, he turned to his colleague Berenice Krikler, the resident clinical psychologist at the Atkinson Morley. What condition was he really in?

Krikler knew next to nothing about motor racing (that would change) and therefore lacked any kind of benchmark against which to measure Stirling's attributes. Her speciality was clinical disorders and she needed to know what sort of a personality profile might be the norm. Bashfully, the guinea pigs stepped forward. Innes Ireland, Graham Hill, Bruce McLaren, Roy Salvadori and Jack Brabham offered their services to construct the sort of baseline which she needed as a starting point; faced with this crew, Krikler had a daunting task.

The essence of her study was a series of reactive, cognitive and personality observations, using both the racing drivers and a control sample of intelligent and experienced motorists. She sought some standard by which Stirling (who was not named in the report, but it was leaked anyway) could be judged. She

realised that the results would be meaningful, as it was evident that these men would view the tests as competitive and, sure enough, they did. Her use of ordinary motorists as some sort of control group was a forgivable error; she realised very quickly that what these men did for a living had little to do with anything that happened on the A3.

But as she collated and analysed the results, it became quite clear to Krikler that by these measures Stirling had better not get back into a racing car. On the section of the test which concerned visual co-ordination and concentration, Stirling scored the maximum measurable deficit against the control groups. Two of his key advantages had simply vanished. When she told him, he politely kept his own counsel, but clearly he did not fully appreciate what had happened to him, nor did he (or anyone else, for that matter), have any idea whether this would be a permanent or shifting state.

The report was kept confidential at the time, but was

published in the *British Journal of Psychiatry* in February 1965, nearly three years after Stirling's crash.

So, while the press, as usual pole-axed by the silly season of later summer and early autumn, waxed lyrical about Stirling's imminent return to racing, the cruel reality was that he was having to lean up against a wall in order to put his socks on in the morning, he was unable to see straight, and was virtually incapable of making himself properly understood. One journalist who knew this truth was Basil Cardew of the *Daily Express*, who had been the first Fleet Street reporter to see him after the crash. Cardew's attempt to interview Stirling had left him with the view that the game was up; the interview which emerged was pure fiction, cooked up by himself and Ken Gregory. Honourably, Cardew kept his personal opinion to himself and told anyone who asked that the boy wonder was fine. Krikler's view, that not only was he unlikely to make a success of any return to racing, but that he should not even have left hospital for several more months, is one which she still holds today.

Obviously, when he did leave the Atkinson Morley on 20 July, it was something of a media event. Still on crutches, he and the eleven nurses who had attended him went off to dinner, followed by the theatre. Each nurse received a gift; Sarah Hobson received a pair of Frank Sinatra records which she still has.

Stirling opted to spend as much time as he could in Nassau where his marriage had ended; the low-key life offered there put him under little everyday stress. The climate was agreeable and he was even able to drive a little, although his friend Herb Jones was on hand to act as chauffeur when the public were not looking. As his brain continued to heal itself, so the paralysis of his facial muscles lessened and he became able to articulate more and more. Peter Jackson, the assistant editor of *Today* magazine, was assigned the task of accompanying Stirling out to Nassau. It was a lucrative, *Hello*-style contract for Stirling, which he had negotiated with Ken Gregory. Jackson recalled: 'Even on the aeroplane, he insisted on demonstrating that he was fit – he even did press-ups in the aisle, but I think that we all felt that he hadn't quite got the point.'

He had changed, too. Whereas the Stirling Moss who had climbed into the little Lotus on St George's Day had been an affable, focused and charming man, the person who came close to picking a fight on the dance floor of a Nassau nighclub was not. He would blurt insults, a thing he had never done before. Part of it was anger, part of it injury, and Jones had, on occasion, to be very firm with him.

Stirling was still extremely unwell, but did not realise it. His ability to accept the damage done to him by the Goodwood injuries extended only to the idea that he had been slowed down a little, that his reflexes and concentration had obviously suffered and that he might, one day, readdress the matter of racing. In terms of the effect upon the rest of his activities, he was outwardly dismissive and quite unable to come to terms with the reality of what had happened to him. In truth, the cause of what had happened interested him rather more than the resultant damage which had been inflicted upon him.

But Berenice Krikler's clinical report, which Stirling was most reluctant to read, stated quite firmly and categorically that he was brain-damaged. He was not mad or crazy, but he was severely injured. Those around him, both professionally and personally, could see it; he could or would not. If it made his friends more protective (and they remain so to this day) then this produced in him a form of obstinacy which, when combined with his own natural impulsiveness, could lead him into perilous territory.

As Ken Gregory put it: 'There was absolutely no doubt in my mind that the man who came out of the Atkinson Morley was not the same man who went in.' Brain injuries are terrible things, and not only because of their obvious effects. Their victims frequently cannot grasp what has happened. In Stirling's case, perhaps because the issues were not properly explained to him in physical terms that he could relate to, he chose to press on regardless. It would cost him dear.

By the last days of autumn, he appeared relatively normal, although inwardly he was still very confused, not least by the nagging worry about what on earth had happened. He was also having to attend St. Thomas's again to have corrective surgery on the shattered eye socket. It was a painful process, involving bone grafts (from his hip) but it went a long way towards correcting his uneven focus. As his vision improved, so did his mood.

Predictably, Stirling had entertained the idea of returning to racing just as soon as Berenice Krikler told him that he should not. While his reaction to her advice did not surprise her unduly, she had also observed him well enough to know that his own sense of perfectionism would not allow him to delude himself about any shortcomings in his performance. She had noted in her report that: 'Racing drivers differ significantly from the controls [the regular motorists] in that they are more stable in their judgement of their performance. There is a trend toward a higher level of aspiration.'

By January, though, Stirling was actually working again, albeit not as a racing driver, but as a product promoter. He was not up to it; his co-ordination was still a ragged shadow of its former self, but he felt that he needed to earn a living as well as to concentrate. As winter gave way to spring, he appeared to be much recovered and the inevitable prospect of a test drive with a racing car loomed. Will he, won't he…? There was remorseless media pressure; no one had ever filled the pages like Stirling had; if he gave up, they would miss him, and if he took up his career again, that decision would produce at least a story a week.

Wednesday, 1 May, 1963 saw him at Goodwood, a year and a week after the crash, but his protective amnesia still firmly refused him access to what had happened. The circuit had been booked for him alone and a BRP-owned Lotus 19 sports car, wearing the number seven, was on hand. It was immaculately prepared as ever and Stirling drove himself down from London uncharacteristically early that morning; he simply did not know what to expect.

He drove the damp circuit at lap speeds that were acceptable, about 1 minute 40 seconds or so, but without being particularly startling by his own measure, which mattered more to him than any absolute – he was not *racing*, after all. Passing St Mary's, he felt absolutely nothing. He realised, with a dawning sense of horror, that Berenice Krikler had been exactly right in her assessment (and, later, as they became better acquainted, that her confidence in his own acuity about himself had also been spot on). All the flowing instincts, the unthinking balancing,

unbalancing and rebalancing of the car, all those things which the Maseratis had taught him, were absent. To the uninformed observer, the performance was probably impressive; to Stirling himself it lacked everything which he had come to love about the sport and his own place in it. Gone too was the schoolboyish enthusiasm for the sheer, fierce joy of it. If his relationship with a racing car had once been a sensuous dance, it was now more like a vaguely recalled hop with a mere acquaintance. There was no flow. It was a disjointed, disconnecting experience; thoroughly depressing. He even spun the car at the chicane.

This was a devastating revelation for him. But perhaps more objectively, Stirling finally realised that this was life in the real world; this was what it was like for everyone else and that the

Facing page: Keeping in touch from Nassau. The low-key life there allowed Stirling to recover in a stress-free environment.

Above: Stirling as passenger; Herb Jones acts as chauffeur on the Nassau trip.

Left: Stirling in the BRP Lotus at Goodwood for his self-assessment test, 1 May, 1963.

Top: Stirling with BRP's Tony Robinson at the Goodwood test.

Middle: In the cockpit of the Lotus at Goodwood.

Bottom: Stirling spins the Lotus 19 at the chicane during the Goodwood test.

massive advantages that he had unconsciously enjoyed for so long were now a thing of the past, alien to him and probably impossible to recover. He was now as other men. It was a terrifying prospect. The familiarity of perfect eyesight, both direct and peripheral, for example, is a comforting one. To have it compromised is a shock, particularly when it is tested *in extremis*; dependence upon it is an unstated thing – it is a physical attribute its possessor naturally takes for granted. It did not take him long, no more than a few hours, to make his decision. He says now:

It was an easy decision to take at the time, because it was the only decision to take. I had to think. I had to give orders to myself – here I'll brake, here I must change down, and so on. And another thing; I used to be able to look at the rev counter without taking my eyes off the road – not only that, but I could see the rev counter and a friend waving to me all at the same time. I'd lost that, that had gone.

that he had not fully recovered from his injuries – at best, his great reputation, and at worst, his life.

For those who were merely Stirling's competitors, there was a similar sense of relief. The total dominance that he had exercised over the sport by virtue of his natural advantages was over. Others could now shine; initially, they would be Graham Hill and Jim Clark. So, just as Fangio's retirement had cleared the way for Stirling, as the death of Ayrton Senna would clear the way for Michael Schumacher, the old order changed. Stirling would never be entirely happy about his decision, although to this day he is acutely aware of the analytical common sense behind Berenice Krikler's advice; he would always wonder whether it was a correct one in the long term. Should he have waited longer?

It is a characteristic of Stirling's that he will ask a question many times over, of many different people (provided he thinks their opinion is worth hearing), in order to receive what he

Naturally he was heartbroken
but inside the sport there were sighs of relief

That evening, the press release, penned with a depressed absence of spin by Ken Gregory, went out: 'I have decided to retire; I will not drive again.' Naturally, he was utterly heartbroken, but inside the heart of the sport there were discreet sighs of relief and for very honourable reasons. Those who knew, loved and admired him realised full well that for him to re-enter the sport at such a relative disadvantage could ultimately be the destruction of him. The late, great Peter Garnier, editor of *The Autocar*, his very good friend and sometime navigator, whose sense of this tragedy was never to leave him, wrote:

He had nothing whatever to gain by making a dramatic return. He had inherited world supremacy on Fangio's retirement at the end of 1957 and had held it unchallenged ever since. He had, however, a great deal to lose by continuing with the sport if there was the slightest chance

Facing page: Considering that he had just decided to retire, the bearded Stirling seems quite cheerful.

Following pages: Clippings taken from Stirling Moss's scrapbook, documenting his crash and recovery.

considers to be the 'right' answer, that is to say, the one which he has decided upon. He still asks this question today, which illustrates well the trauma he underwent – indeed still suffers – at the loss of such a career as he had enjoyed. As this was being prepared, he did it again. He asked Professor Sid Watkins, a neurosurgeon as well as an expert on racing, what his opinion was. Unsurprisingly perhaps, to Stirling's chagrin, Watkins was of the same view as Berenice Krikler, that there was 'no way' that he, under similar circumstances, would have let Stirling back into a racing car. Perhaps, after an interval of forty years, Stirling Moss has finally got his answer, for in his mind, there is no higher authority than Watkins.

For motor racing was not only a sport, it was a rapidly evolving technology. For Stirling to re-enter the sport, say, three years later, would have presented challenges to him which he has never subsequently addressed. The fact that the racing public would be denied the prospect of Stirling Moss driving a Ford GT40 or a Porsche 917 is regrettable, but perhaps Peter Garnier was right. Certainly, Stirling was to come to think so, albeit with great reluctance. The intervening period was not easy. As for his friends, they gathered round in a tight defensive circle.

British Car Ace Still Unconscious

LONDON, April 24 (A.A.P.-Reuter). — British racing driver Stirling Moss, who was seriously injured in a crash yesterday, is unconscious in a London neurological hospital.

Rescuers had to hack Moss free from his car after it crashed at more than 100 m.p.h. during a trophy race at Goodwood.

A hospital bulletin today said Moss' condition showed "slight but definite improvement," but he was still unconscious. There was no question of an operation at present.

Doctors said Moss, who was transferred from Chichester Hospital to Atkinson Morley Hospital, Wimbledon, had "quite a severe head injury, with additional damage to the left shoulder and left knee joint as well as a fractured rib."

Moss, 32, crashed on the thirty-fifth lap of the 100-mile Glover Trophy race when his Lotus-Climax went straight on, at a right-hand bend.

Trapped For 30 Minutes

His car hurtled over the grass, swung sideways and hit the bank rear first.

He was trapped in the wreckage for 30 minutes before rescuers, using cutters, sawed the car in half.

He was taken to hospital with blood streaming from facial wounds.

Doctors first described his condition as "fair" and later said he was "seriously ill."

The 42-lap race was won by another British driver, Graham Hill, in a B.R.M. Bruce McLaren, of New Zealand, was second in a works Cooper.

First reports said Moss' brakes had failed. But another driver, John Surtees, said: "You don't use your brakes there. I think his throttle probably stuck wide open."

Hill said Moss was probably "doing 115 to 120 m.p.h. when he left the course."

Just before the crash Moss equalled the lap record set by Surtees the day before.

Moss had a narrow escape at Goodwood in August when his Ferrari spun off the track at more than 100 m.p.h. after a rear tyre burst.

During practice for the Belgian Grand Prix in June last year he crashed at 145 m.p.h., breaking both legs and injuring his back.

Moss, still in a coma, says 'Mum'

Doctors Hold 'Good Hope' for Moss' Recovery

25, 1962 — *New York Herald Tribune*

STIRLING MOSS — Associated Press

Moss' Chances Called 'Good' for Recovery

By Tom Lambert
A Staff Correspondent
LONDON

Stirling Moss was still unconscious yesterday after a mile per hour crack-up Monday but a hospital official "there seems good hope of his recovery."

Moss, Britain's top race driver, suffered a severe head injury, a fractured left knee and injuries to his left shoulder when his V-8 Lotus-Climax span off the track and into a dirt bank during the 100-mile

Moss was trailing by three laps, as the result of a pit stop, when his car hurtled off the track. Pinned in the wreckage he had to be cut loose with metal shears.

"There are no signs suggestive of dangerous bleeding within the skull" said Lawrence Brown, secretary of Atkinson Morley's Hospital.

"There is a serious fracture involving the left knee joint, but the extent of damage to the left shoulder is still unknown. It is thought inadvisable to disturb the patient by further X-ray examinations."

Moss was reported as saying tell my mother I'm all right as he was lifted from his wrecked car.

But his father, Alfred Moss, a dental surgeon, denied his son ever said it.

"He was unconscious, and has remained unconscious ever since," Moss' father said. "It was I who sent the message to his mother.

Unlucky?

smacked tail first into the examination wrecked car showed the steering and throttle were all working properly.

This seemed to kill the throttle linkage down as he roared toward bend. Other competitors race had suggested Moss lifted his foot off accelerator but the car slow down.

OSHAWA, Ont. Officials of Mosport said yesterday that Moss will be here for the mile sports car racing nearby Mosport Park.

Officials of the first operates the racing north of here and phoned England yesterday learned that the British ace was not hurt at first reports he would be here to the race.

SHOULD STIRLING QUIT RACING?

Yes!
SAY MOTHER AND FATHER

No!
SAYS PAT

By BASIL CARDEW

LATEST ON STIRLING —IMPROVING

Express Staff Reporter

How did it happen?

VISION RECONSTRUCTS THE DRAMA
OF LAP 35 . . . AND FINDS TWO CLUES
TO THE MYSTERY OF MOSS'S CRASH

W**HY did it happen?** Why did Stirling Moss, the world's greatest racing driver, crash at 120 m.p.h.?

The mystery may never be solved.

Moss's manager, Mr. Ken Gregory, said yesterday: "It seems likely that Stirling will lose his memory of the events immediately before the impact because of concussion.

"We may never get the details from the one person who really knew what went wrong."

Yesterday mechanics examined Moss's wrecked car, and with racing drivers I reconstructed the drama of Lap 35 in the Glover Trophy race on Goodwood's 2.4 mile travelling circuit.

Two vital questions remained unanswered:

1. Why was so experienced a driver as Moss trying to overtake at such a speed on a bend where no driver should ever attempt to pass?

2. If he was doing so because he could not give warning to mechanical trouble, what was wrong?

Cut out

There were two clues last night.

CLUE No. 1 is the distributor cap of the wrecked car. It was found undone in the bottom of the engine.

It could have been thrown off by the impact.

But if it came undone before the crash it could mean that Stirling was kept from the "sparking plug," causing the engine to cut out.

Moss would have hurtled on by his own momentum, willing the power to drive forward out of trouble.

This theory is supported by driver Graham Hill, who was directly involved in the...

Story by
DENIS HOLMES
Pictures by
FRANK APTHORP
and
PETER ELINSKAS

...dent and who saw flames screaming out of Moss's exhaust.

The flames would be a sign that ignition trouble was stopping fuel burning in the cylinder and instead it was being ignited in the hot exhaust pipes.

Royal Automobile Club experts are examining the distributor cap and hope to report on its condition and this theory later this week.

CLUE No. 2 is that the tyre marks of the Moss car ran unbroken for 150 yards on the grass before he hit a bank. They show no signs of braking.

This may mean that he had a blackout or was knocked unconscious before getting into serious difficulties.

Perfect

The wrecked 1½-litre V8-cylinder rear-engined Lotus No. 7 was taken from Goodwood yesterday to the UDT-Laystall finance company team's racing headquarters in London.

There it was stripped and examined in detail.

The brakes were perfect, the steering was working the throttle was not stuck open and it was in fourth gear showing that Stirling had changed down into the correct gear for the corner.

Speeds in the 100-mile traditional Easter Monday Grand Prix that was high because of the powerful new V8 engines and the dry, smooth track surface.

On Lap 34, the one before he crashed, Moss had set up a new lap record at 100 m.p.h.

He had been forced into the pits earlier with gear...

trouble and was fighting his way back from tenth position.

At the beginning of Lap 35 he was two laps behind the leader, Graham Hill, the eventual winner, in a V8 BRM.

On his way into the right and then left-hand curves of St. Mary's Corner, Hill began to drop speed from 140 m.p.h.

The aerial picture on the right, taken by a *Daily Mail* photographer soon after the crash, sets the scene.

This is Hill's story of what happened.

Suddenly out of the corner of my eye I saw the nose of Stirling's car level with my cockpit and only 2ft. away. I could see him trying to keep on the circuit, but he was already on the grass.

Precision

I can think of no reason at all why he should have tried to overtake on the most difficult corner of the circuit. It is a corner that needs a lot of precision, and there is no room for the slightest mistake.

I cannot believe that a driver of his calibre would try to pass there, particularly when he was two laps behind and out of the running.

You just cannot do it—and that is why there must have been something seriously wrong.

I believe from those exhaust flames that it was ignition.

Thud! Moss hits the bank. See how his car tilts over.

Seconds from disaster. Moss speeds across the grass.

Moss, right, goes off at a tangent, as Hill takes the bend . . . reconstruction of the drama as the cars raced to St. Mary's Corner.

Image labels: 6ft.-HIGH BANK · DITCH · POINT OF IMPACT · ST. MARY'S CORNER · TRACK OF MOSS'S CAR · 150 YARDS · GRAHAM HILL'S LINE · 110 m.p.h. IN 4th GEAR · NOSE OF MOSS'S CAR LEVEL WITH BRM COCKPIT · 2ft.-APART

COCOONED

L**YING** in hospital for weeks, cocooned in surgical dressing, I found that slow learning to appreciate the small pleasures. In hospital the one and only thing to do was...

As he will, above all, get the fantastic feeling, almost a sense of privilege, having survived...

He seemed to be getting a bit before he settled. He had plenty of...

...comes on. There's no name for it. It's just there.

And there you are, trying...

...had lost a wheel in races, something around so I believe it was.

People have suggested that he...

...vigorous, light-hearted pleasures.

"Cor, it's Stirling Moss, someone will say, in a traffic jam, perhaps, or in an hotel.

"Stirling Moss, where, where is he, where?" says Stirling, looking round in mock amazement.

Let's hope it won't be long before we hear that again.

DAILY HERALD Thursday May 2 1963   3

THE HERALD SALUTES STIRLING MOSS

The Uncrowned King of Speed

SUPREME ARTIST AT THE WHEEL OF A RACING CAR

By ARTHUR EPERON

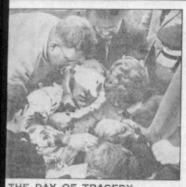

THE DAY OF TRAGEDY

Easter last year, Moss is set to win the world championship in 1962. Then this crash at Goodwood.

THE DAY OF HOPE

Months in hospital follow the crash. But at last Moss is up. And beginning to hope that he will race again.

MOSS IN TRIUMPH, BRITISH GRAND PRIX WINNER, 1955.

STIRLING MOSS swore a gold watch given him by the great Fangio. It was inscribed "To the next world champion."

And that is what everyone always expected him to be.

Then that tragic day at Goodwood 13 months ago.

As Stirling Moss was about to overtake another car his Lotus Climax shot off the track and trapped him in its crumpled body.

He survived, almost miraculously, but to most people it seemed the end of his racing career.

Hoped on

But not to Moss. He hoped on, talked bravely. Until yesterday.

Then he gave the answer to the question which drivers, mechanics and crowds have been asking—and dreading.

But though he was robbed of the final crown, Stirling has the consolation of having won almost every important race.

In the world drivers' championship he was runner-up four times.

The British public named him Sportsman of the Year. Enzo Ferrari, the Italian racing boss, called him "one of the greatest drivers of all time."

His secret of success? Perhaps Alfred Neubauer, of the German Mercedes team, had the answer.

Having named him the greatest-ever racing driver after Fangio, Neubauer said: "He is a supreme *artist*."

The Patriot

Why then did the title to which all his talents laid claim, escape him?

His business manager once told why: "*Because he is a patriot. He has always insisted on driving a British car.*"

And the irony of the Stirling Moss story is that Stirling crashed as British cars did become good enough to beat the Ferraris and the Porsches.

World Champion Graham Hill last night telephoned this tribute from Indianapolis:

"To my mind he is the greatest driver the world has ever seen."

Finishing line

Stirling Moss, the master of motor racing, decides never to race again *(this page and P3). A wise decision though the sport will not be the same without him.*

The Day of Decision

Stirling Moss at his desk last night. He has been out again on Goodwood track, 13 months after his crash. It was his try-out. The old magic was there, the old thrill. He covers 2.4 miles in 1 minute 39.5 seconds. Good going. But not good enough for Moss. "I will never race again," he says.

Was this why Moss crashed?

STIRLING MOSS has decided to retire without trying to discover what was the reason for his accident.

I watched the race on TV and saw that the car appeared to shudder just a lap before the accident.

I remarked to my son at the time that the car seemed to be breaking up—end of course the crash came in the next lap.

A look at the film of the race should soon show whether I am right or not. —H. WILLIAMS, Empire-road, Liverpool.

AND STIRLING?

NOW Stirling Moss is retiring from motor-racing, would it not be a fitting end to his tense career if he were given a knighthood in the next Birthday Honours List?

—(Miss) F. TYLEY,
Barking, Essex.

Daily Mail 6·5·63

Daily Mail 3·5·63

Moss Retires From Car Racing

Stirling Moss is to retire from car racing. He announced his decision yesterday afternoon after a private test at Goodwood, where he was badly injured in an accident while racing just over a year ago.

Scotsman 3·5·63

Stirling's lesson

THE RETIREMENT of Stirling Moss has been regretted the world over . . . and not least by the men of the Warwickshire police force.

In their monthly commentary, an article says that in many ways Stirling made a special contribution to better driving.

"He closes his career with the recognition that his reactions do not meet the needs of a racing driver," says the writer.

"What a lesson for the many drivers on the public roads! What a wonderful example!"

Express 14·5·63

QUOTE

— By Mr. P. E. Brodie, Chief Constable of Warwickshire, in his monthly Commentary For Road Users magazine :

WE are sorry to hear of the retirement of Stirling Moss from motor racing. In many ways during his professional career he made a special contribution to better driving.

He closes that career with the recognition that his reactions do not match the needs of a racing driver. What a lesson for many drivers on the public roads. What a wonderful example.

Stirling Moss retires

Stirling Moss, the racing driver, has decided to retire from motor racing. He was seriously injured on Easter Monday last year when he crashed at 120 m.p.h. at Goodwood.

After trying a few laps at Goodwood in a two-and-a-half litre sports car yesterday, he made his decision.

At his London home last night he said: "I came to the conclusion while driving that it would be foolish to continue because I have lost a certain amount of dexterity. My reactions are down a little."

Asked if he had any regrets at not having won the world championship, he replied: "None at all. Fangio did it five times. If I won it six would it make me better than Fangio? I know it would not, because I am not."

Scotsman 2·5·63

8

A Life Reinvented

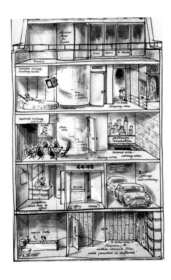

The prospect of enforced retirement stretched ahead of him as a dull, bleak and featureless plain. He had, over his career, established a host of new benchmarks, the standards by which others would now be measured, but the prospect of any return to racing was, if not impossible, then certainly unlikely. Had his retirement been a matter of *Anno Domini*, perhaps it would have been easier to accept, for as he had said to John Freeman in the summer of 1960:

I would retire if somebody passed me on a corner in a similar car – in other words if I felt that somebody was going definitely considerably faster than me and my car was right, then I would retire…I'm not really qualified to go into any particular business, so it is going to be very, very difficult to give up racing.

The hardest thing for a competitor to do is to stop. History has never been short of examples of those who left the big question unanswered, and who made fools of themselves as someone else answered it for them. This particularly applies to sports of physical prowess, as the essential toughness and the will to push both the self and the opposition starts to atrophy. One day it is simply not there. Stirling was denied this experience, indeed denied a choice.

He was now 32. Apart from the brief time he had spent as a management trainee, he had never had a proper job in the sense that most people understood it and neither was he remotely equipped to cope with life outside racing. Outside the sphere of racing, he was a celebrity, but also perhaps something of a curiosity. It was clear even to those who affected little or no interest in motor sport that he was still an important figure, quite simply because he was Stirling Moss. He had gradually inserted himself into the national consciousness in a way that no other sportsman had ever done, and he would discover this soon.

Flippantly, he says now: 'I had to work for a living,' but it must have seemed rather different in that early summer of 1963. Critically, Alfred and Ken Gregory had had the foresight to insure

his career from itself by two strategies. One was an insurance policy taken out by Stirling Moss Ltd, which paid out in the event of an accident preventing him from carrying on his career. In the event of him returning to racing, he would gladly repay the money. The second lay in the form of words of the sponsorship contract with ShellMex-BP, which bound that company to a measure of support should his career be terminated for similar reasons. This second arrangement would offer him something of a lifeline, as it would also mandate a certain amount of work; a displacement activity.

As the ShellMex-BP cartel started to break up and the operators of the petrol stations had to decide whether they would become Shell or BP sites, Stirling started to find himself very busy indeed. In effect, he became the public face of BP as he was helicoptered around the country to open yet another petrol station. It was a modest start to what would evolve into a public relations career of some complexity.

As he hurtled about the country, he realised something very reassuring; whereas he had always been a huge draw for race organisers, and was always sought-after in the paddock, the reception he received as he went about his business now was altogether of a different order. Basically, he discovered that he was loved and not merely by motor racing fans. If he was to snip a ribbon on a forecourt, he was usually accompanied by hundreds, if not thousands of people who merely wanted a glimpse of him. This was the sort of reception usually accorded to royalty and later to pop stars.

That many of his fans simply turned out to see him as a way of expressing regret at what had happened to him was also clear. For others it was a way of expressing their simple pleasure at his survival as well as endorsing with relief, as Peter Garnier had done, his decision to retire. It was, despite his misgivings about that decision, a very warming experience. Such a foundation and the confidence that it

Previous page: With Herb Jones at Nassau, July 1963.

This page top and middle: The house at 46 Shepherd Street, Mayfair; bottom: Stirling in a light moment.

Facing page: Stirling in his office at 46 Shepherd Street.

detail which they show in their profession is at variance with the view of them as extroverted personalities...one gets the impression that they often assume the façade of an extrovert socially.

That observation was certainly true of Stirling Moss (although Innes Ireland was perhaps rather different in that respect). She had also noted that: 'If one considers what is involved with driving in general, control is an important aspect and this seems to be a considerable personality need in motor racing drivers.'

The pair married very quietly in 1964 and immediately the realisation hit that they were two very different people with absolutely nothing in common. It was to be an acrimonious marriage, its tensions quite unrelieved by the arrival of a baby daughter, Allison, on Christmas Day, 1967. David Haynes was the pleased godfather. Within a year the couple had separated, Elaine, as Victorian lady novelists would have it, had been driven to seek solace in the arms of another. Stirling sued for divorce, and while he won (the terms of the divorce action would ensure that) it was a Pyrrhic victory. The whole business had been distressing beyond belief. Was there something wrong with him? That, of course, was a relative rather than an absolute question.

engendered allowed him to start to reinvent himself.

As a result of his success as a PR asset, it was not long before he was off to America again. On one of his many expeditions he met Elaine Barbarino, who worked in the public relations industry. The pair (in the reassuringly artificial environment of an expense-account lifestyle) started to see more and more of each other and as the prospect of something more permanent emerged, Stirling invited her to experience England. For some of his close friends, his relationship with Elaine set some alarm bells going. They knew him as a conservative, retiring man, who attended night-clubs to meet people, invariably when he was safely in the company of others. In short, he looked like a swinger, could act like a swinger, but he wasn't really one at all. That he had very well-developed views on how his life should be ordered was not a matter that was necessarily clear when he was performing on the public relations circuit. His chronic shyness and the desire for an ordered life entirely on his own terms meant that he could be very ill-at-ease indeed when outside his own precisely controlled environment.

Berenice Krikler (who had by then become a good if concerned friend) had spotted this tendency when she wrote the report on her challenging little universe of racing drivers:

They certainly impress one as having a high level of drive in general. The tremendous dedication and attention to

When Johnson's Wax, as a leading sponsor of that extraordinary tournament, the Canadian–American Challenge Cup (Can-Am) needed a spokesman for their interest in it, their advertising agency unerringly picked Stirling. It was an association that would last as long as the series itself, until 1974. The Can-Am series marked the ascendancy of Bruce McLaren and Denny Hulme, as their mighty McLaren Chevrolets tore the air asunder. Can-Am marked something of a high point in the evolution of racing and whatever misgivings Stirling had about not participating, they were nothing as to the disappointment of his fans at not being able to see him doing it, for these were some of the most powerful machines to appear on a race track.

Ken Gregory and Stirling had parted company professionally by now; Gregory's main interest, the British Racing Partnership, had established itself as a promising constructor by the summer of 1963 as Tony Robinson, the chief designer, had managed to do what Alf Francis had not – build a competitive *Grand Prix* car. This suggested that Robinson had been hiding his light under a bushel, for in the

Above: Stirling and Elaine, his second wife.

Facing page: Becoming reacquainted with the MG record car at Snetterton in 1967.

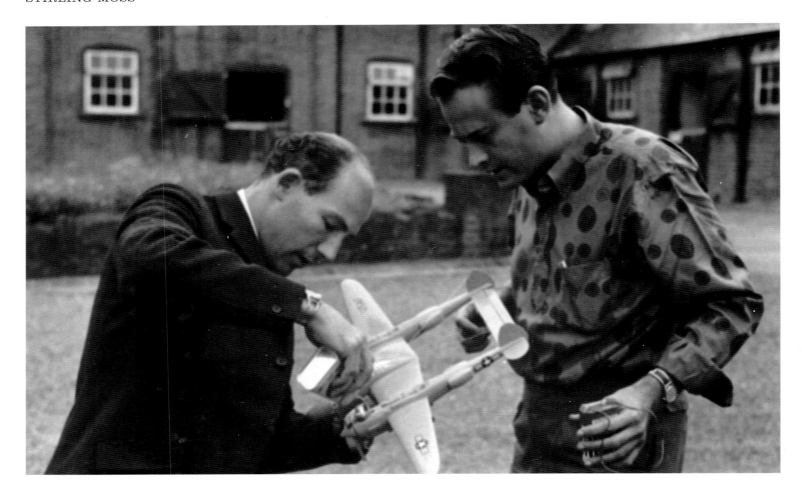

hands of Innes Ireland, this first effort had done well, with a fourth place on only its second outing at Zandvoort. But the politics of the sport, spurred on by the rapid growth of commercial interest in it, were by then coming to the forefront and within a year of that startling Dutch *Grand Prix*, the BRP was informed that it was not to be included in the revenue arrangements agreed by the Formula 1 Constructor's Association – the organisation that would later become FOCA. It was held, with no justification whatsoever, that the BRP was not a full constructor, and was thus ineligible in terms of qualifying for a share of the spoils.

The BRP was by then short of money, having funded its own development costs and Gregory was too distracted to take issue. He had resigned as Stirling's manager in the spring of 1964 and was not minded to press his case to the other constructors, however unfairly he knew that BRP had been treated. Stirling was too distracted by the unhappiness of his second marriage to take any particular interest. Alfred, practical as ever, but acutely aware that the closure of the team was potentially a tragedy for its members, took the view that the firm could tick over for the moment, and Gregory and Tony Robinson concurred. It was as well that they did.

BRP enjoyed a swansong in 1965, with the construction of two Indianapolis cars for Masten Gregory, but the death knell of the firm in the long term had been well and truly sounded. By the beginning of 1966, Ken Gregory had become fully committed to his airline and publishing businesses, and resigned his directorship in SM Ltd.

After his second experience of marriage had proved to be so traumatic, Stirling resolved to change his life and 46 Shepherd Street reverted to the purpose for which it had originally been intended. It became again the definitive bachelor pad and, via the good offices of *The Lady* magazine's classified ad pages, Stirling secured the services of a series of redoubtable housekeepers to look after his every need. He is very good at appearing helpless, a trick he probably learned at home during exeats from Haileybury. It was a technique that had certainly proved effective on his

Above: Boyish pursuits with Herb Jones at the White Cloud Farm.

Right: Advising the actor who would play him in Athol Fugard's 1968 play, *Mille Miglia*. Despite his enthusiasm for the project, Stirling did not like the finished product at all.

mother; Aileen, who could be quite formidable, was always something of a pushover for him.

And so began for him a relatively blissful period of confirmed bachelorhood. 46 Shepherd Street had always been full of gadgets since its construction, but its redefinition as campaign headquarters for what was to become an extremely complicated love life would change its appearance somewhat. No one would be in any doubt as to the true purpose of this extra-ordinary structure, replete with all its famous gadgetry that rather served to give the game

away. Quite soon, Stirling's life veered back to an agreeable norm, balanced very neatly between work and play.

Perhaps his model came from the film *Pillow Talk* (1959) in which a serial seducer, played by Rock Hudson, occupies a Manhattan apartment equipped with every (then) conceivable device to aid trouble-free seduction. Concealed switch-gear operates lights, hi-fi, even removes the bedspread, all at the touch of a button. It seemed to work in the film, and it was certainly to work for a revitalised Stirling as he set about 'spreading happiness' as best he could.

By and large, he has enjoyed excellent relations with all his girlfriends over time, even

after their affairs ended. One reason for this was his transparently clear motivation, coupled with a straightforward honesty. There were occasional moments when he confused himself as to sequence and was hoist by his own petard, but typically the women involved in these rare errors of timing would blame each other rather than him. There were indeed occasional fights which he, tickled pink, would not even attempt to referee

But then Stirling needed a complicated love life, because his business life was the way it was. He had become, through the contract with Johnson's Wax, more or less a transatlantic commuter, and as that relationship would wind down with the demise of Can-Am, it would be replaced with a similar arrangement with Citicorp, who would investigate the practicality of motor racing sponsorship. These commitments were coupled with a host of advertising and endorsement deals. Suddenly, he found his public profile higher than ever as the appreciation of motor sport, fuelled by heavy commercial sponsorship, started to increase.

Despite the fact that he was now enjoying himself immensely, there were irritations. When he heard in 1968 that the eminent South African playwright Athol Fugard was writing a play about his great adventure in the 1955 *Mille Miglia*, he was not unnaturally quite flattered. Typically, he assisted as best he could, advising the actor, Michael Bryant, who would play him, on some of the finer points of preparing for a race, but when he saw the finished product, he was quite appalled.

Particularly irksome to him was the portrayal of himself in a scene where he and 'Jenks' are in a restaurant and a priest approaches to wish him luck. The Stirling Moss of real life would have shyly stood up and extended the schoolboyish courtesy which had become a trademark. Instead, he is portrayed as remaining seated, in his opinion, insolently.

It portrayed me as a slob, and I'm not a slob; I was cross about it because I would

Above: At the Playboy Club.

Right: Behind a different wheel.

never have dreamed of not standing up if a priest came over to talk to me. Perhaps it was a small thing, but dammit, it would have been bloody rude.

And he is not, bar a certain tactical tetchiness, a rude man. The play, dramatically opaque though it was, went out to some critical success (some of it downright sycophantic) but it had missed the point. The Moss portrayed in it was a *chetif*, reduced figure – chain-smoking, clipped, tense and humourless. Almost as bad as the scene with the priest was that the Moss of the play seemed to affect no enthusiasm for girls, which, given the fully aerobatic nature of his sex-life at the time, was irony indeed. He had a reputation to maintain, after all...Denis Jenkinson came across as a very junior and faintly bumbling figure, and it was as much for this as any other reason that Stirling slapped an injunction on the BBC, banning it from ever showing the play again. It never has, in fact, although it can be seen privately at the National Film and Television Archive.

Oddly perhaps, in the light of the above comments concerning the priest, Stirling, rather like his father, holds no particular brief for organised religion, he merely respects the office or more probably the responsibility which goes with it. He does, however, have a belief in God, or at least a God whose points of reference he himself can grasp, God on his terms. It rather misses the point, of course, and revolves more around his sense of equity: 'I believe in God insofar as I don't believe it's fair that I should be killed because a wheel falls off a car built by some ***** like Colin Chapman,' he says. When this writer pointed out that this was exactly what had nearly happened several times, his response was: 'Yes, that's true, but actually it didn't, did it?' Hence, I realised, his sense of being lucky.

This writer remembered the play very well and often wondered why it was not rebroadcast, for it had something of an impact; for the viewing public it was very much the image onto which they fastened and this distressed him, (hence the legal action), for the truth about Stirling is really rather different. His manners are distinctly antediluvian, for which read exquisite, and he is certainly not ashamed of that, although he realises that his natural courtesy can isolate him, particularly now, because his sense of regret at the collapse of common courtesy is palpable.

The episode of the play demonstrates very well what damage the external perception of a character can do; without diligent research, it must seem inevitable that a racing driver under stress must be seen as a clichéd figure from central casting. In reality nothing could be further from the truth. His essentially sunny and optimistic disposition

(although serial acquaintance with the real *Mille Miglia* had rather tested that) marks him out as being really rather well-adjusted. For a control freak, that is.

But this aspect of Stirling's personality should not be considered surprising. Given the mishaps that have befallen him when he was in the hands of other people (many of them seriously life-threatening – wheels falling off or steering sheared, or brakes disappearing) then it would be very odd indeed for him to be relaxed about not being in control. The fact that there are no examples in his résumé of any racing

accident that was actually caused by him, and very few retirements that were not the result of some sort of component failure, then a desire, even a need, to direct one's own life must fall naturally to hand.

Far left: On yet another PR assignment.

Above: One that got away.

In contrast, as the episode of the con-man at Dundrod illustrates, there has always been within him a willingness to trust as well. Just as he was perfectly content to drive cars prepared by people for whom he had a deep respect, he has, all his life, displayed a tendency to assume that the high ethical standards which characterised Rob Walker's activities or those of the BRP, are invariably shared by rather more people than perhaps it is wise to assume. This tendency has, over the years, led him up the odd blind alley.

the toy giraffe which had been Stirling's first gift to her, and despite the fact that she rapidly built up her own circle of friends through her work in advertising (preceded by a stint at Harrod's), it was certain that their paths would cross, for Stirling had stayed in touch with the family, even to the extent of having had a brief romance with Susie's elder sister Christina after his divorce from Elaine.

As a child of the Orient (she had been born in Japan and educated in Hong Kong), her initial response to London was

It was certain that their paths would cross once again. . .

One thing Stirling is very good at is committing; his impulsiveness (or perhaps his sense of curiosity), combined with his tenacity for a given project will often leave him disappointed with an outcome, should that prove to be somewhat less than perfect by his own measure. The Wall Street aphorism, 'Give me half the facts – I want to make a quick decision,' could under some circumstances have been coined for him. This is, of course, one of the reasons why Stirling Moss Ltd was established in the first place, so that the experience of the ERA G-type would not be repeated.

The Paine family had arrived in London from Hong Kong in 1968 and set up house in Chelsea. Susan Paine still had

that it was quite the most appalling place she had ever seen. Insipid food, even worse weather and a resolutely hopeless attitude to service. Hers was a depressing experience undergone by many who came West for the first time.

Stirling, who firmly believed (and still believes) that 'everywhere in the world is a suburb of London', was eager to point out that it was not necessarily how it appeared. For Susie, this had all the impact of Mark Twain's comment, that 'Mr Wagner's music is not as bad as it sounds.' She remained unconvinced. As her career developed, she became more inured to the difficulties of living in London, which for someone from a place as efficient, vibrant and well-mannered

as Hong Kong (or many other places in Asia) is a considerable achievement.

Stirling's bachelor idyll was further interrupted, indeed comprehensively wrecked, exactly ten years after the Goodwood crash. Alfred, who had never really retired, but merely eased his rate of work a little, suddenly developed colonic cancer. He went downhill fast; after a mercifully short illness he died at Stoke Mandeville hospital on 23 April, 1972. He had been a man who had filled every crevice of a room with his friendly bear-like presence and his unexpected death was disorienting for Stirling in the extreme. To any man, the death of his father is perhaps the last rite of passage, and it is the one that most men dread. To Stirling, his very closeness to Alfred, even by some measure his dependence upon him, had not prepared him for this. Stirling without Alfred was a boat without an anchor. Touchingly, his death certificate listed him as a 'retired farmer'.

When Alfred's will was read, some of his astonishing

generosity was revealed. He had, quite spontaneously, offered Stirling's friend Herb Jones a loan to assist with a property transaction with which Herb was struggling. He had taken the trouble, despite his illness, to issue instructions that the debt be written off by his estate. Alfred clearly did not want financial complications impinging on his son's friendships, as Alfred realised that there were comparatively few of them.

The heartbroken Aileen made a very unhappy widow. Swiftly, the family pulled together and a house was built for her in the grounds of the White Cloud Farm, while Pat and her husband Eric Carlsson moved into the old family home. Stirling would visit her as often as his schedule allowed, but was distressed to see that Aileen was quite inconsolable.

Far left: Stirling and Susie.

Above: With Lord Montagu on the London to Brighton run.

Overleaf: Old habits die hard. Stirling waves to the crowd at Watkins Glen, 1998.

Overleaf (pages 334–5):Stirling demonstrates the P25 BRM at Silverstone, 1999.

About this, of course, he could do nothing, just as she could do little to assuage his own grief.

It was initially the departure of Stirling's housekeeper and secretary in 1976 that prompted his cry for help to Susie Paine. When anyone leaves his circle he is vexed, but to find himself without either domestic or commercial help was something of a blow, particularly as he had been so well looked after.

He knew that Susie had business qualifications because he had occasionally given her hair-raising lifts to the secretarial school she had attended in Hong Kong, and so she began a period of moonlighting, as she would go from work to 46 Shepherd Street where she would assist him with sundry business and domestic matters, while he, in turn, feigned helplessness. She was in no doubt (and never had been) as to the nature of his lifestyle: 'I used to tidy up all the hairpins that I would find scattered about.'

Susie and Stirling became an 'item' in 1977. As Susie puts it now: 'I knew we were *the* item on the eve of our wedding, and only then because he took me out to dinner and I knew exactly where he was!'

At least she knew where he was on every Sunday he could manage; she started to accompany him out to the little house within sight of the White Cloud Farm where Aileen lived. Aileen had found adjustment to life without her beloved Alfred almost impossible, and her health, always fairly robust before, was starting to fail. A home was briefly considered, but so independently minded was she, that she proved to be a less than ideal resident, as the Craufurd genes asserted themselves to the last. She died on 22 January, 1980.

Susie and Stirling married on 17 April, 1980, and later that year Susie gave birth to their son Elliot. The pair had been perfectly content to live together, but fully appreciated that should a baby appear, they would marry. Due to the fact that they were unaware of the sex of their forthcoming baby, they provisionally christened it 'Tadpole', and indeed it was 'Tadpole Moss' who issued the wedding invitations. But for Susie there had been some unpleasantness; a no-account hack, making his way on the gossip column of a paper that should have known

better, assumed that this was a shotgun wedding. It was not; it was merely a neatly executed plan B.

There is no doubt in anyone's mind that she is the best thing that ever happened to him; all the doubts he may have had about his ability to sustain a relationship evaporated when he realised that she understood him completely and that there was nothing at all odd about his apparent need to control. He is not, by his own admission, particularly easy to live with, but Susie's view, that she married the 'total package', reflects both her practicality and the truth that the state of bliss in which she has found herself for more than twenty years has had only a very small (and very occasional) price attached to it. Early on, she realised that Stirling was not perhaps quite as other men, when she found herself helping him clean the common parts of a property which he owned and managed. He is quite likely to carry out such tasks on Christmas Day, in fact, as London traffic is less obstructive for the scooter he rides.

As his sense of security established itself, so the compulsive side of his nature receded slightly. He still likes to set his own agenda, he still craves company and hates being alone, but the eight-year-old school boy who set off on that optimistic journey to reach America is still lurking in there somewhere. He has always, for example, been fascinated by illusion, magic and conjuring tricks. He knows that much of it is pure practiced sleight of hand, but that does not put him off. The sheer skill of it fascinates him, even though he realises that it is inevitably something of a con. Oddly enough, he still bears no particular ill-will to the silver-tongued scamp who so effortlessly relieved him of £1000 all those years ago, either.

Stirling's marriage to Susie also coincided with a return to racing, albeit for only two seasons. It was a new experience in more ways than one; Audi saloon cars racing on slicks was new to him and initially it showed a bit too. As for some of the tactics employed in saloon car racing, as close to fairground dodgems as one

Far left and right: Back in the Frazer-Nash at Monaco after 48 years.

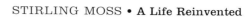

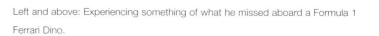

Left and above: Experiencing something of what he missed aboard a Formula 1
Ferrari Dino.

can get, he was not particularly comfortable with it. It was not a safety issue, but rather one of skill; in his previous career, he had only intentionally made contact with another car once at a sports car race in Denmark, when a dawdling Ferrari simply would not get out of the way. He realised, very quickly, that the physical strength of the cars, combined with their extraordinary grip, afforded their drivers a cavalier attitude to risk which had been quite unknown to him, and which left him, despite the thrill of competition, with some rather mixed feelings. Despite the misgivings he had as a professional driver, both Susie and Stirling had tremendous fun and expanded their circle of friends considerably.

But the advent of historic racing, the revisiting of his own sport, has kept him very busy indeed. As the fallout from the 1974 oil shock subsided, the interest in all things to do with historic motor racing suddenly exploded. Of course, this was not a new phenomenon, but the exponential growth of interest in old machinery (with its natural effect on prices),

stamped the historic racing movement with the imprimatur of authenticity; the punter could now wander about the paddock at Goodwood or Silverstone and even engage his modest heroes in casual conversation. These were not men who spent their time cocooned away in some improbable mobile home; these were real racing drivers.

Historic racing did not reinvent Stirling Moss; even without Susie's matchless assistance, he had already done that for himself. But the exposure that he received, as he emerged as the mascot of the sport, went a long way to helping him over any uncertainties he had felt about the nature and the timing, of his retirement. In many ways, his sense of luck stems from this – as Alfred Neubauer was granted the gift of two careers, so was Stirling Moss. Suddenly, the post bag started to swell again, reminding him that he was still regarded as a national treasure.

But there is more to his life than public relations now. He has over forty tenants in the properties which he owns and

The advent of historic racing
has kept him very busy indeed. . .

allowed several well-heeled collectors to justify the vast expense of rebuilding a Maserati, an Aston Martin or a Vanwall and putting them back on the track where they properly belonged.

Naturally, to witness Stirling Moss back in the cockpit was a privilege that people were prepared to pay for; frequently more than the original owners had paid for these *anciens pilotes* to drive in the first place. But there was an agreeable democracy about the reinvented sport: it was accessible, whereas the iron grip of FOCA and the FIA on the modern sport was having entirely the opposite effect, with drivers of really quite modest ability being propelled into the limelight in a way which had simply never happened before.

So a pleasant reinvention of the 1950s sport took place – even the dreaded BRM V16, saved by Tom Wheatcroft from a scrapyard, was recommissioned and a modern public was able to see and understand why it had caused such a sensation in the first place. Ironically, the BRM has become something of an icon, which would have both pleased and confused Raymond Mays. Stirling still thinks it is a rotten car, although he does own that it probably goes rather better now than it did when he and Fangio drove it.

Of course, the mere presence of these senior drivers

unsurprisingly, he carries out much of the work on them himself. He will frequently turn out himself to fix a domestic appliance or a plumbing problem rather than call in outside help, as he believes, probably correctly, that he can do just as competent a job himself. Given the cost of his time in other arenas, this is possibly another example of a 'penny wise, pound foolish' approach to life, but the simple truth of it is that he simply enjoys it for its own sake as much as for the relatively trivial amount of money which might be saved, although that is pleasing, too.

He is not actually a tightwad (although he thinks he is); the reason that he would always prefer to host a dinner party at home than eat out is not primarily an economic one; it is more due to his (by now) instinctive dread of possibly walking unaccompanied into a room full of strangers. As he dislikes solitude, so he dislikes saying, 'Hello, I'm Stirling Moss,' because even he, with all his legion accomplishments, is simply not cocky enough to think that the person he is addressing will be aware of that fact already. At bottom, he is still a very shy man, although probably not for the same reasons as he was fifty years ago. Then his diffidence was to

Left: At Road Atlanta, 1988,

do with his own sense of being an outsider; now, ironically, it has as much to do with his celebrity as anything else.

A thing which impressed David Haynes, when the two first met, and which still impresses him now, is Stirling's total lack of side. Some men (particularly public figures) will hide behind a wall of anonymity and deputise others to do their bidding; Stirling does not. If a recalcitrant tenant needs taking to court, Stirling will do it; if rent needs collecting, he will do that, too on his scooter. He is an extraordinary man who takes pleasure in doing ordinary things.

So, whereas many people navigate a full circle in life and arrive back more or less where they started, with some lessons learned and others never even observed, Stirling has become, from his underachieving schooldays, through a perilous career, nothing less than a national institution; his rôle in the nation's consciousness is unique.

He is a man of infinite small courtesies and works very hard to put people at their ease. By his own admission, people do not interest him very much (unless they are people who do something – literally anything – well), a fact that he is quite happy to point out to them when he meets them, but he is also acutely aware that the rôle he plays now is an important balancing one. He is to many people the most important link there is between motor sport then and now and it is a job he does very well. He is an ambassador for what he considers to be the best aspects of a sport which he also considers to be under threat from the unavoidable forces of commercialism and presentation. This has, in his view, simply gelded it. The *jejune* bafflement in his voice when he explained to me that it now takes the presence of up to seven people to start a Formula 1 car now reflects more his sense of wonder than anything else; as he is a dedicated follower of technology and gadgetry, this is perhaps surprising, but the realisation that the sport at which he reigned supreme has now changed irrevocably is lowering for him. Despite the huge and casual risks of 1950s motor racing, he considers that he 'had the best of it'.

He remains a racer, a competitor. To him, there are drivers, there are racing drivers and there are racers. He considers one or two contemporary drivers to be in the same class as Tony Brooks, Jean Behra, Phil Hill, Dan Gurney and Mario Andretti (racers all) but not many. It is a matter of mind-set as much as anything else. There is, he avers, no modern Fangio and probably never will be.

As we prepared this book, I did my best to compare the Stirling Moss with whom I had had all these fascinating conversations, with the young prodigy who had fixated the media when he erupted on the scene all those years ago.

I came to the conclusion that he probably needs adult supervision and of course he gets it. Part of him is comfortable with the role of *ancien pilote*; part of him hates it. Nothing, for example, would persuade him to even get into a racing car driven by someone else, although it would probably be quite difficult to find a driver prepared to do it, such is the grip his reputation still has upon the exponents of the modern sport. He will drive with his brother-in-law Eric Carlsson, indeed has even been his passenger on a rally, and he will be Susie's passenger ('only because my driving is so boring', she says), but that is the extent of his confidence about being driven. thus his admiration for Denis Jenkinson, his passenger in three *Mille Miglias*, is total.

A few years ago, I accompanied him on a railway journey to Cambridge; he was opening a new factory which belonged to Lister Engineering, whose racing cars he had driven years before. The train left at 4. At 3.57 (he is the only man I know who actually owns a Bradshaw's railway guide) he hove into sight on platform 9 of King's Cross station, where I had been waiting for him. People immediately started to stare, a thing to which he was quite used, but made me somehow uneasy and when we alighted at Cambridge, there was a car waiting. I have never seen a driver more nervous of his passenger – the poor man simply gibbered. Stirling didn't notice (or affected not to) which, given his core feelings about being driven by others, was thoughtful of him.

The opening went well, and the next day many of us descended upon Basildon in Essex. Canon Lionel Webber, then chaplain to both the BRDC and the Queen, had organised with commendable efficiency a fund-raising historic car event for a rather avant-garde architectural addition to his church there. He had somehow persuaded the local police to close the roads around the nearby industrial estate. In doing so, of course, they had unwittingly also suspended the speed limit. Many of the great and the good of historic motor racing were there and many had brought their machinery with them. Stirling was in a Maserati. In the paddock, as he climbed aboard, I remember thinking what a privilege it was to witness, at close hand, Stirling Moss actually in a Maserati racing car. His concentration was total; instrument check, enquiry as to gear ratios, 'Good luck, darling' from Susie, then off. Just like a race.

A few minutes later, he was back; he trotted through the noisy, improvised and crowded paddock: 'Lionel, this is no ******** good,' he announced, 'They're telling everyone to

Right: Back in a 'Birdcage'.

Overleaf: Juan Manuel Fangio in Jenkinson's place in Stirling's 1955 *Mille Miglia* winner. Innes Ireland is alongside in a Lotus 18.

slow down; what on earth's the point?'

Quite unfazed, Canon Webber pointed out firmly to the harassed police what Stirling knew, that a decommissioned road is not subject to the highway code, which is why it was perfectly legal for Chris Amon to drive a 1000-bhp Ferrari Can-Am car round the course on smooth, slick tyres. This had led a deafened, disbelieving and nervous traffic cop to contemplate issuing him a fixed-penalty ticket; the vehicle was even untaxed! No; you must know the rules. When Stirling went out again, much happier now that he was allowed to let rip and 'have a go,' he started to wave airily to the crowd. No one who has read this story will be remotely surprised to learn that almost unanimously, they waved back. When I saw that, I quite marvelled. It was that spectacle that made me realise something; that I simply had to write a book about this extraordinary man.

Early in 2001, at the suggestion of Jackie Stewart, Stirling went to the Mayo Clinic for a routine check, during which it was found that he had prostate cancer. On 6 January, he underwent a six-hour operation which hit him very hard indeed. As he put it: 'It took more out of me than 40 laps round the Nurburgring.' He and his family are deeply indebted to Dr Robert Myers and his team at the clinic, even if, to Stirling's horror, they proved to be rather less flexible than Mr Urquhart had been all those years ago. They would not even let him ride his beloved scooter for two months after his return to London. It is a tribute to their skill, not to say Stirling's own undimmed powers of recovery, that less than seven weeks after this major operation he was on his way to Australia for the first *Grand Prix* of the season in Melbourne.

This writer, ringing the bell at Shepherd Street in late January in order to continue our interrupted conversations, was not sure what to expect. I had never seen Stirling in adversity and although he had thoughtfully telephoned from America while recuperating to keep me posted, indeed he had even read a draft of the manuscript – I was nervous about how he would respond to what had happened to him. I needn't have been concerned, as it transpired. He opened the door and said: 'Christ boy, think how many books you'd have sold if I'd snuffed it.'

This remark confirmed to me that my thoughts at Basildon had not been mistaken. It has been both a great pleasure and a privilege.

These pages are taken from his extensive scrapbooks. His recovery and his life as a celebrity have been well-documented. His wonderful house has featured in many magazine articles.

Automatiskt tjuvlarm vid kudden

FRAMTIDSHUS forts.

I Stirling Moss' sängkammare i rätt och lila (t. h.) finns ett manöverbord intill sängen. Där kan Moss släcka och tända överallt i huset, koppla på tjuvlarmet, beställa väckning, spola vatten i badkaret och hissa ner en TV på bekväm höjd över sängen.

Med en knapp vid sängen kan han hissa ner en TV i bekväm höjd

Ingen får röra hans hi-fi-verk

Hi-fi-anläggningen (bilden ovan) är det enda som ingen annan än Moss får röra. Han vill lyssna på sina favoriter Frank Sinatra, Sammy Davis och Peggy Lee i perfekt återgivning. »Minsta svajning i musiken gör mej galen», säjer han.

RACE NO.	RACE DATE	EVENT, VENUE & COUNTRY	DURATION	CAR	CAPACITY	ENTRANT OR OWNER	WIN NO.*	RESULT	SPEEDS, TIMES, NOTES AND COMMENTS
	1947								
				BMW 328	1971 cc.	A.E.Moss		Winner, Cullen Cup.	
	2/3/1947	Harrow Car Club Trial, GB		BMW 328	1971 cc.	A.E.Moss		Retired.	Broken half-shaft.
	6/4/1947	N.W.London Motor Club Trial, GB		BMW 328	1971 cc.	A.E.Moss		1st Class award.	1st, easy-starting test, 1st steering test.
	28/6/1947	Junior Car Club rally, Eastbourne, GB		BMW 328	1971 cc.	A.E.Moss		7th, standard sports class.	
	1/9/1947	Brighton Speed Trials, GB	1 km. S/start	BMW 328	1971 cc.	A.E.Moss		3rd in class.	
	6/9/1947	Poole speed trials, GB	1 km. S/start	BMW 328	1971 cc.	A.E.Moss			
	20/9/1947	Chichester Speed Trials, Merston, GB		BMW 328	1971 cc.	A.E.Moss		UNC.	
	1948								
	9/5/1948	Prescott Hill Climb, GB	1,127 yds.	Cooper-JAP 500 MkII	498 cc.	S.C.Moss		4th in class.	51.01", Initially set NCR.
	5/6/1948	Stanmer Park Hill Climb, GB	c. 1,200 yds.	Cooper-JAP 500 MkII	498 cc.	S.C.Moss		FTD in class.	58.78"
1	7/4/1948	Brough Aerodrome races, GB	1,144 yds.	Cooper-JAP 500 MkII	498 cc.	S.C.Moss	1	1st in heat, BPT, FL.	48.90 mph
2	7/4/1948	Brough Aerodrome races, GB	1,144 yds.	Cooper-JAP 500 MkII	498 cc.	S.C.Moss	2	1st in Final.	
3	7/4/1948	Brough Aerodrome races, GB	1,144 yds.	Cooper-JAP 500 MkII	498 cc.	S.C.Moss	3	1st in Handicap race.	
	15/7/1948	Bouley Bay Hill Climb, CI		Cooper-JAP 500 MkII	498 cc.	S.C.Moss		FTD in class, NCR.	58.00 mph
	18/7/1948	Prescott Hill Climb, GB	1,127 yds.	Cooper-JAP 500 MkII	498 cc.	S.C.Moss		FTD in class.	49.5"
	25/7/1948	Great Auclum Hill Climb, GB	c.600 yds.	Cooper-JAP 500 MkII	498 cc.	S.C.Moss		FTD in class, 2nd o/a.	23.46"
	7/8/1948	Boscombe Speed Trials, GB	1 km. S/start	Cooper-JAP 500 MkII	498 cc.	S.C.Moss		FTD in class.	31.4"
	5/9/1948	Brighton Speed Trials, GB	1 km. S/start	Cooper-JAP 500 MkII	498 cc.	S.C.Moss		4th in class.	34.14" (Sick engine)
	12/9/1948	Prescott Hill Climb, GB	1,127 yds.	Cooper-JAP 500 MkII	498 cc.	S.C.Moss		3rd in class.	53.67" (Heavy rain)
4	18/9/1948	Goodwood 500cc race, GB	3 laps.	Cooper-JAP 500 MkII	498 cc.	S.C.Moss	4	1st, BPT.	71.92 mph Inaugural Goodwood race.
	25/9/1948	Shelsley Walsh Hill Climb, GB	½ mile.	Cooper-JAP 500 MkII	498 cc.	S.C.Moss		FTD (in 750 class)	43.84"
5	2/10/1948	Silverstone 500cc race, GB	3 laps.	Cooper-JAP 500 MkII	498 cc.	S.C.Moss		PP. Retired.	66.98 mph Engine blew up.
6	9/10/1948	Dunholme Lodge Aerodrome, GB	8 laps.	Cooper-JAP 500 MkII	498 cc.	S.C.Moss	5	1st.	78.56 mph
	1949								
7	18/4/1949	Goodwood Easter Handicap, GB	5 laps.	Cooper-JAP 1000 Mk III	996 cc.	S.C.Moss	6	1st, BPT, FL.	BPT 79.76 mph., FL 82.44 mph
8	18/4/1949	Goodwood 500 cc race, GB	5 laps.	Cooper-JAP 500 Mk III	498 cc.	S.C.Moss		Retired.	Piston failure.
9	14/5/1949	Silverstone 500 cc race, GB (GP meet)	56 miles.	Cooper-JAP 500 Mk III	498 cc.	S.C.Moss	7	1st, FL.	70.95mph
				Cooper-JAP 1000 Mk III	996 cc.	S.C.Moss		Retired.	Magneto.
10	26/5/1949	Manx Cup, Douglas, IoM		Cooper-JAP 500 Mk III	498 cc.	S.C.Moss		FTD in class.	36.62"
	28/5/1949	Blandford Hill Climb, GB	½ mile.	Cooper-JAP 1000 Mk III	996 cc.	S.C.Moss		2nd, 1100 cc class.	38.57"
	11/6/1949	Shelsley Walsh Hill Climb, GB	½ mile.	Cooper-JAP 1000 Mk III	996 cc.	S.C.Moss		2nd, 1100 cc class.	36' 10". 4th overall.
	25/6/1949	Bo'ness Hill Climb, GB	½ mile.	Cooper-JAP 1000 Mk III	996 cc.	S.C.Moss		3rd in heat.	First overseas event.
11	10/7/1949	IX Circuito del Garda, I	68 miles.	Cooper-JAP 1000 Mk III	996 cc.	S.C.Moss	8	1st in class.	
12	10/7/1949	IX Circuito del Garda, I	68 miles.	Cooper-JAP 1000 Mk III	996 cc.	S.C.Moss		9th. UNC.	Broken drive chain.
13	17/7/1949	Reims-Gueux race, F		Cooper-JAP 1000 Mk III	996 cc.	S.C.Moss		2nd, 1100 cc class.	3rd overall.
	21/7/1949	Bouley Bay Hill Climb, CI		Cooper-JAP 1000 Mk III	996 cc.	S.C.Moss		1st, PP.	66.92 mph
14	31/7/1949	Zandvoort 500 cc race, NL	26 miles.	Cooper-JAP 500 Mk III	498 cc.	S.C.Moss	9	2nd.	
15	20/8/1949	BRDC Silverstone, GB	30 miles.	Cooper-JAP 500 Mk III	498 cc.	S.C.Moss		Retired.	Engine failure. Gold Cup for most 'meritorious performance'.
16	27/8/1949	Prix du Leman, Lausanne, CH		Cooper-JAP 1000 Mk III	996 cc.	S.C.Moss		1st, NCR.	44.7"
	11/9/1949	Prescott Hill Climb, GB	1,127 yds.	Cooper-JAP 1000 Mk III	996 cc.	S.C.Moss	10	1st, FL.	84.7 mph
17	17/9/1949	Madgwick Cup, Goodwood, GB	5 laps.	Cooper-JAP 1000 Mk III	996 cc.	S.C.Moss		Retired.	Reason unclear.
18	17/9/1949	Goodwood Trophy, GB	5 laps.	Cooper-JAP 1000 Mk III	996 cc.	Works		Retired.	
	24/9/1949	Shelsley Walsh Hill Climb, GB	½ mile.	Cooper-JAP 1000 Mk III	996 cc.	S.C.Moss		FTD.	38.19"
19	2/10/1949	Brough Aerodrome races, GB	1,144 yds.	Cooper-JAP 500 Mk III	498 cc.	S.C.Moss		3rd in heat 2.	Engine tired-
20	2/10/1949	Brough Aerodrome races, GB	1,144 yds.	Cooper-JAP 500 Mk III	498 cc.	S.C.Moss		3rd in final.	Engine very tired-
21	2/10/1949	Brough Aerodrome races, GB	1,144 yds.	Cooper-JAP 500 Mk III	498 cc.	S.C.Moss		Retired in handicap.	Engine finally gives up.
	1950								
22	10/4/1950	Easter meeting, Goodwood, GB	15 miles.	HWM-Alta 'offset'	1960 cc.	Works		6th.	
23	10/4/1950	Easter meeting, Goodwood, GB	15 miles.	HWM-Alta 'offset'	1960 cc.	Works		2nd.	
24	16/4/1950	500 cc race, Brands Hatch, GB	20 miles.	Cooper-JAP 500 Mk IV	498 cc.	S.C.Moss		Retired.	Piston holed.
25	30/4/1950	Paris GP, Montlhéry, F	103 miles.	HWM-Alta 'offset'	1960 cc.	Works		Retired.	Con-rod broken.
26	13/5/1950	BRDC 500 cc, Silverstone, GB	30 miles.	Cooper-JAP 500 Mk IV	498 cc.	S.C.Moss	11	1st, BPT, FL in heat 1.	77.40 mph
27	13/5/1950	BRDC 500 cc, Silverstone, GB	30 miles.	Cooper-JAP 500 Mk IV	498 cc.	S.C.Moss		2nd.	Piston holed. Leading.
28	14/5/1950	Prix de Mons, B	37 miles	HWM-Alta 'offset'	1960 cc.	Works		6th, heat 1.	
29	14/5/1950	Prix de Mons, B	37 miles.	HWM-Alta 'offset'	1960 cc.	Works		7th, final.	
30	20/5/1950	Prix de Monte Carlo, MON	30 miles.	Cooper-JAP 500 Mk IV	498 cc.	S.C.Moss	12	1st in heat, BPT, FL.	56.55 mph
31	20/5/1950	Prix de Monte Carlo, MON	30 miles.	Cooper-JAP 500 Mk IV	498 cc.	S.C.Moss	13	1st in final, FL.	55.68 mph
32	28/5/1950	Circuit du Lac, Aix-les-Bains, F		HWM-Alta 'offset'	1960 cc.	Works		Retired.	Food poisoning.
33	28/5/1950	500 cc race, Aix-les-Bains, F		Cooper-JAP 500 Mk IV	498 cc.	S.C.Moss		Retired.	Engine.
34	4/6/1950	Swiss GP, Bremgarten, CH	190 miles.	HWM-Alta 'offset'	1960 cc.	Works		DNS	Illness - hepatitis?
35	11/6/1950	Rome GP, Caracalla Baths, I	60 laps.	HWM-Alta 'offset'	1960 cc.	Works		Retired, FL.	1.58". Stub axle broke, ran 3rd.
36	17/6/1950	Goodwood 1500 cc race, GB	7 laps.	Cooper-MG	1250 cc.	Works		5th, FL.	74.50 mph
37	25/6/1950	Brands Hatch 500 cc races, GB	3 miles.	Cooper-JAP 500 Mk IV	498 cc.	S.C.Moss	14	1st, FL, heat 1.	65.94 mph
38	25/6/1950	Brands Hatch 500 cc races, GB	3 miles.	Cooper-JAP 500 Mk IV	498 cc.	S.C.Moss	15	1st, final.	63.98 mph
39	25/6/1950	Brands Hatch 500 cc races, GB	3 miles.	Cooper-JAP 500 Mk IV	498 cc.	S.C.Moss	16	1st, 500 car heat.	
40	25/6/1950	Brands Hatch 500 cc races, GB	3 miles.	Cooper-JAP 500 Mk IV	498 cc.	S.C.Moss	17	1st, 500 prod.car final.	63.31 mph
41	25/6/1950	Brands Hatch 500 cc races, GB	3 miles.	Cooper-JAP 500 Mk IV	498 cc.	S.C.Moss	18	1st, '10 fastest' race.	64.00 mph
42	2/7/1950	Coupe des 'Racers 500', Reims, F	63 miles.	Cooper-JAP 500 Mk IV	498 cc.	S.C.Moss		6th.	
43	2/7/1950	Coupé des Petits Cylindres, Reims, F	126 miles.	HWM-Alta 'offset'	1960 cc.	Works		3rd.	
44	9/7/1950	Bari Grand Prix, I	200 miles.	HWM-Alta 'offset'	1960 cc.	Works		3rd, final. (F1 race).	
45	22/7/1950	Naples GP, Posillipo, I	127 miles.	HWM-Alta 'offset'	1960 cc.	Works	19	1st heat 1, FL.	
46	22/7/1950	Naples GP, Posillipo, I	127 miles.	HWM-Alta 'offset'	1960 cc.	Works		Crashed in final.	Teeth, knee etc.
47	7/8/1950	500 Trophy, Brands Hatch, GB	35 miles.	Cooper-JAP 500 Mk IV	498 cc.	S.C.Moss	20	1st, heat 2.	
48	7/8/1950	500 Trophy, Brands Hatch, GB	35 miles.	Cooper-JAP 500 Mk IV	498 cc.	S.C.Moss		2nd, final, LR.	67.54 mph
49	7/8/1950	*Daily Telegraph* Trophy, Brands Hatch	35 miles.	Cooper-JAP 500 Mk IV	498 cc.	S.C.Moss	21	1st in heat.	

#	Date	Event	Distance	Car	cc	Entrant	No.	Result	Notes
50	7/8/1950	*Daily Telegraph* Trophy, Brands Hatch	35 miles.	Cooper-JAP 500 Mk IV	498 cc.	S.C.Moss		Retired in final.	Carburettor.
51	12/8/1950	Prix de Berne, Bremgarten, CH	95 miles.	HWM-Alta 'offset'	1960 cc.	Works		Retired, FL, LR.	67.67 mph Gearbox broken.
52	26/8/1950	BRDC, Silverstone meeting, GB	101 miles.	HWM-Alta 'offset'	1960 cc.	Works		9th, heat 2.	
53	26/8/1950	BRDC, Silverstone meeting, GB	101miles.	HWM-Alta 'offset'	1960 cc.	Works		6th, final.	
54	26/8/1950	BRDC, Silverstone meeting, GB	29 miles.	Cooper-Norton 500Mk V	498 cc.	S.C.Moss	22	1st, PP FL.	79.87 mph
55	10/9/1950	Circuit de Mettet, B	98 miles.	HWM-Alta 'offset'	1960 cc.	Works		4th, heat 1.	
56	10/9/1950	Circuit de Mettet, B	98 miles.	HWM-Alta 'offset'	1960 cc.	Works	23	1st, heat 2.	2nd on aggregate.
57	16/9/1950	RAC Tourist Trophy, Dundrod, GB (NI)	3 hours.	Jaguar XK120	3442 cc.	T. Wisdom	24	1st, FL, LR.	77.61 mph (in wet).
58	17/9/1950	500 cc races, Brands Hatch, GB	3 miles.	Cooper-Norton 500Mk V	498 cc.	S.C.Moss	25	1st, heat 2.	
59	17/9/1950	500 cc races, Brands Hatch, GB	3 miles.	Cooper-Norton 500Mk V	498 cc.	S.C.Moss		Retired, final.	Gearbox broken.
60	24/9/1950	Circuit de Perigeux, F	85 miles.	HWM-Alta 'offset'	1960 cc.	Works		2nd, heat 1.	
61	24/9/1950	Circuit de Perigeux, F	85 miles.	HWM-Alta 'offset'	1960 cc.	Works		3rd, final.	
62	30/9/1950	B.A.R.C., Goodwood, GB	10 laps.	HWM-Alta 'offset'	1960 cc.	Works		3rd, final.	
63	30/9/1950	B.A.R.C., Goodwood, GB	5 laps.	Cooper-Norton 500Mk V	498 cc.	S.C.Moss		7th.	
64	7/10/1950	Castle Combe race meeting, GB	20 laps.	HWM-Alta 'offset'	1960 cc.	Works	26	2nd, FL.	72.39 mph Engine rebuilt in paddock.
65	7/10/1950	Castle Combe race meeting, GB	7 laps.	Cooper-Norton 500Mk V	498 cc.	S.C.Moss		1st.	
66	7/10/1950	Castle Combe race meeting, GB	10 laps.	Cooper-Norton 500Mk V	498 cc.	S.C.Moss	27	1st in heat.	
67	7/10/1950	Castle Combe race meeting, GB	20 laps.	Cooper-Norton 500Mk V	498 cc.	S.C.Moss		Retired, final.	Carburettor.
68	7/10/1950	Castle Combe race meeting, GB	20 laps.	Frazer-Nash	1971 cc.	Works	28	1st.	
	7/10/1950	Castle Combe race meeting, GB	20 laps.	Frazer-Nash	1971 cc.	Works		Team h'cap prize.	
69	15/10/1950	X Circuito del Garda, I	68 miles.	HWM-Alta 'offset'	1960 cc.	Works		Retired.	Stub axle failure.
	24/10/1950	Endurance run, Montlhéry, F	2,579 miles.	Jaguar XK120	3442 cc.	Works		2,579.16 miles/24 hours.	107.46 mph Co-driver Leslie Johnson.
	17/11/1950	*Daily Express* Rally GB		Aston Martin DB2	2580 cc.	Works		'Clear' on road, but:	Failed final tests. Co-driver Lance Macklin.
	21/11/1950	Montlhéry record attempts, F	See right.	Kieft-Norton 350	349 cc.	Works		Class J 50km	78.44 mph Driving shared with Ken Gregory.
	21/11/1950	Montlhéry record attempts, F	See right.	Kieft-Norton 350	349 cc.	Works		50miles	78.75 mph"
	21/11/1950	Montlhéry record attempts, F	See right.	Kieft-Norton 350	349 cc.	Works		100km	79.08 mph"
	21/11/1950	Montlhéry record attempts, F	See right.	Kieft-Norton 350	349 cc.	Works		1 hour	79.37 mph"
	21/11/1950	Montlhéry record attempts, F	See right.	Kieft-Norton 350	349 cc.	Works		100 miles	79.62 mph"
	21/11/1950	Montlhéry record attempts, F	See right.	Kieft-Norton 350	349 cc.	Works		200km	77.11 mph"
	23/11/1950	Montlhéry record attempts, F	See right.	Kieft-Norton 500	498 cc.	Works		Class I 50km	90.06 mph Driving shared with Gregory and Jack Neill.
	23/11/1950	Montlhéry record attempts, F	See right.	Kieft-Norton 500	498 cc.	Works		50miles	90.63 mph"
	23/11/1950	Montlhéry record attempts, F	See right.	Kieft-Norton 500	498 cc.	Works		100km	90.87 mph"
	23/11/1950	Montlhéry record attempts, F	See right.	Kieft-Norton 500	498 cc.	Works		1 hour	91.34 mph"
	23/11/1950	Montlhéry record attempts, F	See right.	Kieft-Norton 500	498 cc.	Works		100 miles	91.40 mph"
	23/11/1950	Montlhéry record attempts, F	See right.	Kieft-Norton 500	498 cc.	Works		200km	88.60 mph"
	23/11/1950	Montlhéry record attempts, F	See right.	Kieft-Norton 500	498 cc.	Works		200miles	86.99 mph"

1951

#	Date	Event	Distance	Car	cc	Entrant	No.	Result	Notes
	10/2/1951	Chiltern night trial, GB		Morris Minor saloon	919 cc.	A.Woods		Lost!	
70	26/3/1951	Lavant Cup, Goodwood, GB	7 laps.	HWM Formula 2	1960 cc.	Works		1st.	
71	26/3/1951	Richmond Trophy, Goodwood, GB	20 laps.	HWM Formula 2	1960 cc.	Works	29	1st.	
72	8/4/1951	Marseilles GP, F	150 miles.	HWM Formula 2	1960 cc.	Works		5th.	Formula 1 race.
73	22/4/1951	San Remo GP, Ospedaletti, I	120 miles.	HWM Formula 2	1960 cc.	Works		3rd.	
74	29/4/1951	*Mille Miglia*, Brescia, I	992 miles.	Jaguar XK120	3442 cc.	Works		CRA.	Skidded on oil. With F. Rainbow.
75	3/5/1951	Luxembourg 500cc GP, Fundel, LU		Kieft-Norton 500	498 cc.	S.C.Moss		Retired.	
76	5/5/1951	BRDC Int'l Trophy, Silverstone, GB	15 laps.	HWM Formula 2	1960 cc.	Works		6th, heat 1.	
77	5/5/1951	BRDC Int'l Trophy, Silverstone, GB	30 laps.	HWM Formula 2	1960 cc.	Works		14th, final.	Formula 1 race.
78	5/5/1951	BRDC 1 hour production car race		Jaguar XK120	3442 cc.	Works	30	1st, FL. Team prize.	84.50 mph
79	13/5/1951	Monza Autodrome GP, I		HWM Formula 2	1960 cc.	Works		4th, heat 1.	
80	13/5/1951	Monza Autodrome GP, I		HWM Formula 2	1960 cc.	Works		3rd, heat 2.	3rd on aggregate.
81	14/5/1951	Whitsun meeting, Goodwood, GB	3 laps.	Kieft-Norton 500	498 cc.	S.C.Moss		9th in heat.	
82	14/5/1951	Whitsun meeting, Goodwood, GB	3 laps.	Kieft-Norton 500	498 cc.	S.C.Moss	32	1st in final, FL, LR.	Speed unknown.
83	20/5/1951	Columbus Centenary GP, Genoa, I		HWM Formula 2	1960 cc.	Works		Retired.	Differential seized. Leading.
84	20/5/1951	500 cc race, Genoa, I		Kieft-Norton 500	498 cc.	S.C.Moss		Retired.	Suspension failure.
85	27/5/1951	Swiss GP, Bremgarten, CH	190 miles.	HWM Formula 2	1960 cc.	Works		8th.	Broken 'screen, ran out of fuel.
86	3/6/1951	Circuit du Lac, Aix-les-Bains, F	100 miles.	HWM Formula 2	1960 cc.	Works	33	1st, FL, heat 2.	62.76 mph
87	3/6/1951	Circuit du Lac, Aix-les-Bains, F	100 miles.	HWM Formula 2	1960 cc.	Works		2nd, final.	
88	10/6/1951	Rome GP, Baths of Caracalla, I	100 miles.	HWM Formula 2	1960 cc.	Works		4th.	
89	14/6/1951	British Empire Trophy, Douglas, IoM	200 miles.	Frazer-Nash Le Mans	1971 cc.	Gilby Eng.	34	1st, FL. Team prize.	69.78 mph
90	24/6/1951	Le Mans 24 hours, Sarthe, F		Jaguar C-type	3442 cc.	Works		Retired, LR.	105.85 mph, Engine, 92 laps. Leading. C/d Fairman.
91	1/7/1951	AVUSRennen, Berlin, D	200 miles.	HWM Formula 2	1960 cc.	Works		Retired.	Crankshaft snapped, 3 laps.
92	8/7/1951	Rouen GP, Les Essarts, F	200 miles.	HWM Formula 2	1960 cc.	Works		Retired.	Gearbox, 27 laps.
93	14/7/1951	British GP 500 cc race, Silverstone, GB	60 miles.	Kieft-Norton 500	498 cc.	S.C.Moss	35	1st, PP, FL, NR.	2.02"-85.23 mph
94	15/7/1951	Circuit de Mettet, F	210 miles.	HWM Formula 2	1960 cc.	Works		4th.	
95	22/7/1951	Dutch GP 500 cc race, NL	44 miles.	Kieft-Norton 500	498 cc.	S.C.Moss	36	1st, PP, FL.	73.14 mph
96	22/7/1951	Dutch GP, Zandvoort NL	235 miles.	HWM Formula 2	1960 cc.	Works		3rd.	
97	29/7/1951	German GP 500cc race, Nurburgring, D	5 laps.	Kieft-Norton 500	498 cc.	S.C.Moss		PP, FL. Retired,	72.7 mph Steering arm broken.
	5/8/1951	Freibourg Hill Climb, D		HWM Formula 2	1960 cc.	Works		4th (F2 Class).	
	5/8/1951	Freibourg 500 cc Hill Climb, D		Kieft-Norton 500	498 cc.	S.C.Moss		1st.	
98	12/8/1951	GP OstSchweitz, Erlen CH		HWM Formula 2	1960 cc.	Works		Retired.	Suspension. Leading.
99	2/9/1951	GP of Bari, I		Ferrari 166	1992 cc.	D. Murray		DNS.	Accident in practice.
100	8/9/1951	Wakefield Trophy, Curragh, EI		HWM Formula 2	1960 cc.	Works	37	1st, LR.	83.96 mph
101	8/9/1951	O'Boyle Trophy, Curragh, EI		HWM Formula 2	1960 cc.	Works	38	1st.	
102	15/9/1951	RAC Tourist Trophy, Dundrod, GB (NI)	319 miles.	Jaguar C-type	3442 cc.	Works	39	1st, BPT, team prize.	
103	23/9/1951	Modena GP, I	200 miles.	HWM Formula 2	1960 cc.	Works		Retired	Magneto and sparking plug.
104	29/9/1951	Madgwick Cup, Goodwood, GB	10 laps.	HWM Formula 2	1960 cc.	Works	40	1st, FL. Team prize.	
105	29/9/1951	Sports car race, Goodwood, GB	10 laps.	Jaguar C-type	3442 cc.	Works	41	1st, PP FL.	84.83 mph
106	29/9/1951	2nd Sept. Handicap, Goodwood, GB	10 laps.	Jaguar C-type	3442 cc.	Works	42	1st, FL. Team prize.	86.02 mph
107	29/9/1951	3rd Sept. Handicap, Goodwood, GB	10 laps.	HWM Formula 2	1960 cc.	Works		2nd.	
108	29/9/1951	*Daily Graphic* Trophy, Goodwood, GB	15 laps.	HWM Formula 2	1960 cc.	Works		5th.	Formula 1 race.
109	13/10/1951	Winfield races, Scotland, GB	25 laps.	HWM Formula 2	1960 cc.	Works	43	1st, FL. Team prize.	82.1 mph

No.	Date	Event	Distance	Car	Capacity	Entrant	#	Result	Notes
110	20/10/1951	Brands Hatch 500 cc races, GB	3 miles.	Kieft-Norton 500	498 cc.	S.C.Moss	44	1st, heat 3, DNS final.	Gearbox casing cracked.
111	20/10/1951	Brands Hatch Championship, GB	3 miles.	Kieft-Norton 500	498 cc.	S.C.Moss	45	1st, heat 2.	
112	20/10/1951	Brands Hatch Championship, GB	3 miles.	Kieft-Norton 500	498 cc.	S.C.Moss	46	1st, final.	
	1952								
	22/1/1952	Monte Carlo Rally	c.2000 miles.	Sunbeam-Talbot 90	2267 cc.	Works		2nd.	With Navigators D. Scannell & J.A.Cooper.
	17/2/1952	Kitching Trophy Trial, GB		Harford III special	1172 cc.	C. Harrison		7th.	With J.A.Cooper.
	24/3/1952	Lyons-Charbonnieres Rally, F		Jaguar XK120	3442 cc.	S.C.Moss		2nd in class, 15th overall.	With Gregor Grant.
113	12/4/1952	Castle Combe 500 cc races, GB	10 laps.	Kieft-Norton 500	498 cc.	S.C.Moss	47	1st, LR, FL.	77.9 mph
114	12/4/1952	Castle Combe 500 cc races, GB	10 laps.	Kieft-Norton 500	498 cc.	S.C.Moss	48	1st, FL.	77.39 mph
115	12/4/1952	Castle Combe relay race, GB	10 laps.	Frazer-Nash Le Mans	1971 cc.	Gilby Eng.		UNC.	Shared car with R. Salvadori.
116	14/4/1952	Earl of March Trophy, Goodwood, GB	5 laps.	Kieft-Norton 500	498 cc.	S.C.Moss	49	1st, PP,LR.	First outing with disc brakes.
117	14/4/1952	Easter Handicap, Goodwood, GB	6 laps.	Jaguar C-Type	3442 cc.	Works		4th, FL.	Steering, dampers, split fuel tank. With N.Dewis.
118	4/5/1952	*Mille Miglia*, Brescia, I	992 miles.	Jaguar C-Type	3442 cc.	Works		Retired.	
119	10/5/1952	BRDC Silverstone 500 cc race, GB	15 laps.	Kieft-Norton 500	498 cc.	S.C.Moss		3rd, PP, FL.	75.27 mph
120	10/5/1952	BRDC Silverstone Touring car race, GB	17 laps.	Jaguar Mk VII	3442 cc.	Works	50	1st, PP, FL.	75.22 mph
121	10/5/1952	BRDC Silverstone Sports car race, GB	17 laps.	Jaguar C-Type	3442 cc.	Works	51	1st, PP, FL.	87.08 mph
122	10/5/1952	BRDC Silverstone Champions race, GB	5 laps.	Jaguar XK120	3442 cc.	Works	52	1st, FL.	79.83 mph
123	11/5/1952	Brussels GP, Bois de la Cambre, B		Kieft-Norton 500	498 cc.	S.C.Moss		Retired; collision.	Car written off.
124	18/5/1952	Swiss GP, Bremgarten, CH	280 miles.	HWM Formula 2	1960 cc.	Works		DNS; withdrawn.	Generic suspension failure; team withdrawn.
125	22/5/1952	Luxembourg GP, Findel, LU	58 miles.	Kieft-Norton 500	498 cc.	D. Annable	53	1st, heat 2.	
126	22/5/1952	Luxembourg GP, Findel, LU	58 miles.	Kieft-Norton 500	498 cc.	D. Annable		6th, final.	Magneto problem.
127	25/5/1952	Eifelrennen, Nurburgring, D	7 laps.	HWM Formula 2	1960 cc.	Works		2nd.	
128	25/5/1952	500 cc race, Nurburgring, D	71 miles	Kieft-Norton 500	498 cc.	D. Annable		PP. Retired,	Broken hub - lying second.
129	29/5/1952	British Empire Trophy, Douglas, IoM	200 miles	Frazer-Nash Le Mans	1971 cc.	Gilby Eng.		Retired.	Ignition.
130	2/6/1952	Monaco GP, MON	100 laps.	Jaguar C-Type	3442 cc.	Works		PP, Disq.	Received "outside assistance".
131	2/6/1952	Prix de Monte Carlo MON		Frazer-Nash Le Mans	1971 cc.	Works		PP, Retired.	Hub damage.
132	7/6/1952	Ulster Trophy, Dundrod, GB	34 laps.	BRM V16	1488 cc.	Works		Retired.	3 laps. Overheating, clutch, gearknob fell off!
133	14/6/1952	Le Mans 24 hours, Sarthe, F		Jaguar C-Type	3442 cc.	Works		Retired.	Overheating. All cars retired.
134	22/6/1952	Belgian GP, Spa-Francorchamps, B	315 miles.	ERA G-type	1971 cc.	Works		Retired.	Crash after engine failure.
135	29/6/1952	Sports Car race, Reims, F	50 laps.	Jaguar C-Type	3442 cc.	T. Wisdom	54	1st.	1st win with Dunlop discs.
136	29/6/1952	Marne GP, Reims, F	200 miles.	HWM Formula 2	1960 cc.	Works		UNC.	Broken oil pipe.
	11/7/1952	Alpine Rally. Int'l	2055 miles.	Sunbeam-Talbot 90	2267 cc.	Works		1st in class.	With J. Cutts.
137	19/7/1952	British GP, Silverstone, GB	249 miles.	ERA G-type	1971 cc.	Works		Retired.	Overheating.
138	19/7/1952	British GP 500 cc race, Silverstone, GB	45 miles.	Kieft-Norton 500	498 cc.	D. Annable	55	1st, PP, eq. FL.	84.98 mph, shared with Don Parker.
139	20/7/1952	Namur GP, B		Kieft-Norton 500	498 cc.	D. Annable	56	1st in heat.	
140	20/7/1952	Namur GP, B		Kieft-Norton 500	498 cc.	Works		Retired in final.	Suspension.
141	27/7/1952	Fairwood Aerodrome, Wales, GB		Kieft-Norton 500	498 cc.	Works		Retired.	Collision.
142	27/7/1952	Fairwood Aerodrome, Wales, GB		Kieft-Norton 500	498 cc.	D. Annable		3rd.	
	28/7/1952	Prescott Hill Climb, GB	1,127 yds.	Kieft-Norton 500	498 cc.	D. Annable		2nd.	
143	2/8/1952	*Daily Mail* Trophy, Boreham, GB	67 laps.	ERA G-type	1971 cc.	Works		3rd.	
144	2/8/1952	Boreham Sports Car race, GB	34 laps.	Jaguar C-Type	3442 cc.	T. Wisdom	57	1st, PP, FL.	90.00 mph
145	2/8/1952	Boreham 500 cc race, GB	10 laps.	Cooper-Norton 500	498 cc.	Works		3rd.	
146	4/8/1952	Sprint meeting, Brands Hatch, GB	10 laps.	Kieft-Norton 500	498 cc.	D. Annable		2nd in heat 4.	
147	4/8/1952	Sprint meeting, Brands Hatch, GB	10 laps.	Kieft-Norton 500	498 cc.	D. Annable		2nd in final.	
148	4/8/1952	Telegraph Trophy, Brands Hatch, GB	30 laps.	Kieft-Norton 500	498 cc.	D. Annable	58	1st, heat 3, LR.	71.43 mph
149	4/8/1952	Telegraph Trophy, Brands Hatch, GB	30 laps.	Kieft-Norton 500	498 cc.	D. Annable		Retired in final.	Con-rod.
	5/8/1952	7-day records, Montlhéry, F	16, 851.73 miles.	Jaguar XK120	3442 cc.	Works			10,000miles@100.66mph, with Fairman, Hadley & Johnson.
150	16/8/1952	9-hour race, Goodwood, GB		Jaguar C-type	3442 cc.	Works		5th, PP.	Co-driver Peter Walker.
151	17/8/1952	Dutch GP, Zandvoort, NL	90 laps.	ERA G-type	1971 cc.	Works		Retired.	Engine, 74 laps.
152	17/8/1952	Dutch GP 500 cc race, Zandvoort, NL	17 laps.	Cooper-Norton 500 Mk V	498 cc.	Works	59	1st.	
152	23/8/1952	Turnberry meeting, GB	10 laps.	Jaguar C-type	3442 cc.	T. Wisdom	60	1st, heat 2.	
154	23/8/1952	Turnberry meeting, GB	10 laps.	Jaguar C-type	3442 cc.	T. Wisdom	61	1st in final.	
155	23/8/1952	Turnberry meeting, GB	10 laps.	Cooper-Norton 500 Mk V	498 cc.	Works	62	1st, PP.	
156	31/8/1952	Grenzlandring, NL		Cooper-Norton 500 Mk V	498 cc.	Works		3rd.	
157	7/9/1952	Italian GP, Monza, I	313 miles.	Connaught A-type	1496 cc.	Works		Retired.	Engine, 46 laps.
158	27/9/1952	500 cc race, Goodwood, GB	5 laps.	Cooper-Norton 500 Mk V	498 cc.	Works	63	1st.	
159	27/9/1952	Sports car race, Goodwood, GB	5 laps.	Jaguar C-type	3442 cc.	T. Wisdom		2nd, PP, LR.	85.37 mph
160	27/9/1952	Madgwick Cup, Goodwood, GB	7 laps.	ERA G-type	1971 cc.	Works		Retired.	Collision.
161	27/9/1952	Formule libre Trophy, Goodwood, GB		ERA G-type	1971 cc.	Works		5th.	
162	4/10/1952	500 cc race, Castle Combe, GB	7 laps.	Cooper-Norton 500 Mk V	498 cc.	Works	64	1st, heat 1.	
163	4/10/1952	500 cc race, Castle Combe, GB	10 laps.	Cooper-Norton 500 Mk V	498 cc.	Works	65	1st, PP, LR in final.	80.58 mph
164	4/10/1952	Formula 2 race, Castle Combe, GB	20 laps.	ERA G-type	1971 cc.	Works		PP. Retired,	Steering.
165	11/10/1952	Sports car race, Charterhall, GB	20 laps.	Jaguar C-type	3442 cc.	T. Wisdom		2nd.	
166	11/10/1952	500 cc race, Charterhall, GB	25 laps.	Cooper-Norton 500 Mk V	498 cc.	Works		2nd, FL, BPT. 76.9 mph	
167	11/10/1952	Formula 2 race, Charterhall, GB	40 laps.	ERA G-type	1971 cc.	Works		4th.	
	12/11/1952	*Daily Express* Rally, GB	1250 miles.	Jaguar XK 120 Coupé	3442 cc.	Works		13th.	With Navigator J.A Cooper.
	2/12/1952	15 Countries demonstration run.	3,352 miles.	Humber Super Snipe	4086 cc.	Works		Finished.	With J. Cutts, L. Johnson, D. Humphrey.
	1953								
	20/1/1953	Monte Carlo Rally	2000 miles.	Sunbeam-Talbot 90	2267 cc.	Works		6th.	With Navigators D.Scannell and J.A.Cooper.
	17/3/1953	Record attempt, Jabbeke, B	See right.	Sunbeam-Talbot Alpine	2267 cc.	Works			120.459 mph
	18/3/1953	Record attempt, Montlhéry, F	See right.	Sunbeam-Talbot Alpine	2267 cc.	Works			116 mph
168	6/4/1953	Lavant Cup, Goodwood, GB	7 laps.	Cooper-Alta Special	1960 cc.	S.C.Moss.		7th.	
169	6/4/1953	Earl of March Trophy, Goodwood, GB	5 laps.	Cooper-Norton 500	498 cc.	S.C.Moss.		3rd.	
170	26/4/1953	*Mille Miglia*, Brescia, I	992 miles.	Jaguar C-type	3442 cc.	Works		Retired.	Rear axle. With Navigator M. Morris-Goodall.
171	9/5/1953	BRDC Int'l Trophy, Silverstone, GB	15 laps.	Cooper-Alta Special	1960 cc.	S.C.Moss.		2nd, heat 1, FL.	
172	9/5/1953	BRDC Int'l Trophy, Silverstone, GB	30 laps.	Cooper-Alta Special	1960 cc.	S.C.Moss.		9th in final.	
173	9/5/1953	Touring car race, Silverstone, GB	17 laps.	Jaguar Mk VII	3442 cc.	Works	66	1st, PP, FL.	76.36 mph
174	9/5/1953	Sports car race , Silverstone, GB	17 laps.	Jaguar C-type	3442 cc.	Works		7th.	Rolled car in practice.

#	Date	Race	Distance	Car	cc	Entrant		Result	Speed	Notes
175	16/5/1953	Ulster Trophy, Dundrod, GB	10 laps.	Connaught A-type	1496 cc.	Works		2nd, heat 1, PP, FL.	84.46 mph	
176	16/5/1953	Ulster Trophy, Dundrod, GB	10 laps.	Connaught A-type	1496 cc.	Works		DNS final;		disqualified after substitute (Salvadori's) car offered.
177	25/5/1953	Coronation Trophy, Crystal Palace, GB	17 laps.	Cooper-Alta Special	1960 cc.	S.C.Moss.		4th, heat 1.		
178	25/5/1953	Coronation Trophy, Crystal Palace, GB	10 laps.	Cooper-Alta Special	1960 cc.	S.C.Moss.		5th in final.		
179	25/5/1953	500 cc race, Crystal Palace, GB	10 laps.	Cooper-Norton 500	498 cc.	S.C.Moss.	67	1st, FL.	70.68 mph	
180	31/5/1953	Eifelrennen, Nurburgring, D	5 laps.	Cooper-Alta Special	1960 cc.	S.C.Moss.		6th.		
181	31/5/1953	500 cc race, Nurburgring, D	5 laps.	Cooper-Norton 500	498 cc.	S.C.Moss.	68	1st.	66.55 mph	
182	6/6/1953	Dutch GP, Zandvoort, NL	90 laps.	Connaught A-type	1496 cc.	Works		9th.		
183	13/6/1955	Le Mans 24 hours, Sarthe, F		Jaguar C-type	3442 cc.	Works		2nd.		Co-driver Peter Walker.
184	18/6/1953	British Empire Trophy, Douglas, IoM	16 laps.	Jaguar C-type	3442 cc.	Works		2nd, heat 3.		
185	18/6/1953	British Empire Trophy, Douglas, IoM	16 laps.	Jaguar C-type	3442 cc.	Works		4th in final.		
186	28/6/1953	Rouen GP, Les Essarts, F	60 laps.	Cooper-Alta Special	1960 cc.	S.C.Moss.		UNC.		Gearbox - no first gear.
187	5/7/1953	French GP, Reims-Gueux, F	311 miles.	Cooper-Alta Special	1960 cc.	S.C.Moss.		Retired.		Clutch.
188	5/7/1953	12 hour race, Reims, F		Jaguar C-type	3442 cc.	Works	69	1st.		With Peter Whitehead.
	10/7/1953	Alpine Rally	1947 miles.	Sunbeam-Talbot Alpine	2267 cc.	Works		Coupe des Alpes.		
189	18/7/1953	British GP 500cc race, Silverstone, GB	15 laps.	Cooper-Norton 500	498 cc.	S.C.Moss.	70	1st, PP, eq. FL.	86.37 mph, FL shared with Stuart Lewis-Evans.	
190	26/7/1953	Jubilee GP, Lisbon, P		Jaguar C-type	3442 cc.	Works		2nd.		
191	2/8/1953	German GP Nurburgring, D	18 laps.	Cooper-Alta Mk2	1960 cc.	S.C.Moss.		6th.		
192	9/8/1953	GP of Sables d'Ollone, F	90 laps.	Cooper-Alta Mk2	1960 cc.	S.C.Moss.		4th, heat 1.		
193	9/8/1953	GP of Sables d'Ollone, F	90 laps.	Cooper-Alta Mk2	1960 cc.	S.C.Moss.		5th, heat 2.		3rd on aggregate.
194	15/8/1953	F2 meeting, Charterhall, GB	50 laps.	Cooper-Alta Mk2	1960 cc.	S.C.Moss.		PP, Retired.		Fuel injection.
195	15/8/1953	Formule libre, Charterhall, GB	50 laps.	Cooper-Alta Mk2	1960 cc.	S.C.Moss.		Retired.		Engine.
196	15/8/1953	500cc race, Charterhall, GB	20 laps.	Cooper-Norton 500	498 cc.	S.C.Moss.	71	1st.		
197	22/8/1955	9-hours race, Goodwood, GB		Jaguar C-type	3442 cc.	Works		Retired.		Engine. Co-driver Peter Walker.
198	5/9/1953	RAC Tourist Trophy, Dundrod, GB (NI)	823 miles.	Jaguar C-type	3442 cc.	Works		4th. 1st, 3 litre class		Co-driver Peter Walker.
199	7/9/1953	Italian GP, Monza, I	313 miles.	Cooper-Alta Mk2	1960 cc.	S.C.Moss.		13th.		
200	19/9/1953	London Trophy, Crystal Palace, GB		Cooper-Alta Mk2	1960 cc.	S.C.Moss.	72	1st, PP, heat 1.		
201	19/9/1953	London Trophy, Crystal Palace, GB		Cooper-Alta Mk2	1960 cc.	S.C.Moss.	73	1st, PP, heat 2.		1st on aggregate.
202	19/9/1953	Redex Trophy, Crystal Palace, GB		Cooper-Norton 500	498 cc.	S.C.Moss.		2nd, heat 1.		
203	19/9/1953	Redex Trophy, Crystal Palace, GB		Cooper-Norton 500	498 cc.	S.C.Moss.		Retired.		Engine.
	20/9/1953	Prescott Hill Climb, GB	1,127 yds.	Cooper-Alta Mk2	1960 cc.	S.C.Moss.		1st F2 class..		
	20/9/1953	Prescott Hill Climb, GB	1,127 yds.	Cooper-JAP 1100 MkVII	1097 cc.	S.C.Moss.			46.48 mph	
204	26/9/1953	Madgwick Cup, Goodwood, GB	7 laps.	Cooper-Alta Mk2	1960 cc.	S.C.Moss.		2nd.		
205	26/9/1953	Woodcote Cup, Goodwood, GB	5 laps.	Cooper-Alta Mk2	1960 cc.	S.C.Moss.		2nd, F2 race.		
206	26/9/1953	Goodwood Trophy, Goodwood, GB	10 laps.	Cooper-Alta Mk2	1960 cc.	S.C.Moss.		4th.		
207	26/9/1953	500 cc race, Goodwood, GB	3 laps.	Cooper-Norton 500	498 cc.	S.C.Moss.		Retired.		Magneto drive.
208	3/10/1953	500cc race, Castle Combe, GB		Cooper-Norton 500	498 cc.	S.C.Moss.	74	Retired.		Oil on clutch.
209	3/10/1953	Fry memorial race, Castle Combe, GB		Cooper-JAP 1100 MkVII	1097 cc.	S.C.Moss.		1st, heat 2 LR.	81.19 mph	
								Retired.		Collision with A.P.Rolt.
	1954^									
	18/1/1954	Monte Carlo Rally	2000 miles.	Sunbeam-Talbot 90	2267 cc.	Works		15th.		With Navigators D.Scannell and J.A.Cooper.
210	7/3/1954	12-hour race, Sebring, USA	170 laps.	OSCA sports	1452 cc.	Cunningham	75	1st.		With Bill Lloyd.
211	10/4/1954	British Empire Trophy, Oulton Park, GB	20 laps.	Leonard-MG	1250 cc.	L. Leonard		3rd, heat 1.		
212	10/4/1954	British Empire Trophy, Oulton Park, GB	30 laps.	Leonard-MG	1250 cc.	L. Leonard		Retired.		Engine.
213	17/4/1954	500cc race, Goodwood, GB	3 laps.	Beart-Cooper MkVIIA	498 cc.	F. Beart		7th.		
214	9/5/1954	GP of Bordeaux, F	200 miles.	Maserati 250F	2493 cc.	S.C.Moss.		4th, FL.	67.67 mph	
215	15/5/1954	BRDC Int'l Trophy, Silverstone, GB	15 laps.	Maserati 250F	2493 cc.	S.C.Moss.		3rd, heat 1.		
216	15/5/1954	BRDC Int'l Trophy, Silverstone, GB	15 laps.	Maserati 250F	2493 cc.	S.C.Moss.		Retired in final.		Broken de Dion tube.
217	15/5/1954	BRDC Touring car race, Silverstone, GB	17 laps.	Jaguar Mk VII	3442 cc.	Works		3rd, PP, eq. FL, LR.	77.48 mph, shared with Rolt and Appleyard.	
218	15/5/1954	BRDC 500 cc race, Silverstone, GB	10 laps.	Beart-Cooper MkVIIA	498 cc.	F. Beart	76	1st, eq. FL	86.37 mph, shared with Les Leston.	
219	23/5/1954	Eifelrennen F3 race, Nurburgring, D	61 miles.	Beart-Cooper MkVIIA	498 cc.	F. Beart	77	1st.		
220	29/5/1954	Formule Libre 200 mile race, Aintree, GB	17 laps.	Maserati 250F	2493 cc.	S.C.Moss.		3rd, heat 1.		
221	29/5/1954	Formule Libre 200 mile race, Aintree, GB	34 laps.	Maserati 250F	2493 cc.	S.C.Moss.		1st in final.		
222	29/5/1954	500 cc race, Aintree, GB	10 laps.	Beart-Cooper MkVIIA	498 cc.	F. Beart	79	1st, FL.	70.92 mph	
223	6/6/1954	Rome GP, Castelfusano, I	60 laps.	Maserati 250F	2493 cc.	S.C.Moss.		UNC.		Transmission, 54 laps.
224	12/6/1954	Le Mans 24-hour race, Sarthe, F		Jaguar D-type	3442 cc.	Works		Retired.		Brakes. C/d Peter Walker.
225	20/6/1954	Belgian GP, Spa-Francorchamps, B	300 miles.	Maserati 250F	2493 cc.	S.C.Moss.		3rd.		First F1 World Championship points.
226	4/7/1954	12-hour race, Reims, F		Jaguar D-type	3442 cc.	Works		Retired.		Transmission.
	9/7/1954	Alpine Rally	c. 2500 miles.	Sunbeam-Talbot Alpine	2267 cc.	Works		Coupe des Alpes d'Or.		With Navigator John Cutts.
227	17/7/1954	British GP, Silverstone, GB	90 laps.	Maserati 250F	2493 cc.	S.C.Moss.		Retired, FL.		Broken drive shaft, lap 81.
228	17/7/1954	500 cc race, Silverstone, GB	17 laps.	Beart-Cooper MkVIIA	498 cc.	F. Beart	80	1st		
229	25/7/1954	GP of Caen, F	60 laps.	Maserati 250F	2493 cc.	S.C.Moss.		2nd, LR.	92.4 mph	
230	1/8/1954	German GP, Nurburgring, D	22 laps.	Maserati 250F	2493 cc.	S.C.Moss.		Retired.		Engine, lap 2. SM 'works' driver in his own car.
231	2/8/1954	500cc races, Brands Hatch, GB	10 laps.	Beart-Cooper MkVIIA	498 cc.	F. Beart		2nd, heat 4.		
232	2/8/1954	500cc races, Brands Hatch, GB	40 laps.	Beart-Cooper MkVIIA	498 cc.	F. Beart		2nd in final.		
233	7/8/1954	Gold Cup, Oulton Park, GB	36 laps.	Maserati 250F	2493 cc.	S.C.M/Works	81	1st, FL.	85.11 mph	
234	7/8/1954	Formule Libre race, Oulton Park, GB	20 laps.	Maserati 250F	2493 cc.	S.C.M/Works	82	1st, LR.	85.4 mph	
235	7/8/1954	500cc race, Oulton Park	27 laps.	Beart-Cooper MkVIIA	498 cc.	F. Beart	83	1st.		
236	15/8/1954	GP of Pescara, I	254 laps.	Maserati 250F	2493 cc.	S.C.M/Works		PP. Retired.		Oil pipe. SM works driver in his own car.
237	22/8/1954	Swiss GP, Bremgarten, CH	66 laps.	Maserati 250F	2493 cc.	Works		Retired.		Oil pump.
238	5/9/1954	Italian GP, Monza, I	80 laps.	Maserati 250F	2493 cc.	S.C.M/works		Retired.		Oil tank split, 78 laps. Leading.
239	11/9/1954	RAC Tourist Trophy, Dundrod, GB	680 miles.	Jaguar D-type	3442 cc.	Works		18th.		Lost oil pressure. Co-driver Peter Walker.
240	25/9/1954	Goodwood Trophy, Goodwood, GB	21 laps.	Maserati 250F	2493 cc.	S.C.M/Works	84	1st, PP, FL.	92.9 mph	
241	25/9/1954	Woodcote Cup, Goodwood, GB	10 laps.	Maserati 250F	2493 cc.	S.C.M/Works		3rd.		Formule Libre race.
241	25/9/1954	Sports Car race, Goodwood, GB	5 laps.	Lister-Bristol	1971 cc.	Works		2nd, FL.	83.72 mph	
242	25/9/1954	500cc races Goodwood, GB	5 laps.	Beart-Cooper MkVIIA	498 cc.	F. Beart		2nd, LR.	85.88 mph	
243	2/10/1954	*Daily Telegraph* Trophy, Aintree, GB	17 laps.	Maserati 250F	2493 cc.	S.C.Moss.	85	1st, PP eq. FL.	86.54 mph, shared with Hawthorn.	
244	2/10/1954	Formule Libre race, Aintree, GB	17 laps.	Maserati 250F	2493 cc.	S.C.Moss.	86	1st, PP, LR.	89.55 mph	
245	2/10/1954	500cc race, Aintree, GB	17 laps.	Beart-Cooper MkVIIA	498 cc.	F. Beart	87	1st, PP, eq. FL.	78.72, shared with J Russell.	
246	10/10/1954	Coupé du Salon, Montlhéry, F	24 laps.	Connaught ALSR	1496 cc.	P. Bell	88	1st, 1500 class.		

247	24/10/1954	Spanish GP, Barcelona. ES	80 laps.	Maserati 250F	2493 cc.	S.C.M/Works		Retired.	Oil pump, lap 21.
	29/11/1954	Great American Mountain Rally, USA	1100 miles.	Sunbeam-Talbot Alpine	2267 cc.	Works		Team award.	With Navigator Ron Kessel.

1955

248	16/1/1955	Argentine GP, Buenos Aires, ARG	96 laps.	MB W196	2498 cc.	Works		4th.	Shared with Kling and Herrmann.
249	30/1/1955	City GP, Buenos Aires, ARG	30 laps.	MB W196	2982 cc.	Works		3rd, FL heat 1.	
250	30/1/1955	City GP, Buenos Aires, ARG	30 laps.	MB W196	2982 cc.	Works	89	1st, heat 2. eq. FL.	75.48 mph, shared with Farina, 2nd on aggregate.
251	13/3/1955	12-hour race, Sebring, USA		Healey 100S	2660 cc.	Works		6th.	Co-driver Lance Macklin.
252	11/4/1955	Glover Trophy, Goodwood, GB	21 laps.	Maserati 250F	2493 cc.	SM Ltd.**		PP. Retired,	Fuel injection blocked, lap 13.
253	11/4/1955	Chichester Cup, Goodwood, GB	7 laps.	Maserati 250F	2493 cc.	SM Ltd.		3rd.	
254	11/4/1955	Sports car race, Goodwood, GB	5 laps.	Beart-Rodger-Climax	1098 cc.	F. Beart		Retired.	Throttle.
255	24/4/1955	GP of Bordeaux, F	123 laps.	Maserati 250F	2493 cc.	SM Ltd.		4th, FL.	67.67 mph
256	1/5/1955	*Mille Miglia*, Brescia, I	992 miles.	M-B300SLR	2982 cc.	Works	90	1st, NR.	97.96 mph With D. Jenkinson. All-time course record.
257	7/5/1955	BRDC Int'l Trophy Silverstone, GB	60 laps.	Maserati 250F	2493 cc.	SM Ltd.		Retired.	Engine.
257	7/5/1955	BRDC Sports car race, Silverstone, GB	17 laps.	Beart-Rodger-Climax	1098 cc.	F. Beart		Last.	Ignition, door flew open, etc...
259	22/5/1955	Monaco GP, Monte Carlo, MON	100 laps.	MB W196	2498 cc.	Works		UNC.	Valve damage. Leading for 80 laps.
260	29/5/1955	Eifelrennen, Nurburgring, D	10 laps.	M-B300SLR	2982 cc.	Works		2nd.	
261	5/6/1955	Belgian GP, Spa-Francorchamps, B	36 laps.	MB W196	2498 cc.	Works		2nd.	
262	11/6/1955	Le Mans 24-hours race, Sarthe, F		M-B300SLR	2982 cc.	Works		Withdrawn.	Team withdrawn; Moss/Fangio 3 laps in lead.
263	19/6/1955	Dutch GP Zandvoort, NL	100 laps.	MB W196	2498 cc.	Works		2nd.	
264	16/7/1955	British GP, Aintree	90 laps.	MB W196	2498 cc.	Works	91	1st, PP, LR.	89.7 mph, First Championship GP win.
265	24/7/1955	Civil Governor's Cup, Lisbon, P	25 laps.	Porsche 550	1498 cc.	Works	92	1st, PP, FL.	83.53 mph
267	7/8/1955	Swedish Sports Car GP, Råbelöv, S	32 laps.	MB300SLR	2982 cc.	Works		2nd, eq. FL.	2' 24.5", shared with Fangio.
268	13/8/1955	Redex Trophy, Snetterton, GB	25 laps.	Maserati 250F	2493 cc.	SM Ltd.		3rd, FL.	83.79 mph
269	20/8/1955	9-hours race, Goodwood, GB	309 laps.	Porsche 550	1498 cc.	Works		Retired.	Collision. Driving with von Hanstein; leading.
270	27/6/1955	*Daily Herald* Trophy, Oulton Park, GB	80 laps.	Connaught	1496 cc.	P. Bell		7th, 1500 class.	
271	27/8/1955	*Sporting Life* Trophy, Oulton Park, GB	15 laps.	Standard 10	948 cc.	?		2nd, 1100 class.	
272	3/9/1955	*Daily Telegraph* Trophy, Aintree, GB	17 laps.	Maserati 250F	2493 cc.	SM Ltd.		Retired.	Engine.
273	11/9/1955	Italian GP, Monza, I	50 laps.	MB W196	2498 cc.	Works		Retired, LR.	134.04 mph piston, lap 28.
274	17/9/1955	RAC Tourist Trophy, Dundrod, GB (NI)	84 laps.	M-B300SLR	2982 cc.	Works	93	1st, BPT.	Co-driver John Fitch.
275	24/9/1955	Gold Cup, Oulton Park, GB	54 laps.	Maserati 250F	2493 cc.	SM Ltd.	94	1st, LR.	87.81 mph
276	16/10/1955	Targa Florio, Madonie, Sicily, I	13 laps.	M-B300SLR	2982 cc.	Works	95	1st, LR.	62.2 mph, Co-driver Peter Collins.
277	9/12/1955	Governor's Trophy, Nassau.	30 laps.	Healey 100S	2660 cc.	Works		6th.	
278	9/12/1955	Nassau Trophy, Nassau	60 laps.	Healey 100S	2660 cc.	Works		Retired.	F. Suspension failed.

1956

279	7/1/1956	NZ GP, Ardmore, NZ	210 miles.	Maserati 250F	2493 cc.	SM Ltd.	96	1st, PP, LR.	78.4 mph
280	7/1/1956	Sports car handicap, Ardmore, NZ	32 miles.	Porsche 550	1498 cc.	Works	97	1st.	
281	22/1/1956	Argentine GP, Buenos Aires, ARG	238 miles.	Maserati 250F	2493 cc.	Works		Retired.	Engine.
282	29/1/1956	1000km race, Buenos Aires, ARG	1000 km.	Maserati 300S	2991 cc.	Works	98	1st.	Co-driver Carlos Menditeguy.
283	5/2/1956	Buenos Aires GP, Mendoza, ARG	60 laps.	Maserati 250F	2493 cc.	Works		2nd.	
284	24/3/1956	12-hour race, Sebring, USA	194 laps.	Aston Martin DB3S	2922 cc.	Works		Retired.	Engine. Co-driver Peter Collins.
285	2/4/1956	Glover Trophy, Goodwood, GB	32 laps.	Maserati 250F	2493 cc.	Works	99	1st, PP, LR.	95.79 mph
286	2/4/1956	Sports Car race, Goodwood, GB	15 laps.	Aston Martin DB3S	2922 cc.	Works	100	1st, PP FL.	90.95 mph
287	14/4/1956	British Empire Trophy, Oulton Park, GB	16 laps.	Cooper Bobtail	1460 cc.	Works		4th, FL in heat.	84.23 mph
288	14/4/1956	British Empire Trophy Oulton Park, GB	25 laps.	Cooper Bobtail	1460 cc.	Works	101	1st, FL in final.	84.95 mph
289	23/4/1956	200 mile race, Aintree, GB	67 laps.	Maserati 250F	2493 cc.	SM Ltd.	102	1st.	
290	23/4/1956	Sports Car Race, Aintree, GB	30 laps.	Cooper Bobtail	1460 cc.	SM Ltd.		5th.	
291	29/4/1956	*Mille Miglia*, Brescia, I	992 miles.	Maserati 350S	3483 cc.	Works		CRA.	Skid. With Denis Jenkinson.
292	5/5/1956	BRDC Int'l Trophy, Silverstone, GB	60 laps (174 miles)	Vanwall	2490 cc.	Works	103	1st, PP eq. LR.	102.3 mph, shared with Hawthorn.
293	5/5/1956	BRDC Sports Car race, Silverstone, GB	25 laps.	Aston Martin DB3S	2922 cc.	Works		2nd.	
294	13/5/1956	Monaco GP, Monte Carlo, MON	195 miles.	Maserati 250F	2493 cc.	Works	104	1st.	
295	21/5/1956	London Trophy, Crystal Palace, GB	10 laps.	Maserati 250F	2493 cc.	SM Ltd.	105	1st, PP, FL, heat 1.	79.4 mph
296	21/5/1956	London Trophy, Crystal Palace, GB	10 laps.	Maserati 250F	2493 cc.	SM Ltd.	106	1st, LR, heat 2.	79.94 mph, 1st on aggregate.
297	21/5/1956	Anerley Trophy, Crystal Palace, GB	10 laps.	Cooper Bobtail	1460 cc.	SM Ltd.		2nd.	
298	21/5/1956	Norbury Trophy, Crystal Palace, GB	10 laps.	Cooper Bobtail	1460 cc.	SM Ltd.	107	1st, LR.	77.22 mph
299	27/5/1956	1000km race, Nurburgring, D	44 laps.	Maserati 300S	2991 cc.	Works	108	1st.	Co-driver Jean Behra.
300	3/6/1956	Belgian GP, Spa-Francorchamps, B	36 laps.	Maserati 250F	2493 cc.	Works		3rd, LR.	124.15 mph Took over C. Perdisa's car.
301	24/6/1956	Supercortemaggiore GP, Monza I	1000 km.	Maserati 200S	1993 cc.	Works		2nd.	Co-driver C. Perdisa.
302	1/7/1956	12-hour race, Reims, F	1,226 miles.	Cooper Bobtail	1460 cc.	SM Ltd.		Retired.	Engine overheating. Co-driver Phil Hill.
303	1/7/1956	French GP, Reims, F	515 miles	Maserati 250F	2493 cc.	Works		5th.	Gear lever broke off, lap 22.Took over Perdisa's car.
304	8/7/1956	Rouen GP, Les Essarts, F	205 miles.	Aston Martin DB3S	2922 cc.	Works		2nd.	
305	14/7/1956	British GP, Silverstone, GB	303 miles.	Maserati 250F	2493 cc.	Works		Retired, PP FL.	102.104 mph Gearbox. Led for 68 laps.
306	14/7/1956	GP Sports race, Silverstone, GB	25 laps.	Maserati 300S	2991 cc.	Works	109	1st, PP FL.	96.67 mph
307	22/7/1956	Sports Car GP, Bari, I	124 miles.	Maserati 300S	2991 cc.	Works	110	1st PP, FL.	83.11 mph
308	28/7/1956	Le Mans 24-hour race, Sarthe, F		Aston Martin DB3S	2922 cc.	Works		2nd.	Co-driver Peter Collins 298 laps.
309	5/8/1956	German GP, Nurburgring, D	22 laps.	Maserati 250F	2493 cc.	Works		2nd.	
310	5/8/1956	1500cc Sports car race, Nurburgring, D	7 laps.	Maserati 150S	1484 cc.	Works		2nd, PP, FL.	83.2 mph
311	12/8/1956	Swedish Sports Car GP, Råbelöv, S	153 laps.	Maserati 300S	2991 cc.	Works		PP, Retired,	Fire, then brakes. 2 cars used.
312	18/8/1956	*Daily Herald* Trophy, Oulton park, GB	40 laps.	Aston Martin DB3S	2922 cc.	Works	111	1st, PP, FL.	78.39 mph
313	18/8/1956	*Sporting Life* Trophy, Oulton Park, GB	10 laps.	Cooper Bobtail	1460 cc.	Willment	112	1st, FL.	77.41 mph
314	2/9/1956	Italian GP, Monza, I	50 laps.	Maserati 250F	2493 cc.	Works	113	1st, FL.	135.4 mph
	3/9/1956	Record attempts, Monza, I	50 km.	Lotus XI	1098 cc.	Works			50km @ 135.54 mph
	3/4/1956	Record attempts, Monza, I	50 miles.	Lotus XI	1098 cc.	Works			50miles @ 132.77 mph
	17/9/1956	Tour de France, F		MB 300SL	2996 cc.	SM Ltd.		2nd.	With Georges Huel.
315	4/11/1956	GP of Caracas, VE	85 laps.	Maserati 300S	2991 cc.	Works	114	1st, PP, FL.	85.53 mph
316	25/11/1956	T.T. race, Melbourne, AUS	100 miles.	Maserati 300S	2991 cc.	Works	115	1st, LR.	1' 55.8"
317	02/23/56	Australian GP, Melbourne, AUS	248 miles.	Maserati 250F	2493 cc.	Works	116	1st, PP, LR.	100.26 mph
318	9/12/1956	Nassau Trophy, Bahamas	210 miles.	Maserati 300S	2991 cc.	Cunningham	117	1st, FL.	

1957

No.	Date	Event	Distance	Car	cc	Entrant	Win	Result	Notes
319	12/1/1957	Argentine GP, Buenos Aires, ARG	100 laps.	Maserati 250F	2493 cc.	Works		8th, PP, FL.	83.58 mph
320	20/1/1957	1000km race, Buenos Aires, ARG	98 laps.	Maserati 450S/300S	4477/2991	Works		2nd, FL.	105.95 mph 450S broke, took over 300S
321	27/1/1957	Buenos Aires City GP, Autodrome, ARG	30 laps.	Maserati 250F	2493 cc.	Works		Retired heat 1.	Heat exhaustion.
322	27/1/1957	Buenos Aires City GP, Autodrome, ARG	30 laps.	Maserati 250F	2493 cc.	Works		6th.	6th on aggregate. Took over C. Menditiguy's car.
323	24/2/1957	Sports car GP of Cuba, Havana, CU	90 laps.	Maserati 200S/300S	1993/2991	Chimeri/Pines		Retired.	Both engines failed.
324	24/3/1957	12-hour race, Sebring, USA	197 laps.	Maserati 300S	2991 cc.	Works		2nd 4th in Index.	Co-driver Harry Schell.
325	7/4/1957	Syracuse GP, I	80 laps.	Vanwall	2490 cc.	Works		3rd, LR.	107.39 mph
326	22/4/1957	Glover Trophy, Goodwood, GB	32 laps.	Vanwall	2490 cc.	Works		PP. Retired.	Throttle linkage, lap 13. Leading.
327	12/5/1957	*Mille Miglia*, Brescia, I	992 miles.	Maserati 450S	4477 cc.	Works		Retired.	Brake pedal snapped at 7 miles. With Denis Jenkinson.
328	19/5/1957	Monaco GP, Monte Carlo, MON	105 laps.	Vanwall	2490 cc.	Works		CRA.	Brake failure, Lap 4. Leading.
329	26/5/1957	1000km race, Nurburgring, D	44 laps.	Maserati 450S/300S	4477/2991	Works		5th FL.	86.43 mph, lost wheel; took over Scarlatti then Godia 300.
330	22/6/1957	Le Mans 24 hour race, Sarthe, F		Maserati 450S Zagato	4477 cc.	Works		Retired.	Transmission. Co-driver Harry Schell.
331	20/7/1957	British GP, Aintree, GB	90 laps.	Vanwall	2490 cc.	Works	118	1st, PP, LR.	90.60 mph Swapped cars with Tony Brooks.
332	4/8/1957	German GP, Nurburgring, D	22 laps.	Vanwall	2490 cc.	Works		5th.	
333	11/8/1957	Swedish Sports Car GP, Ràbelöv	145 laps.	Maserati 450S & 300S	4477/2991	Works	119	1st (& 3rd).	Co-drove with both Behra/Schell & Bonnier/Schell/Scarlatti.
334	18/8/1957	GP of Pescara, I	18 laps.	Vanwall	2490 cc.	Works	120	1st, LR.	97.87 mph
	23/8/1957	Record attempts, Bonneville, USA	see right.	MG EX181	1500 cc.	Works			1km @ 254.64 mph,
									1mile @ 245.11mph,
									5km @ 243.08 mph,
									5miles @ 235.69 mph,
									10km @ 234.70 mph
335	8/9/1957	Italian GP, Monza, I	87 laps.	Vanwall	2490 cc.	Works	121	1st.	120.28 mph
	15/9/1957	Tour de France, F		MB 300 SL	2996 cc.	SM Ltd.		4th.	With Peter Garnier.
336	27/10/1957	Moroccan GP, Casablanca	250 miles.	Vanwall	2490 cc.	Works		PPP, DNS.	Flu. Provisional Pole Position.
337	3/11/1957	Venezuelan GP Caracas, VE	101 laps.	Maserati 450S (X2)	4477 cc.	Works		PP, FL. Retired.	3' 38". Collision with Dressler, took over Behra's car; Retired.
338	3/12/1957	Tourist Trophy, Nassau, BA.	60 laps.	Aston Martin DBR2	3670 cc.	Works		24th.	Fuel pump failing.
339	3/12/1957	Governor's Trophy, Nassau	30 laps.	Aston Martin DBR2	3670 cc.	Works		4th.	
340	8/12/1957	100 mile race, Nassau, BA	100 miles.	Ferrari 290S	3480 cc.	J. de Vroom	122	1st.	DBR2 wrecked by another entrant; borrowed de Vroom car.
341	8/12/1957	Nassau Trophy, Nassau, BA	210 miles.	Ferrari 290S	3480 cc.	J. de Vroom	123	1st.	

1958

No.	Date	Event	Distance	Car	cc	Entrant	Win	Result	Notes
342	19/1/1958	Argentine GP, Buenos Aires, ARG	194 miles.	Cooper-Climax	1960 cc.	RRC Walker	124	1st.	First GP win for Cooper. 1st. rear-engined win since 1939.
343	26/1/1958	1000km race, Buenos Aires, ARG	106 laps.	Porsche 500ARSK	1588 cc.	Works		3rd, 1st in class.	Co-driver Jean Behra.
344	2/2/1958	Buenos Aires City GP, Mendoza, ARG	89 miles.	Cooper-Climax	1960 cc.	RRC Walker		Retired.	Rammed by Iglesias.
345	23/2/1958	Sports Car GP of Cuba, Havana, CU	310 miles.	Ferrari 335S	4100 cc.	N.A.R.T.	125	1st.	Race stopped. Split purse with Masten Gregory.
346	22/3/1958	12-hour race, Sebring, USA	200 laps.	Aston Martin DBR1	2922 cc.	Works		LR. Retired,	93.6 mph Transmission, 90 laps. Co-driver Tony Brooks..
347	7/4/1958	Sussex Trophy, Goodwood, GB	21 laps.	Aston Martin DBR2	3910 cc.	Works	126	1st, PP LR.	92.5 mph
348	7/4/1958	Glover Trophy, Goodwood, GB	42 laps.	Cooper-Climax	1960 cc.	RRC Walker		Retired, eq. LR.	89.7 mph Stalled, lap 22. Shared LR with Hawthorn.
349	12/4/1958	British Empire Trophy, Oulton Park, GB	20 laps.	Aston Martin DBR2	3910 cc.	Works	127	1st, heat 3.	
350	12/4/1958	British Empire Trophy, Oulton Park, GB	25 laps.	Aston Martin DBR2	3910 cc.	Works	128	1st, final.LR.	
351	19/4/1958	200 mile race, Aintree, GB	67 laps.	Cooper-Climax	2015 cc.	RRC Walker	129	1st.	
352	3/5/1958	BRDC Int'l Trophy, Silverstone, GB	50 laps.	Cooper-Climax	2015 cc.	RRC Walker		Retired.	Gearbox.
353	3/5/1958	BRDC Sports car race, Silverstone, GB	25 laps.	Aston Martin DBR3/300	2992 cc.	Works		Retired.	Engine bearings, lap 14. First 3-litre car to lap over 100 mph.
354	11/5/1958	Targa Florio, Madonie, Sicily, I	13 laps.	Aston Martin DBR1	2992 cc.	Works		Retired, LR.	63.33 mph Transmission, 5 laps. Co-driver Tony Brooks.
355	5/18/58	Monaco GP, Monte Carlo, MON	200 miles.	Vanwall	2490 cc.	Works		Retired.	Valve gear, 38 laps. Leading.
356	26/5/1958	Dutch GP, Zandvoort, NL	195 miles.	Vanwall	2490 cc.	Works	130	1st, FL.	94.84 mph
357	1/6/1958	1000km race, Nurburgring, D	44 laps.	Aston Martin DBR1	2922 cc.	Works	131	1st, LR.	87.5 mph Co-driver Jack Brabham.
358	15/6/1958	Belgian GP, Spa-Francorchamps, B	24 laps.	Vanwall	2490 cc.	Works		Retired.	Error! Over-revved engine after missing gear.
359	21/6/1958	Le Mans 24 hour race, Sarthe, F		Aston Martin DBR1	2922 cc.	Works		Retired.	Engine, lap 30. Co-driver Jack Brabham.
360	29/6/1958	Two Worlds Trophy, Monza I Prix Esso	500 miles.	Maserati Special	4190 cc.	Zanetti		4th, heat 1.	
361	29/6/1958	Two Worlds Trophy, Monza I Prix Mobil	500 miles.	Maserati Special	4190 cc.	Zanetti		5th, heat 2.	
362	29/6/1958	Two Worlds Trophy, Monza I	500 miles.	Maserati Special	4190 cc.	Zanetti		CRA, heat 3.	Steering sheared off at 165 mph
363	6/7/1958	Coupé de Vitesse, Reims, F	30 laps.	Cooper-Climax F2	1475 cc.	RRC Walker		Retired, FL, LR.	118.51 mph Engine Oil pressure.
364	6/7/1958	French GP, Reims-Gueux, F	50 laps.	Vanwall	2490 cc.	Works		2nd.	Front brake locking up.
365	13/7/1958	Sports Car race, Villa Real, P	35 laps.	Maserati 300S	2991 cc.	Works	132	1st, PP, LR.	88.28 mph
366	19/7/1958	British GP, Silverstone, GB	255 miles.	Vanwall	2490 cc.	Works		PP. Retired.	Valve gear, lap 26
367	19/7/1958	Sports Car race, Silverstone, GB	75 miles.	Lister-Jaguar	3781 cc.	Works	133	1st, PP eq. FL.	99.41 mph, shared with Cliff Allison.
368	20/7/1958	GP of Caen, F	188 miles.	Cooper-Climax F1	2495 cc.	RRC Walker	134	1st, PP, FL.	
369	3/8/1958	German GP, Nurburgring, D	15 laps.	Vanwall	2490 cc.	Works		Retired, LR.	92.9 mph Magneto, lap 3.
370	10/8/1958	Kannonloppet, Karlskoga, S	50 laps.	Maserati 300S	2991 cc.	Works	135	1st, PP, FL.	
371	15/8/1958	Copenhagen GP, Roskilde, DK	16 laps.	Maserati 300S	2991 cc.	Works		PP, Retired, heat 1.	Engine.
372	15/8/1958	Copenhagen GP, Roskilde, DK	16 laps.	JBW-Maserati	1993 cc.	B.Naylor	136	1st, heat 2 LR.	46.7"
373	16/8/1958	Copenhagen GP, Roskilde, DK	16 laps.	Maserati 300S	2991 cc.	Works		"Data inexact".	2nd on aggregate.
374	24/8/1958	Portuguese GP, Oporto, P	230 miles.	Vanwall	2490 cc.	Works	137	1st, PP.	
375	30/8/1958	100 mile races, Brands Hatch, GB	42 laps.	Cooper-Climax F2	1475 cc.	RRC Walker		2nd, heat 1, FL.	77.23 mph
376	30/8/1958	100 mile races, Brands Hatch, GB	42 laps.	Cooper-Climax F2	1475 cc.	RRC Walker	138	1st, heat 2, LR.	77.77 mph, 1st on aggregate.
377	7/9/1958	Italian GP, Monza, I	250 miles.	Vanwall	2490 cc.	Works		PP. Retired.	Gearbox, lap 18. Leading.
378	13/9/1958	RAC Tourist Trophy, Goodwood, GB	355 miles.	Aston Martin DBR1	2992 cc.	Works	139	1st, PP, LR.	93.33 mph Co-driver, Tony Brooks.
379	19/10/1958	Moroccan GP, Ain Diab, Casablanca, MO	259 miles.	Vanwall	2490 cc.	Works	140	1st, FL.	117.8 mph
380	29/11/1958	Melbourne GP, Albert Park, AUS	225 miles.	Cooper-Climax F1	2495 cc.	RRC Walker	141	1st, PP, FL, heat 1.	99.6 mph
381	29/11/1958	Melbourne GP, Albert Park, AUS	100 miles.	Cooper-Climax F1	2495 cc.	RRC Walker	142	1st, PP, LR in final.	102.26 mph

1959

No.	Date	Event	Distance	Car	cc	Entrant	Win	Result	Notes
382	10/1/1959	New Zealand GP, Ardmore, NZ	150 miles.	Cooper-Climax F1	2495 cc.	RRC Walker		PP, heat 2. Retired.	Broken half-shaft.
383	10/1/1950	New Zealand GP, Ardmore, NZ	150 miles.	Cooper-Climax F1	2495 cc.	RRC Walker	143	1st, LR in final.	85 m.p.h; Started at back of grid.
384	21/3/1959	12-hour race, Sebring, USA		Lister-Jaguar	3781 cc.	Cunningham		Disq &15th.	Outside help - shared Cunningham car.
385	30/3/1959	Glover Trophy, Goodwood, GB	101 miles.	Cooper-Climax F1	2495 cc.	RRC Walker	144	1st, FL.	94.12 mph
	8/4/1959	GP d'Europe, Paris F		Micromil		Organisers	145	1st.	

386	18/4/1958	200 mile race, Aintree	67 laps.	Cooper-BRM	2491 cc.	RRC Walker		Retired, FL, LR.	90.01 mph, Gearbox, lap c.31. Leading.
387	25/4/1959	GP of Syracuse, I	188 miles.	Cooper-Borgward F2	1493 cc.	RRC Walker	146	1st, PP.	
388	2/5/1959	BRDC Int'l, Silverstone, GB	50 laps.	BRM P25	2491 cc.	Works		PP, Retired.	Brakes, lap 5. Leading.
389	2/5/1959	BRDC GT race, Silverstone, GB	12 laps.	Aston Martin DB4GT	3670 cc.	Works	147	1st, PP, FL.	88.7 mph
390	2/5/1959	BRDC Sports car race, Silverstone, GB	12 laps.	Aston Martin DBR1	2992 cc.	Works		2nd.	
391	10/5/1959	Monaco GP, Monte Carlo MON	198 miles.	Cooper-Climax F1	2495 cc.	RRC Walker		PP. Retired.	Gearbox, lap 82. Leading.
392	31/5/1959	Dutch GP, Zandvoort, NL	195 miles.	Cooper-Climax F1	2495 cc.	RRC Walker		Retired, FL, LR.	96.99 mph, Gearbox, lap 63. Leading.
393	7/6/1959	1000km race, Nurburgring, D	44 laps.	Aston Martin DBR1	2992 cc.	Works	148	1st, LR.	89.16 mph, Co-driver Jack Fairman.
394	20/6/1959	Le Mans 24-hour race, Sarthe, F		Aston Martin DBR1	2992 cc.	Works		Retired.	Valves. Co-driver Jack Fairman.
395	5/7/1959	French GP, Reims-Gueux, F	258 miles.	BRM P25	2491 cc.	BRP		Retired.	Spin, stalled.
396	5/7/1959	Coupé de Vitesse, Reims-Gueux, F	129 miles.	Cooper-Borgward F2	1493 cc.	RRC Walker	149	1st, PP, LR.	130.21 mph
397	12/7/1959	Rouen GP, Les Essarts, F	143 miles.	Cooper-Borgward F2	1493 cc.	RRC Walker	150	1st, LR.	100.98 mph
398	12/7/1959	Coupé Delamere, Les Essarts, F	35 laps.	Maserati Tipo 60	1989 cc.	Works	151	1st, PP, FL.	95.00 mph
399	18/7/1959	British GP, Aintree, GB	225 miles.	BRM P25	2491 cc.	BRP		2nd, eq.LR.	92.31 mph, shared with Bruce McLaren.
400	18/7/1959	Sports Car race, Aintree, GB	17 laps.	Cooper-Monaco	2495 cc.	SM Ltd.		Retired, LR.	87.60 mph, Fire, lap 13.
401	26/7/1959	Circuit d'Auvergne, Clermont-Ferrarnd, F	130 miles.	Cooper-Borgward F2	1493 cc.	RRC Walker	152	1st, PP, LR.	78.73 mph
402	2/8/1959	German GP, Avusring, Berlin, D	2X30 laps.	Cooper-Climax F1	2495 cc.	RRC Walker		Retired, heat 1.	Gearbox, lap 2.
403	9/8/1959	Kannonloppet, Karlskoga, S	30 laps.	Cooper-Monaco	2495 cc.	SM Ltd	153	1st, LR.	68.41 mph
404	15/8/1959	Copenhagen GP, Roskilde, DK	140 km.	Cooper-Monaco	2495 cc.	SM Ltd	154	1st in 4 heats.	
405	16/8/1959	Copenhagen GP, Roskilde, DK	140 km.	Cooper-Monaco	2495 cc.	SM Ltd	155	1st o/agg, eq.LR.	46.2", LR shared with David Piper.
406	23/8/1959	Portuguese GP, Monsanto, P	210 miles.	Cooper-Climax F1	2495 cc.	RRC Walker	156	1st, PP, FL.	
407	29/8/1959	100-mile race, Brands Hatch, GB	42 laps.	Cooper-Borgward F2	1493 cc.	RRC Walker		3rd, PP, heat 1.	
408	29/8/1959	100-mile race, Brands Hatch, GB	42 laps.	Cooper-Borgward F2	1493 cc.	RRC Walker		4th, heat 2.	3rd on aggregate.
409	5/9/1959	RAC Tourist Trophy, Goodwood, GB	224 laps.	Aston Martin DBR1	2992 cc.	Works	157	1st, PP.	Co-Driver Brooks, then took over Shelby car.
410	13/9/1959	Italian GP, Monza, I	257 miles.	Cooper-Climax F1	2495 cc.	RRC Walker	158	1st, PP.	Gives Cooper F1 World Constructors' Championship.
411	26/9/1959	Gold cup, Oulton Park, GB	150 miles.	Cooper-Climax F1	2495 cc.	RRC Walker	159	1st, PP, LR.	97.64 mph
412	10/10/1959	LA Times GP, Riverside, USA	200 miles.	Aston Martin DBR2	4180 cc	Elisha Walker		Retired.	Engine oil pressure.
413	18/10/1959	Formule Libre GP, Watkins Glen, USA	230 miles.	Cooper-Climax F1	2495 cc.	BRP	160	1st, PP, FL.	97.1 mph
414	29/11/1959	Governor's Trophy, Nassau, BA.	54 miles.	Aston Martin DB4GT	3670 cc	F de Arellano	161	PP, 1st in heat.	
415	29/11/1959	Governor's Trophy, Nassau, BA.	54 miles.	Aston Martin DB4GT	3670 cc	F deArellano		Retired, LR in final.	82.78 mph Brakes.
416	2/12/1959	Nassau Trophy, Nassau, BA	30 laps.	Aston Martin DBR2	4180 cc	Elisha Walker	162	1st in heat.	
417	2/12/1959	Nassau Trophy, Nassau, BA	30 laps.	Aston Martin DBR2	4180 cc	Elisha Walker	163	1st in Race.	
418	12/12/1959	US GP, Sebring, USA	218 miles.	Cooper-Climax F1	2495 cc.	RRC Walker		PP, Retired.	Gearbox, lap 6.

1960

419	1/1/1960	South African GP, East London, SA	150 miles.	Cooper-Borgward F2	1493 cc.	Yeoman Cred.		2nd, PP, FL.	88.51 mph
420	9/1/1960	New Zealand GP, Ardmore, NZ	30 miles.	Cooper-Climax F1	2495 cc.	Yeoman Cred.	164	1st, FL, heat 1.	1' 21.7"
421	9/1/1960	New Zealand GP, Ardmore, NZ	150 miles.	Cooper-Climax F1	2495 cc.	Yeoman Cred.		PP, LR .Retired.	1' 21.2". Clutch.
422	7/2/1960	Argentine GP, Buenos Aires, ARG	80 laps.	Cooper-Climax F1	2495 cc.	RRC Walker		3rd, PP, FL.	88.43 mph, Took over M. Trintignant's car.
423	28/2/1960	Cuban Sports car GP, Havana, CU	50 laps.	Maserati Tipo 61	2890 cc.	Camoradi	165	1st, PP, LR.	82.02 mph
424	19/3/1960	GP of Syracuse, I	56 laps.	Porsche F2	1482 cc.	RRC Walker		PP, FL, LR. Retired.	103.56 mph, Valve, lap 27. Leading.
425	26/3/1960	4-hour race, Sebring, USA	57 laps.	Austin-Healey Sprite	994 cc.	Works		2nd.	
426	26/3/1960	12-hour race Sebring, USA		Maserati Tipo 61	2890 cc.	Camoradi		Retired, FL.	94.47 mph, Gearbox, 9hours. C/d Gurney. Leading.
427	10/4/1960	Brussels GP, Heysel, B	35 laps.	Porsche F2	1482 cc.	RRC Walker	166	1st, LR, heat 1.	82.11 mph
428	10/4/1960	Brussels GP, Heysel, B	35 laps.	Porsche F2	1482 cc.	RRC Walker		3rd, PP, FL, heat 2.	74.23 mph, 2nd on aggregate.
429	18/4/1960	Glover Trophy, Goodwood, GB	42 laps.	Cooper-Climax F1	2495 cc.	RRC Walker		PP, 2nd, LR.	102.13 mph
430	18/4/1960	Lavant Cup, Goodwood, GB	15 laps.	Porsche F2	1482 cc.	RRC Walker		2nd.	
431	18/4/1960	Fordwater Trophy, Goodwood, GB	10 laps.	Aston Martin DB4GT	3670 cc.	RRC Walker	167	1st, PP, FL.	84.05 mph
432	30/4/1960	200 mile race, Aintree, GB	150 miles!	Porsche F2	1482 cc.	RRC Walker	168	1st, FL.	88.41 mph (winning speed).
433	14/5/1960	BRDC Int'l Trophy, Silverstone, GB	50 laps.	Cooper-Climax F1	2495 cc.	RRC Walker		PP, Retired.	F. suspension, lap 34. Leading.
434	14/5/1960	Touring car race, Silverstone, GB	36 miles.	Jaguar 3.8 saloon	3781 cc.	E. Endeavour		2nd, PP.	
435	22/5/1960	1000km race, Nurburgring, D	44 laps.	Maserati Tipo 61	2890 cc.	Camoradi	169	1st, LR.	88.48 mph, Co-driver, Dan Gurney.
436	29/5/1960	Monaco GP, Monte Carlo, MON	100 laps.	Lotus-Climax 18	2495 cc.	RRC Walker	170	1st, PP.	First GP victory for Lotus.
437	6/6/1960	Dutch GP, Zandvoort, NL	75 laps.	Lotus-Climax 18	2495 cc.	RRC Walker		4th, PP, LR.	99.36 mph, Wheel wrecked .
438	18/6/1960	Belgian GP, Spa-Francorchamps	315 miles.	Lotus-Climax 18	2495 cc.	RRC Walker		DNS.	Crashed in practice (hub failure) SM hurt.
439	7/8/1960	Kannonloppet, Karlskoga, S	25 laps.	Lotus-Climax 19 Sports	2495 cc.	Yeoman Cred	171	1st, LR.	69.4 mph
440	14/8/1960	Portuguese GP, Oporto, P	55 laps.	Lotus-Climax 18	2495 cc.	RRC Walker		Disq.	Lap 51- spin; pushed car the wrong way.
441	20/8/1960	RAC Tourist Trophy, Goodwood, GB	108 laps.	Ferrari 250 SWB	3000 cc.	RRC Walker	172	1st, PP, LR.	89.44 mph
442	27/8/1960	100 mile race, Brands Hatch, GB	40 laps.	Porsche F2	1482 cc.	RRC Walker		11th.	Carburettors.
443	27/8/1960	Redex Trophy, Brands Hatch, GB	10 laps.	Ferrari 250 SWB	2953 cc.	RRC Walker	173	1st, PP, LR.	82.09 mph
444	10/9/1960	Copenhagen GP, Roskilde, DK	87 miles.	Porsche F2	1482 cc.	RRC Walker		4th.	Gear selection difficulties.
445	18/9/1960	Austrian GP, Zeltweg, OST	59 laps.	Porsche F2	1482 cc.	RRC Walker	174	1st, FL.	93.9 mph
446	24/9/1960	Gold cup meeting, Oulton Park, GB	60 laps.	Lotus-Climax 18	2495 cc.	RRC Walker	175	1st, PP, eq. FL.	94.3 mph, shared with Bruce McLaren.
447	2/10/1960	GP of Modena, I	100 laps.	Lotus-Climax 18 F2	1475 cc.	R Parnell		Retired.	Broken tappet.
448	9/10/1960	Formule Libre GP, Watkins Glen, USA	230 miles.	Lotus-Climax 18 F1	2495 cc.	RRC Walker	176	1st, PP, FL.	109 mph
449	16/10/1960	LA Times GP, Riverside, USA	200 miles.	Lotus-Climax 19 Sports	2495 cc.	Yeoman Cred.		PP, Retired.	Transmission, fire.
450	23/10/1960	Pacific GP, Laguna Seca, USA	100 miles.	Lotus-Climax 19 Sports	2495 cc.	Yeoman Cred.	177	1st, heat 1.	
451	23/10/1960	Pacific GP, Laguna Seca, USA	100 miles.	Lotus-Climax 19 Sports	2495 cc.	Yeoman Cred	178	1st, LR, heat 2.	1' 17.2"
452	20/11/1960	US GP, Riverside, USA	75 laps.	Lotus-Climax 18 F1	2495 cc.	RRC Walker	179	1st, PP.	
	25/11/1960	Nassau go-kart race, Nassau BA.		Bultaco go-kart	100 cc.	Organisers		13th.	
453	27/11/1960	Nassau Tourist Trophy, Nassau, BA	200 miles.	Ferrari 250 SWB	2953 cc.	RRC Walker	180	1st, FL.	84.35 mph
454	3/12/1960	Int'l Trophy, Nassau, BA		Lotus-Climax 19 Sports	2495 cc.	Yeoman Cred.		Retired.	Bonnet mechanism broken. Leading.
455	4/12/1960	Governor's Trophy, Nassau, BA	54 miles.	Lotus-Climax 19 Sports	2495 cc.	Yeoman Cred.		Retired.	Front suspension, lap 12.
456	17/12/1960	Cape GP, Killarney, SA	75 laps	Porsche F2	1482 cc.	RRC Walker	181	1st, PP.	
457	27/12/1960	South African GP, East London, SA	80 laps.	Porsche F2	1482 cc.	RRC Walker	182	1st.	

1961

458	7/1/1961	New Zealand GP, Ardmore, NZ	15 laps.	Lotus-Climax 18 2.5litre	2495 cc.	RRC Walker	183	1st, PP, LR, heat 1.	90.1 mph, 'Intercontinental Formula'.
459	7/1/1961	New Zealand GP, Ardmore, NZ	75 laps.	Lotus-Climax 18 2.5litre	2495 cc.	RRC Walker		Retired.	Half-shaft Cracked, lap 30. Leading.
460	21/1/1961	Lady Wigram Trophy, Christchurch, NZ	47 laps.	Lotus-Climax 18 2.5litre	2495 cc.	RRC Walker		2nd.	

461	29/1/1960	Australian GP, Warwick Farm, AUS	45 laps.	Lotus-Climax 18 2.5litre	2495 cc.	RRC Walker	184	1st, PP, FL.	80.68 mph
462	24/3/1961	4-hour race, Sebring, USA		Austin-Healey Sprite	994 cc.	Works		4th.	
463	25/3/1961	12-hour race, Sebring, USA		Maserati Tipo 61	2890 cc.	Camoradi		Retired, I.R.	3' 13". Exhaust fell apart. Co-driver Graham Hill.
464	3/4/1961	Lavant Cup, Goodwood, GB	21 laps.	Cooper-Climax 2.5litre	2495 cc.	RRC Walker	185	1st.	90.47 mph 'Intercontinental' Formula.
465	3/4/1961	Glover Trophy, Goodwood, GB	42 laps.	Lotus-Climax 18 F1	1495 cc.	RRC Walker		4th, PP.	
466	3/4/1961	Sussex Trophy, Goodwood, GB	15 laps.	Lotus-Climax 19 Sports	2495 cc.	UDT-Laystall	186	1st, PP.	
467	3/4/1961	Fordwater Trophy, Goodwood, GB	10 laps.	Aston Martin DB4GT	3679 cc.	Essex Racing		3rd, PP.	
468	9/4/1961	Brussels GP, Heysel, B	22 laps.	Lotus-Climax 18 F1	1495 cc.	RRC Walker		Unc heat 1.	Carburation.
469	9/4/1961	Brussels GP, Heysel, B	22 laps.	Lotus-Climax 18 F1	1495 cc.	RRC Walker		8th, heat 2.	Carburation.
470	9/4/1961	Brussels GP, Heysel, B	22 laps.	Lotus-Climax 18 F1	1495 cc.	RRC Walker		2nd, heat 3.	7th on aggregate.
471	16/4/1961	Vienna GP, Aspern, OS	55 laps.	Lotus-Climax 18 F1	1495 cc.	RRC Walker	187	1st, PP, FL, I.R.	84.57 mph
472	22/4/1961	200 mile race, Aintree, GB	50 laps.	Cooper-Climax F2	1475 cc.	RRC Walker		Retired.	Bearings, 3 laps.
473	22/4/1961	Sports car race, Aintree, GB	17 laps.	Lotus-Climax 19 Sports	2495 cc.	UDT-Laystall	188	1st, I.R.	90 mph
474	25/4/1961	GP of Syracuse, I	56 laps.	Lotus-Climax 18 F1	1495 cc.	RRC Walker		8th.	Magneto.
475	30/4/1961	Targa Florio, Madonie, I	450 miles.	Porsche RS60	1966 cc.	Camoradi/works		Retired.	Differential split. Leading - 8km to go. Co-driver G. Hill.
476	6/5/1961	BRDC Int'l Trophy, Silverstone, GB	80 laps.	Cooper-Climax 2.5litre	2495 cc.	RRC Walker	189	1st, FL.	93.75 mph
477	6/5/1961	Sports Car race, Silverstone, GB	25 laps.	Lotus-Climax 19 Sports	2495 cc.	UDT-Laystall	190	1st, PP, I.R.	106.22 mph
478	14/5/1961	Monaco GP, Monte Carlo, MON	100 laps.	Lotus-Climax 18 F1	1495 cc.	RRC Walker	191	1st, PP, eq. FL.	73.05 mph shared with Ginther's Ferrari.
479	22/5/1961	Dutch GP, Zandvoort, NL	75 laps.	Lotus-Climax 18 F1	1495 cc.	RRC Walker		4th.	
480	28/5/1961	1000km race, Nurburgring, D	44 laps.	Porsche RS61/Carrera	1605 cc.	Works		8th & 1st in class.	Took over Carrera, co-driver G. Hill.
481	3/6/1961	Silver City Trophy, Brands Hatch, GB	76 laps.	Lotus-Climax '18-21' F1	1495 cc.	UDT-Laystall	192	1st, PP, I.R.	93.52 mph
482	10/6/1961	Le Mans 24-hour race, Sarthe, F		Ferrari250 SWB	2953 cc.	RRCW/NART		Retired.	Fan broke. Leading class, 3rd overall.
483	18/6/1961	Belgian GP, Spa-Francorchamps, B	36 laps.	Lotus-Climax '18-21' F1	1495 cc.	RRC Walker		8th.	No explanation!
484	24/6/1961	Player's 200 mile race, Mosport, CAN	40 laps.	Lotus-Climax 19 Sports	2495 cc.	UDT-Laystall	193	1st, heat 1. FL.	
485	24/6/1961	Player's 200 mile race, Mosport, CAN	40 laps.	Lotus-Climax 19 Sports	2495 cc.	UDT-Laystall	194	1st, heat 2.	1st on aggregate.
486	2/7/1961	French GP, Reims-Gueux, F	52 laps.	Lotus-Climax '18-21' F1	1495 cc.	RRC Walker		Retired.	Collision damage, lap 31.
487	8/7/1961	British Empire Trophy, Silverstone, GB	52 laps.	Cooper-Climax 2.5litre	2495 cc.	RRC Walker	195	1st, FL.	109.3 mph
488	8/7/1961	GT race, Silverstone, GB	25 laps.	Ferrari 250 SWB	2953 cc.	RRC Walker	196	1st, PP, FL.	95.95 mph
489	15/7/1961	British GP, Aintree, GB	75 laps.	Lotus-Climax '18-21' F1	1495 cc.	RRC Walker		Retired & Disq.	Retired (brake pipe). Took over Ferguson 4X4, disq.
490	23/7/1961	Solitude GP, Stuttgart, D	25 laps.	Lotus-Climax '18-21' F1	1495 cc.	UDT-Laystall		10th.	Gearbox, lap 22.
491	6/8/1961	German GP, Nurburgring, D	15 laps.	Lotus-Climax '18-21' F1	1495 cc.	RRC Walker	197	1st.	Final Grand Epreuve F1 victory.
492	7/8/1961	Peco Trophy, Brands Hatch, GB	20 laps.	Ferrari 250 SWB	2953 cc.	RRC Walker	198	1st, PP, I.R.	83.53 mph
493	7/8/1961	Guards Trophy, Brands Hatch, GB	76 laps.	Cooper-Climax 2.5litre	2495 cc.	RRC Walker		PP.Retired.	Gearbox, lap 24. Leading.
494	19/8/1961	RAC Tourist Trophy, Goodwood, GB	109 laps.	Ferrari 250 SWB	2953 cc.	RRC Walker	199	1st.	Final (7th) RAC T.T. win.
495	20/8/1961	Kannonloppet, Karlskoga, S	30 laps.	Lotus-Climax '18-21' F1	1495 cc.	UDT-Laystall	200	1st, eq. FL.	1' 30.4", shared with J. Surtees.
496	26/8/1961	Copenhagen GP, Roskilde, DK	20 laps.	Lotus-Climax '18-21' F1	1495 cc.	UDT-Laystall	201	1st, PP, FL, heat 1.	47.00"
497	26/8/1961	Copenhagen GP, Roskilde, DK	30 laps.	Lotus-Climax '18-21' F1	1495 cc.	UDT-Laystall	202	1st, PP, FL, heat 2.	42.8"
498	26/8/1961	Copenhagen GP, Roskilde, DK	30 laps.	Lotus-Climax '18-21' F1	1495 cc.	UDT-Laystall	203	1st, PP, FL, heat 3.	43.1", 1st on aggregate.
499	3/9/1961	GP of Modena, I	100 laps.	Lotus-Climax '18-21' F1	1495 cc.	RRC Walker	204	1st, PP, FL.	89.4 mph
500	10/9/1961	Italian GP, Monza	43 laps.	Lotus-Climax 21 F1	1495 cc.	Works/Walker		Retired.	Wheel bearing, lap 37. Innes Ireland's works car.
501	23/9/1961	Gold Cup meeting, Oulton Park, GB	60 laps.	Ferguson-Climax 4X4	1495 cc.	RRC Walker	205	1st, I.R.	93.42 mph Only ever F1 victory by 4X4 car.
502	30/9/1961	Pepsi-Cola Trophy, Mosport, CAN	100 laps.	Lotus-Climax 19 Sports	2495 cc.	ex-UDT		3rd, PP, I.R.	91.72 mph, Gearbox, radiator problems.
503	8/10/1961	US GP, Watkins Glen, USA	100 laps.	Lotus-Climax '18-21' F1	1495 cc.	RRC Walker		Retired.	Engine, lap 58. Leading.
504	13/10/1961	LA Times GP, Riverside, USA	200 miles.	Lotus-Climax 19 Sports	2495 cc.	ex-UDT		UNC heat 1.	Brake fluid loss.
505	15/10/1961	3 hour Production car race, Riverside, USA		Sunbeam Alpine	1592 cc.	Works		3rd, 1st in class.	Co-driver Jack Brabham.
506	22/10/1961	Pacific GP, Laguna Seca, USA	100 miles.	Lotus-Climax 19 Sports	2495 cc.	UDT-Laystall	206	1st, heat 1.	Sticking throttle.
507	22/10/1961	Pacific GP, Laguna Seca, USA	100 miles.	Lotus-Climax 19 Sports	2495 cc.	UDT-Laystall	207	1st, heat 2.	Brakes off, 1st on aggregate.
508	3/12/1961	Nassau Tourist Trophy, Nassau, BA	200 miles.	Ferrari 250 SWB	2953 cc.	RRC Walker	208	1st, PP, heat 2.	
509	3/12/1961	Nassau Tourist Trophy, Nassau, BA	200 miles.	Ferrari 250 SWB	2953 cc.	RRC Walker	209	1st, PP in race.	
510	8/12/1961	Governor's Trophy, Nassau, BA	30 laps.	Lotus-Climax 19 Sports	2495 cc.	Rosebud Rac.		Retired.	Rear upright broken.
511	10/12/1961	Nassau Trophy, Nassau, BA	56 laps.	Lotus-Climax 19 Sports	2495 cc.	UDT-Laystall		Retired.	Rear wishbone. Leading.
512	17/12/1961	Natal GP, Westmead, Durban, SA	89 laps.	Lotus-Climax '18-21' F1	1495 cc.	UDT-Laystall		2nd, FL.	
513	26/12/1961	South African GP, East London, SA	80 laps.	Lotus-Climax '18-21' F1	1495 cc.	UDT-Laystall		2nd.	
	1962								
514	6/1/1962	New Zealand GP, Ardmore, NZ	150 laps.	Lotus-Climax 21 2.5litre	2495 cc.	RRC Walker	210	1st, FL.	1' 32.8"
515	13/1/1962	Vic Hudson Memorial Trophy, Levin, NZ	28 laps.	Cooper-Climax 2.5litre	2495 cc.	RRC Walker		2nd in heat.	
516	13/1/1962	Vic Hudson Memorial Trophy, Levin, NZ	28 laps.	Cooper-Climax 2.5litre	2495 cc.	RRC Walker		2nd in race.	Race shortened to 9 laps-rain.
517	20/1/1962	Lady Wigram Trophy, Christchurch, NZ	150 miles.	Lotus-Climax 21 2.5litre	2495 cc.	RRC Walker	211	1st, eq. FL.	1' 20.1"
518	27/1/1962	Teretonga Trophy, Teretonga, NZ	75 miles.	Cooper-Climax 2.5litre	2495 cc.	RRC Walker		2nd, heat 1.	
519	27/1/1962	Teretonga Trophy, Teretonga, NZ	75 miles.	Cooper-Climax 2.5litre	2495 cc.	RRC Walker		2nd in main race.	
520	4/2/1962	100 mile race, Warwick Farm, AUS	45 laps.	Cooper-Climax 2.7litre	2700 cc.	RRC Walker	212	1st, PP.	Last win.
521	11/2/1962	3-hour Continental race, Daytona, USA		Ferrari 250GTB	2953 cc.	NART		4th, 1st in class.	
522	11/3/1962	Formule Libre race, Sandown Pk, AUS	120 miles.	Cooper-Climax 2.7litre	2700 cc.	RRC Walker		5th.	
523	23/3/1962	3-hour race, Sebring, USA		Austin-Healey Sprite	994 cc.	Works		3rd.	
524	25/3/1962	12-hour race, Sebring, USA		Ferrari 250TR/61		UDT/NART		Disq. FL.	"Refueling infringement". Co-driver I. Ireland.
525	1/4/1962	Brussels GP, Heysel, B	62.5 miles	Lotus-Climax '18-21' V8	1495 cc.	RRC Walker		2nd, FL, heat 1.	83.46 mph
526	1/4/1962	Brussels GP, Heysel, B	62.5 miles	Lotus-Climax '18-21' V8	1495 cc.	RRC Walker		Retired heat 2. FL.	84.85 mph, Valvegear.
527	1/4/1962	Brussels GP, Heysel, B	62.5 miles	Lotus-Climax '18-21' V8	1495 cc.	RRC Walker		DNS heat 3.	UNC on aggregate.
528	14/4/1962	Lombank Trophy, Snetterton, GB	50 laps.	Lotus-Climax '18-21' V8	1495 cc.	UDT/Walker		7th, PP, FL.	104.23 mph Sticking throttle.
529	23/4/1962	Glover Trophy, Goodwood, GB	100 miles.	Lotus-Climax '18-21' V8	1495 cc.	UDT/Walker		PP, eq.FL, CRA.	105.37 mph, with Surtees. CRA., lap 36.

RACE RECORD AND STATISTICS - STIRLING CRAUFURD MOSS. 1948–1962.

In compiling this, I would like to thank Doug Nye for allowing me to use so much of his own hard work from *My Cars, my Career*. Other sources include: *Alf Francis*, by Peter Lewis, *All but my life*, by Ken Purdy, *Rob Walker*, by Michael Cooper-Evans, and Ken Gregory, as well as a great box of old journals. Sadly, the records of the RRC Walker team were lost in a works fire, but happily, Stirling is a good record-keeper. Where possible, I have included the entrant or owner of the car, although for certain of the entries it is, at this distance, a complete mystery. All errors or omissions are, of course, mine. Unavoidably, I have had to use some abbreviations:

FL.: Fastest lap. **FTD:** Fastest time of the day. **I.R.:** Lap record. **DNS:** Did not start. **Disq.:** Disqualified. **CRA:** Crashed. **Ret'd.:** Retired. **BPT:** Best practice time. **PP:** Pole position. **NCR:** New course record (Hill Climbs and Sprints). **UNC:** Unclassified.

* Counting all heats and finals, but discounting speed trials, rallies, record attempts and hill climbs, Stirling Moss entered 529 (numbered) racing events. He won 212 of them; 40.075% of those entered.

^ From 1954, when he became a Formula driver, he entered 310 races of all types, winning 138 of them; a 44.52% victory rate. Of those races which he finished in that period, 234 in all, he won 58.97% of them.
  Between 1958 and 1962, he drove in 93 races for Rob Walker. Of the 70 he finished, he won 46 of them, or 65.71%.

** Stirling Moss Limited was formed in late 1954.

At this distance, it has proved difficult to ascertain the exact duration of some events, as they are obscure now. Thus, some details are unavoidably approximate.

First published in the United Kingdom in 2001 by Cassell & Co
Wellington House, Strand, London, WC2R 0BB

Distributed in the United States of America by Sterling Publishing Co., Inc.,
387 Park Avenue South, New York, NY 10016-8810.

Designed by Wherefore Art?
Index by Derek Copson

Printed and bound in Italy

A CIP catalogue record for this book is available from the British Library.

ISBN 0 304 35904 1

Credits

The publishers would like to thank the following for permission to reproduce
this material. Every care has been taken to trace copyright holders. However,
if there are any omissions we will be happy to rectify them in future editions

Stirling Moss Archives: pages 7; 9; 12–13; 14; 16–17; 18; 19; all images 20;
21; 22–23; 24–25; 27; 28; 29; 30–31; 32; 35; 36; 37; 39; 40; 43; 44–45; 46;
47; 48; 49; 50; 52; 53; 54; 55; 59; 62; 63; 64–65; 66; 67; 68; 69; 70; 71;
72–73; 74; 76; 77; 80–81; 83; 84–85; 86; 87; 88–89; 91; 99; 100–101; both
images 102; both images 103; 104; 106–107; 111; 114–115; 116; both images
122; 123; 124–125; 126; 127; 128; 129; 130; 132; 136; 138–139; 140–141;
142; 143; 144–145; 146; 147; 148–149; 150–151; 152–153; 154–155; upper
right 155; 156–157; 158; 160; 163; 164; 165; 166; 167; 168; 169; 170–171;
173; 174–175; 176–177; 180–181; 182; 183; 184; 185; 186–187; upper right
187; middle and bottom images 190; 191; 192–193; upper right 195; upper
left 196; 196–197; 198–199; 202; 204–205; upper right 205; 208; 209; 210;
211; 212; 213; 214; 215; 218–219; 220–221; 222; 223; 225; 226; 230–231;
upper right 231; 235; 237; 238–239; 242–243; 248; 249; 250–251; 252–253;
254–255; 256; 258; 261; 262–263; 264; 266–267; 270; 272; 273; 274; 275;
276; 278; 279; 280; 282; 284; 292; 293; 299; 300; 303; 304; 305; 306–307; 3
small images upper right 307; 308; 310; 311; 312; 313; 314; 315; 316; 317;
318; 3 small images upper left 320; 321; 322; 324; 329; 330; 332–333;
334–335; 336; two small images middle right margin 337; 338–339, 340; 343;
346; 347; 360.
Hulton Getty: pages 6, 10–11; 51; 56–57; 60–61; 74; 90; 94–95; 97; 98; 105;
112–113; 120–121; 131; 133; 134–135; 172; 188; 189; top left 190; 194–195;
206–207; 216–217; 224; 228–229; 233; 245; 246–247; 257; 260; 271;
294–295; 296; 297; 298; 302; 344–345.
Hulton Archives (part of Hulton Getty): pages 240; 301; 323.
LAT; pages 58; 92–93; 118–119; 162; 179; 200–201; 227; 234; 268; 269;
281; 283; 286; 287; 288; 289; 290; 291.
Daily Express: pages 78–79; 108–109; 176–177; 325; 326; 327; 328; 331;
small image upper right margin 39l.
H. Jones 319.

Captions

Front endpapers (i): Windows
Front endpapers (ii): A relic of the crash which nearly killed him; Goodwood,
1962.
Page 359: Moss by Elliot Moss.
Page 360: At the chequered flag in the Aston Martin, 1958 Targa Florio.
On the left, in flat cap, is Mike Hawthorn.
Back endpapers (i): The steering wheel of the Lotus 18, distorted by the
forces of an impact at Spa, June 1960.
Back endpapers (ii): A well-worn pair of racing gloves.

Elliot Moss